MW00353414

Unzipped is a hyper-relevant, compe[...]
and an era few, if any, films or TV show[...]
curtain of her experience, of what she endured, only to see her emerge
through the lens of adaptation more vigilant in a sense is nothing short of
inspiring—for any reader.

— Matt Misetich,
Senior Executive, Pipeline Media Group

After reading the preface of *Unzipped: Chronicles of a Fashion Fit Model*,
I couldn't put it down. Darlene's writing is mesmerizing and her story
is raw and honest. This book exposes the insidious contradictions and
skewed morals of post-war America—an era when even discussing rape
was taboo—it is filled with hope, acceptance with strength, and ultimately,
redemption. I believe that *Unzipped* will become a classic in its genre.

— Debra Poneman,
Professional speaker and bestselling author

Darlene's story of abuse is heartbreaking. In *Unzipped*, she is raw and real
about the effects the abuse had on her life. There is an underlying tone of
hope, healing, and triumph in the pages of this brilliantly written mas-
terpiece. Anyone who has ever been a victim of abuse should read this
book. There is so much wisdom within its pages. Darlene is a fierce warrior
and an advocate of survivors everywhere. This book will leave you feeling
empowered, inspired, and armed with hope. It will remind you that your
healing is worth fighting for.

— Sarah Kacala,
Author of *Little Girl Speak*

Unzipped gives hope to all women who have been victims of abuse and
have struggled to support and raise their children. Darlene's incredible
account of her career as a fashion fit model, overcoming adversity—and
ultimately finding financial and occupational success, as well as love—is
truly inspirational.

— Marci Shimoff,
#1 *New York Times* bestselling author of
Chicken Soup for the Woman's Soul and Happy for No Reason

UNZIPPED

UNZIPPED

Chronicles of a Fashion Fit Model

DARLENE PARRIS YOUNG

WITH

JANICE HARPER

Copyediting: Janice Harper
Proofreading: Nina Shoroplova—ninashoroplova.ca
Book Interior and E-book Design: Amit Dey—amitdey2528@gmail.com
Cover Design: Zizi Iryaspyhra Subiyarta—pagatana.com

Publishing Consultant: Geoff Affleck—geoffaffleck.com

Library of Congress Number:
ISBN:
978-1-7347980-0-5 (Paperback)
978-1-7347980-1-2 (Kindle)
978-1-7347980-2-9 (eBook)

1. BIO035000 BIOGRAPHY & AUTOBIOGRAPHY / Fashion
2. BIO022000 BIOGRAPHY & AUTOBIOGRAPHY / Women
3. BIO026000 BIOGRAPHY & AUTOBIOGRAPHY / Personal Memoirs
4. BUS070090 BUSINESS & ECONOMICS / Industries / Fashion & Textile Industry

Author's Note

The events in this memoir are true to the best of my memory, though some of the dialogue has been reconstructed for dramatic effect. The names of the characters have been changed and, in some cases, identifiable information has been altered to protect their identities. One character, Deborah, who appears in the early chapters of the book, is a composite character of two women who were close friends.

Dedication

There are so many people who helped me bring this book to life. Firstly, I would like to acknowledge my beautiful husband, who came on this path with me. Even though, at times, I became overwhelmed recalling some of my experiences for this book, he continued to contribute his love and patience. Believe me, it was not an easy path for him to read about some of my more difficult experiences.

Many thanks go to my daughter, Shelley, and my son, Michael, who encouraged me to write my memoir. I would not have been able to do this without my amazing children. They were always there to witness my healing process.

I also want to thank my sisters for filling in times and dates as to the different events in this book. I am truly blessed to have my family, my sisters, to help me.

Lastly, I need to especially thank my new and dear friend, Janice Harper. Her editing and counsel were inspirational. Without her wisdom and her patience, this book would not have been possible. From the depths of my soul, I thank her.

To family and friends: *"We Did It!"*

May light be in your lives forever.

Darlene

Table of Contents

Table of Contents

Chapter 1

Milk Stain

I was pressing his pants when I noticed the milk stain. How in God's name did he spill milk on the front of his pants when he doesn't even like milk, I wondered. My neurotic husband couldn't even be persuaded to eat vanilla ice cream, much less anything else that was white. Nonetheless, he had somehow managed to spill milk or ice cream or God knows what all over his pants, and there was no time to send them to the cleaners. I wouldn't even ask him what happened, it would only annoy him. And he was already late to work, thanks to all our fighting. There was nothing to do but clean it up the best I could and send him off. Hopefully, he wouldn't even notice.

I grabbed a clean, wet washcloth and after wringing out the excess water, I blotted the spot clean and pressed it dry, then centered the inseams and pressed the creases as straight as I could. Ironing was soothing and even though I was rushing to get the pants done in time, the feel of the heavy warm iron beneath my hands, smoothing and transforming the soft fabric beneath it, brought me calm. I so needed calm after all that screaming through the house and inside my head.

"Come *on,* Darlene!" Dick hollered from the bedroom, "bring me my damn pants already!"

"I'm just finishing them now, sweetheart!" I called out in the most loving voice I could muster. I didn't dare say anything in any tone that might set him off. I pulled them off the ironing board, shut off the iron and delivered the freshly pressed pants to my husband, the smile pressed on my face as expertly as the crisp crease I'd pressed into his trousers.

Though he worked all day as a lineman, climbing telephone poles and repairing phone lines, Dick had also taken on a part-time evening job in security at the police station, so he could make some extra money. We'd married young—I was only 17 and Dick just a few years older—and now, not four years later, we had a nearly four-year-old son and a baby daughter already walking. It was 1969 and money wasn't easy to come by; we needed all we could get.

As Dick flew out the door I thought how handsome he looked in his uniform. He reminded me of my dad when he had been decked out in his World War II officer's jacket, so impressive with all his medals. Watching my husband walk away, I recalled my father marching with the veterans of World War II in the Tilton, New Hampshire, Memorial Day Parade. It was a sunny day, the snow had finally melted, and I was eight years old, standing with my mother, my sisters, Julie and Donna, and my baby brother, Danny, still in his stroller. We were so excited to see our daddy.

They had many groups marching that day—the Tilton Northfield High School Band, the Cub Scouts, and the Girl Scouts and many different drum and bugle corps that had come from across the state. Each one was more exciting than the last and the music was loud and exhilarating. As I peered between the legs of the adults who were standing in my way, I saw our military men march by us, dressed so elegantly in their uniforms, every one of them looking so proud. I was thrilled when my father passed by, turning and giving us the biggest smile ever. My mother waved back, blowing him a kiss.

She forgave him so much.

Later that afternoon, after we'd come home, I snuck into my parents' bedroom and there it was, resting on their bed. I had watched him take the jacket off, laying it carefully atop the gold and brown floral bedspread, as if it were made of paper-thin glass and would shatter if mistreated. Freed of the jacket that had defined him all those years (and freed from the responsibility of hanging it in the closet, which was my mother's duty), he left the room, no doubt to pour himself a drink.

I ran over to the bed and touched it, as if were a royal garment made of the finest cloth in the kingdom. I could barely lift it; the many medals were like heavy weights. Slipping my arms into it, I turned to the full-length mirror. It was way too big for me and didn't look anything like it did on my dad. It swallowed me up, but on my handsome father, it had looked magnificent, magical even. It completely transformed him, just as I saw it transforming me as I stood there, swallowed by his Eisenhower jacket. I may have looked terribly small inside it, but I felt so big with it draped over me. I was important in that jacket.

Dick hadn't served in the military, but with his bright blue eyes, his strong muscles from working as a lumberjack in his teens, practicing karate, riding his motorcycle and now working on those phone poles, he certainly looked as heroic and strong as any of those men had in that parade. I stood on the porch in the chilly fall evening and smiled as I waved goodbye and wished him a good night. He climbed in the car and didn't glance back.

I went back inside and closed the door and let the smile fade. Smiling no longer came naturally to me. It was what one did to change the subject.

I reached my arm over my shoulder to rub the pain away, but I couldn't reach the spot between my shoulder blades where it still throbbed. He'd pressed that shotgun so deep into my skin I just knew he'd left a bruise.

At least this time it wouldn't show.

Later that night after putting the kids to bed, I wrapped myself up in my favorite blanket and picked up the *Cosmopolitan* magazine that promised to enlighten me on the pros and cons of an open marriage. Do people in New Hampshire even have open marriages, I wondered.

I'd always assumed those kind of marriages only existed in Manhattan or L.A., certainly not in a small New England town like ours, a town so small you couldn't open a jar of pickles without the whole town dropping by with burgers and buns, ready for a potluck. How in the world my husband thought we could open up our marriage without being chased out of town was beyond me. But that's the kind of marriage he was telling me he wanted.

Tammy Wynette's song, "Stand by Your Man," played in the background, and as I listened to the lyrics, it felt as if she was singing straight to me.

I wondered if I was standing by my man or I had given up on him. It sure felt like he had given up on me. He kept telling me I'd put on too much weight since Shelley was born eighteen months earlier, and he thought I was lazy for not losing it faster. He also thought since I was so busy with the kids that he should be able to date other women; he wouldn't be so angry all the time, he explained, if we had an open marriage. Besides, it was what modern marriage was all about, he kept saying, and didn't we want to be modern?

But if he wants an open marriage so he can date other women, I wondered, *why was he so enraged at the thought of me seeing another man today?* Not that I *was* seeing another man, or even that I would if I had wanted to. I'd been out shopping when my husband got home and saw the duffle bag set inside the door. By the time I walked through that same door with the groceries he was in a rage.

"Who the hell are you fucking, Darlene?" he demanded to know, but nothing I said could convince him that I was as bewildered as he was about the duffle bag in the doorway. Next thing I knew, he'd gone for his shotgun and jammed it hard between my shoulder blades, demanding an answer. As I felt the pressure of the gun's muzzle pressing on my back I started to sweat and the nausea and anxiety just flooded me. All those memories of my dad raging at my mother, beating her so badly on their weekly fights, came rushing through me like a wave of terror. Was he going to pull the trigger?

In those moments, thinking of the gun about to go off, I was para-lyzed. I couldn't move, and it seemed like forever before I could even speak. I prayed to God he wouldn't kill me. What would happen to my babies if he did?

A sound coming up the walk startled us both, and I felt the gun go away. I turned and saw his eyes narrow as he looked out the window, watching a man in a military uniform walk up the drive, framed by the brilliant orange and red autumn leaves, like something out of a Norman Rockwell painting. But it wasn't my dad. He knew better than to come to my home.

Dick's jaw clenched as he thought he was seeing my lover come up the walk, but relaxed and broke into a phony grin when he recognized the man. It was my sister Julie's husband, home from his tour of duty in Vietnam. We opened the door and welcomed him as if we were the happiest couple on earth, thrilled to see him, while Dick nonchalantly set the rifle against the wall, like setting a broom aside. Of course, I *was* thrilled to see my brother-in-law, since he may have just saved my life.

Our unexpected visitor explained that Julie wasn't home, so he came by our place thinking she'd be with me. When he got no answer, he let himself in and dropped off his bag while he went for a walk into town.

I don't remember the conversation after that, just that that's the day I started to recognize the weakness in my husband, who had such terrifying strength.

I mindlessly turned the pages of the *Cosmo* magazine. The pages told me I was supposed to turn my husband on if I wanted to keep him. The magazine said nothing about him turning me on but assured me sex was for my own enjoyment. It said the wife's hang ups caused a cheating husband and gave lots of advice on how to lose weight fast to keep him happy and assured us that every woman could have a career and even seduce our bosses if we impressed them with our cleavage. Tammy Wynette's voice faded into silence, and the words in the maga-zine grew louder. I'd grown too fat. Too ugly. Too unattractive for my husband, who now wanted other women—and my permission to sleep with them.

The pillows pressed into my back but no matter how I moved, I couldn't relieve the tender pain of that gun barrel—or the memory of it shoved into my flesh as I waited to die. Nothing about that in *Cosmo*. No articles on How to Keep Your Husband from Pulling the Trigger or What to Say When the Man You Love Says He's Going to Kill You.

Would he kill me? I wondered. *If not today, another day?*

Nope, death was not an option. Time to grow up, Darlene, I told myself. Time to lose that baby fat, get a job and feel good about myself. I hadn't felt good about myself in a very long time, and I sure hadn't felt like I was pretty. I would definitely do something about that. Tomorrow.

In the meantime, the only thing that would make me feel happy would be to get out of that bed I shared with my husband, where his scent lingered like a bad dream. I put the magazine down and went into my son's room, where he was sleeping soundly, still clutching his little stuffed bear. His poodle, Cinnamon, slept at his feet. I crawled into Michael's narrow bed, putting my arms around his warm little body, and hugged him close. He was the only male I trusted, and I needed his love to help me feel something other than the ugliness I was feeling at that moment.

My son loved me no matter what.

And no matter what, I was going to survive for him and for my daughter.

I just had no idea how I could do that. I had no money, no skills, and I was a high school dropout. Without Dick's income, I wouldn't even have a home.

All I had was my pretty face.

"All you're good for is marriage, Darlene," my dad had told me more times than I could ever count. "Men are fools for a pretty face. And you've got your figure . . ."

The problem was, that figure had just gestated two babies, and the pretty face no longer drew my husband's interest.

Which pretty much left me with nothing. Nothing but my children.

As I thought about my children, Tammy Wynette's other hit from the year before played inside my head.

"D-I-V-O-R-C-E."

Chapter 2

Tips

By the next morning, my conviction to leave my husband had wavered, as it always did. Falling asleep next to my sweet little boy, I realized that leaving my marriage meant taking my children from their father. A boy needs his daddy, I reasoned. I couldn't do that to my son. I couldn't send his daddy away, no matter how much I wanted to for my own sake.

I knew it was up to me to save my marriage. Dick was under tremendous strain having to support us all on his wages—the stress was so great he'd even had to take that second job. Besides, I thought as I searched through my closet for a decent outfit that would fit, I'd let myself go since the babies were born. No wonder he wanted an open marriage.

Squeezing into a pair of hip-hugger jeans that were at least a size too tight, I remained determined to lose the baby fat and get a job. My sisters could watch the kids while I worked and I'd bring in enough extra money that Dick could quit that second job. Once I lost the weight I knew he'd be happy again. Of course, I wasn't qualified to do much other than serve food, but if all I could do was serve food, then that's what I would do. I'd get a job as a waitress.

My mom and my sisters, Julie and Donna, agreed to take turns watching the kids and it didn't take me long to get a part-time job as a waitress in a diner not far from the public service department where Dick worked during the day. That was perfect—he could drop by on his lunchbreaks and see me, and I figured the more we saw each other, the better. It could only improve our marriage.

Unless, of course, it didn't.

"That's my girl!" Dick said when I told him the news. "Now I don't have to work so damned hard all the time. You just be sure to hustle, you hear me? That's how you'll get the good tips."

Dick took me in his arms, swung me around and planted a giant kiss on me, then suggested we go out to dinner. I'd been half afraid of his response since he'd always been against his wife working. But the financial strain of raising a family had changed his views, and I was thrilled. I could get out of the house, bring in some money, and get my marriage back on track. The weight of my shame and all that anxiety lessened almost immediately.

But once I started working, I realized I may have bitten off more than I could chew. The work was exhausting, especially since I usually had to get up once or twice a night for one or both of the kids. On my feet all day, rushing home to get the kids and take care of them, fix dinner, get the dishes done, the kids bathed and put to bed, and then make love to my husband, I was moving constantly. Still, it was worth it. The pounds began to disappear and along with the heavy workload, I'd developed a tremendous willpower to stay away from fatty foods and desserts. The curves that I'd lost were returning and so was Dick's attention.

The tips I was bringing home also made a big difference, and I enjoyed meeting so many people during the day. I quickly learned that the friendlier I was, the bigger the tips, so I did my best to stay upbeat and friendly, even with the occasional letch who I'd just as soon serve a pie in the face than a piece of pie on a plate. But it was all in a day's work, after all.

My husband, however, didn't see it that way. Dick had indeed been coming to the restaurant regularly, just as I'd hoped, but rather than watch me with pride, he watched me with suspicion.

"Why's your skirt so short?" he wanted to know, as if I'd been the one to choose the waitresses' uniforms. When I first started losing the extra weight, Dick was thrilled, but it wasn't long before he resented any man smiling in my direction.

"Don't you notice these men are flirting with you? Why do you have to be so friendly?" The anger in his voice was palpable and I knew that defending myself by telling him I needed to be friendly to get the tips would only enrage him because it would be a confession that I was inviting the attention. So I did my best to play up to his own manhood and keep his temper down.

"The only man who gets my attention is you, sweetheart," I'd tell him, rubbing my body against his. "They can flirt all they want, but the only thing they're getting from me is their lunch and the check that comes with it."

Then I'd take him by the hand and lead him to bed—unless of course I had a child to attend to. It was a constant balancing act between keeping him or the kids happy and it seemed I could never satisfy them all at once, no matter how cleverly I tried to manage everything to everyone's satisfaction.

I was too tired to even argue.

Dick was right about me being extra friendly to the men, of course—because they tipped better than the women, at least that was the case back then. And I was there to make money for our family, which meant forcing a smile when they called me *honey*, winking when they pinched my ass, or complimenting them when they acted like jerks. If I didn't do those things, I didn't get decent tips; I might even get fired—I'd seen other women let go for not being sufficiently "friendly." But I figured it was a small price to pay for making my own money.

The big price to pay was provoking Dick's escalating anger. I'd come to loathe his daily visits. Every step I took was made with care, lest he accuse me of swinging my hips and tempting their attention. Every extra minute serving a male was a risk at inciting his fury for being too friendly. And every guy who grabbed me when Dick was watching me became a guarantee I'd catch hell when I got home for "inviting" the wandering hand.

I had to get out of there. I had to get far enough away that Dick couldn't just drop by and put me under his surveillance.

Fortunately, I wasn't alone. One of the other waitresses, Deborah, also wanted out. I wanted to get out of Dick's watchful eye, and Deborah wanted to move on to a better restaurant, where the tips and the clientele would be better.

"Hey, Darlene," Deborah said to me in a hushed tone one day when we were hustling trays of food back and forth, "I hear they're hiring at the Concord Hotel out on New Hampshire Highway; want to go with me, our next day off?"

"Concord?" I asked, "Isn't that a bit far? It's twenty miles." But far, I realized the moment it came out of my mouth, was just what I was hoping for.

"It's just down Fort Eddy Road, and we can take turns driving so we'll save on gas," she said, grabbing some waters to deliver to her table. "Besides, they've got a liquor license. The tips'll be great!"

I was in. And in two weeks' time, we both started our new jobs. The pay was 90 cents an hour, plus tips.

The very first night I knew I'd made the right decision. The work was no harder than the place I'd been working at, but the clientele was much classier. For the first time I had a bird's-eye view of how "the other half" lived—the ones who could afford to drop thirty bucks on a bottle of wine—a big price back then—and eat Oysters Rockefeller. The hotel was a hotspot for politicians throughout the region, and everyone who was anyone in New Hampshire ate there, poring over newspapers while dining alone, talking politics over steaming bowls of Beef Burgundy with other men in suits, or making high-powered deals over a steady stream of cocktails. I saw how they dressed, how they ate, and how they talked to each other, and began to see a world I'd never seen before, one where people didn't scream at each other or shovel food into their mouths as fast as they could before returning to work to punch a time-clock. It was a world I'd only dreamed of, and now here I was, smiling my way right into it—and into much bigger tips.

But the guys weren't any better than the ones at the diner who'd grabbed my ass while serving them Salisbury steak and mashed potatoes. I had to deal with some of the dirtiest politicians who were traveling through the state, away from their wives for weeks at a time, running their hands up my leg or making crude comments intended to test just what they could get away with. They treated the waitresses at the hotel like horses at the racetrack, literally betting against each other about how far they could go before we would complain. Even though my husband was no longer watching, I had to watch out for myself. I learned early on not to stand too close to the tables as I took a dinner order or there'd inevitably be some jerk who would reach up and pull the big brass loop that dangled from the front zipper of my waitress uniform. I also learned how to talk back in a way that put them in their place but didn't challenge their egos—a skill I'd learned from five years of marriage to a man who'd haul off and backhand me if I challenged him.

"Now, you know better than to talk like that, judge," I'd say with a wink while brushing his hand away, "you know those thoughts are against the law in most states!"

Retorts like that always brought a laugh and as I learned to make them laugh, I started to lose some of my fears about setting boundaries. I also began to lose some of the low self-esteem that had been building for years, first as a teen in my dad's house, then as a young wife in Dick's castle. And as my self-esteem grew I realized that some of my customers were easier to talk to than my own husband, who was growing so moody that nothing I said or did ever pleased him. I hadn't been working at the hotel for long when he knocked me right into a snowbank for no better reason than I asked him to please stay home one evening and spend some time with the family.

About the only time he was happy it seemed was when he was leaving for work in the evenings, a job he said we still couldn't afford for him to give up. Still, crazy as it sounds now, I wasn't ready to give up on my marriage no matter how much I wished I'd never gotten into it.

I was ready to give up on a few of those slimy customers, however. While most could be kept under control with a bit of flirtatious boundary setting, there was always the occasional creep who wouldn't give up. One night a particularly lecherous jerk was really testing my patience.

"Come here, honey," he called from two tables away, long after he'd finished his meal. "Our glasses are half empty and your pitcher's so full! Why don't you come here and pour us all some more water! That's right, honey, bend over while you do it so I can get a good look at those two girls of yours!"

I dutifully poured him and the two men with him some water but did my best to avoid his gaze. He was hideous to look like, with the face of an ostrich and breath like an old sock. He'd been in several times before and all the waitresses knew and feared him. He worked for the Liquor Control Board, and although I was always careful not to serve minors, just knowing he could yank our liquor license at any time made me extra careful to please him, even though I hated every minute of it—something my face could barely conceal.

"Come on, sweetie, let's see your smile! You know you'd better be nicer to me or I could make trouble for you . . ." His bony hand ran up my leg and I felt his fingers press into my thigh, while the other guys laughed loudly. I prayed he didn't leave any bruises or Dick would only add to them when I got home.

I stepped back, brushing his hand away.

"Whoa . . ." he said, his eyes narrowing, "I was just checking to see if you're wearing pantyhose, and I see you're not. You know that's a violation of the hotel rules, don't you?"

"I'll be sure to wear them from now on, sir," I said, hoping he'd just pay the damn bill and be gone.

"I'll tell your boss to overlook it this time," he said, his leer returning. "You know he's a friend of mine, don't you?"

"Thank you," I said, "I appreciate it." The men continued to leer, clearly enjoying the show. "Can I get anything else for you gentlemen?"

"How about a little head?" he asked, and the other two men burst into laughter.

I felt my face burn red and turned and walked away. I went straight to the bar.

"A beer on tap," I asked the bartender. He poured it, the heavy foam floating atop the amber drink. Returning to the man's table, I plopped it in front of him. "Is that enough head for you?" I asked him.

The shock on his face was priceless. Now his friends were laughing *at* him, not *with* him. "I'll tell you what," he said, after slurping the foam like a dog lapping his dinner. By now he was so drunk I feared he'd fall face flat in the beer I knew I'd have to pay for. "I'll wait for you to get off work. We can have a drink together and talk about it, how's that sound?"

It sounded like a threat. But I thanked him again and told him my husband wouldn't like that.

"But we don't have to tell, do we?" he replied, his tongue flapping in his mouth like a foul ribbon of red. *No, not an ostrich,* I thought. *He looks like a snake. A dried, shriveled snake of a man who would slither out the door and return to his cave once he'd finished taunting me.*

"Have a good evening," I said, leaving their bill as I stepped away, praying I hadn't said anything to cost me my job.

A bit later, a man at a nearby table called me over. Not another one, I hoped, I only have the energy for one creep this evening. I forced a smile and went to the table, where I saw a short, cute dark-haired man who'd been in before. He was from Boston and staying at the hotel; I often saw him carrying a heavy canvas bag on his shoulder, which made his hips swing just the slightest. It was a camera bag, he'd once explained, and every time we chatted I thought what a kind, friendly man. I knew he was married, because he'd mentioned his wife and sons before, commenting on how much she spoiled the boys.

"Hey," he said, "I saw that man putting his hand on your knee. You know you don't have to take that from any guy."

I glanced toward the door and watched as the snake-man and his friends slithered away, into the darkness from where they'd come.

"Yeah, I'd like to dump his dinner in his lap, but what can I do? He holds the liquor license to this place, and he keeps threatening to take it away." I told him about the man wanting to wait for me after work, doing my best to make light of it.

The cute guy didn't smile; I liked that. He looked caring and concerned. "Look," he said, "he's just showing off his power to impress the guys he's with. You're gonna run into jerks like that all the time, and you need to give 'em a clear message."

"I do that, and I'm out of a job," I said, relaxing as I began clearing his salad plate away. This guy was nice, but he didn't get it.

"No, here's what you do." A mischievous look crossed his face and I leaned closer to hear more. "One smart way to turn these jerks off is when they start messing with you, just say to them, here's my number."

"Give them my phone number!? How's that going to turn them off? That would only turn them on—and my husband sure wouldn't like it!"

"No, no, the number you give 'em isn't really your own. Let them dial the number—and reach an abortion clinic!"

We howled at the idea, and even though the closest place for a legal abortion was New York, it was close enough that I could pull it off. I thought it was crazy, but I also thought I might give it a try one day (though I never dared).

The rest of the evening as I served the kind man his meal, we chatted about his boat and he told me how much he loved to sail. I felt such a relief to meet a man who treated me with so much respect and compassion.

When he paid his bill, I noticed he'd left a generous tip, along with his business card. His name was George Resnik and his card indicated he was a fashion photographer. I slipped the tip into my pocket and just as I was about to slip the card in, as well, I noticed he'd written something on the back of it.

His hotel room number.

The fury that shot through me was greater than the fury I'd felt when the snake-man ran his bony hand up my leg, greater than the fury I'd felt when all the men had leered and grabbed and suggested that for the pleasure of serving them their dinner I should be thrilled to play with their pricks. I was livid.

After I got off work, I went straight to George Resnik's room, ripped his damn tip in half and slipped it under his door. Then I went home.

But I kept his business card.

To this day I don't know why. But that little business card would change my life forever.

Chapter 3

Beating the Bat

“ichael Garland!” I hollered, racing across the living
room and snatching Cinnamon from my son's hands.
Michael was trying to get the dog to kiss his baby sis-
ter, who was crying at the sight of a giant dog face moving in on her. I
put Cinnamon down and picked up Shelley, patting her back to calm
her as I hurried to get ready for work.

“I want her to kiss Cinnamon!” he protested, annoyed that I'd
spoiled his mission.

“Darlene!” Dick hollered from the bathroom, “When was the last
goddamned time you bought me a new razor?” His temper was rising
and if I didn't get out of the house soon, all hell would break loose.
Since going back to work it was hard to keep up with the shopping,
much less the housekeeping, the laundry, the cooking and everything
else I had to do. Just as he started to bitch about the state of the bathtub
that I hadn't cleaned in a week, Julie came to the door to pick up the
kids. Saved by the bell, I handed both kids off to her along with Shelley's diaper bag and Michael's toys and a change of clothes. No sooner
had they left than Deborah was honking outside and I gave Dick a

quick peck on the lips, told him I loved him and would get him a new razor tomorrow, and jumped in her VW bug.

"Go!" I urged her and we looked at each other like a couple of bank robbers and drove off laughing.

"Oh, Deborah, I love my job but I don't know how much longer I can keep up without collapsing. I don't think I've had five minutes to myself since I started working." It was true; I was burning the candle at both ends and it was our daily commute to work that brought me my only quiet in the day.

"Welcome to the club," she said, glancing at me with a conspiratorial grin. "But at least we're making our own money and not having to ask our husbands for it."

"That's a fact," I agreed, "but it seems like no matter how good the tips are, it all goes faster than it comes in!"

"Well, I find that hard to believe," she said, "seems to me you're flirting your way straight to the bank!"

A flash of shame and anger shot through me. Deborah and I had been friends almost as long as I'd known Dick—our husbands were friends and the four of us socialized fairly often. She knew I was faithful to Dick, and she knew how we were treated at work. But Deborah was quite religious, and as much as I enjoyed her company, there were certain things that she was quick to judge on, and women's behavior was at the top of her list.

She was also a big-boned girl, with a lot of extra weight. While she still took her fair share of harassment, I seemed to get more than my fair share. I did what I could to discourage it. I wore hardly any makeup, kept my long, dark hair tied back in a ponytail and as I've said, I wasn't one for smiling. Still, it wasn't my face they were staring at or reaching for. Deborah knew that if I talked back too harshly, I wouldn't have a job. I wished I'd never told her about delivering the beer to snake-man or reading the message on the back of George Resnik's card.

"You know I'm just trying to survive, Deborah."

"I know; I'm just teasing you, Darlene, don't take it personal. I know you need the money, God bless you."

"Yes, and I know you need it, too. We both do."

"Amen to that! Pete's talking about expanding his business now that I'm working, and that just means we'll both be working that much harder."

"I don't know how you do it, Deborah," I said, "no matter how crazy it gets at work, you seem to stay so calm. It must be your faith."

"That and a little of mother's little helper," she said, glancing again at me, this time with a wink.

"With *what?*" I couldn't believe what she just said. Was Deborah taking drugs?

"Relax! They're harmless. I get them from my doctor. Here, hand me my purse."

I reached down on the floor of the car where she'd set her macraméd purse and as she drove with her left hand, she reached over with her right and riffled through her bag, pulling out a small prescription bottle.

"Here, you can have these. Take a couple of these and you won't care what the kids are doing, or Dick is screaming about."

I held the bottle in my hand and noted they were Valium. I'd heard about those, but I didn't want to start taking drugs to keep me going.

"No, Deborah, I can't. Besides, these are yours."

"Don't worry about it, Darlene, I've got plenty! Really, take them. You'll thank me."

I had no plans to take them but, like George Resnik's business card, I slipped the bottle into my pocket.

We drove the rest of the way in peaceful, blissful silence.

I hadn't been on my shift long before George Resnik appeared at one of my tables. I was determined not to chat with him, but to just take his order and earn my tip. Rather than being embarrassed or upset, however, it was clear he was delighted to see me.

"Why'd you rip up my tip?" he chided me, clearly having enjoyed my little temper tantrum on the other side of his door.

"I'm here to work, not go up to some guy's hotel room," I said. "You acted like you were concerned about the way that guy was treating me, and then you hand me that great big tip and your room number like I'm some call girl!"

He laughed softly and shook his head, then apologized, explaining that he left the room number on his card in case the guy from the Liquor Control Commission had been waiting for me outside when I got off work.

"Darlene, I wasn't hitting on you; I love my wife. It just sounded like he might've been trouble and I thought you might need some help. And I left that big tip so you could get some pantyhose!" He winked, and the gentle look on his face was enough to convince me he was being sincere. I softened and took his order, but before he left, he asked if I'd ever done any modeling.

"Who, me?" I asked, laughing. "I'm not that glamorous, I'm afraid."

"Don't sell yourself short," he said, "You're very photogenic. You could make good money modeling. You've got a great face and figure, and I can put you in touch with the right people."

I was flattered, but assured him I enjoyed my job and besides, I'd heard that line so many times before. Any girl with a pretty face and figure gets told by guys that she could be a model. Still, it made me feel good.

"Look, you could use a break. I'll even take the headshots for free."

"Thank you, I'm flattered, I really am, but I don't think it's for me."

"Well, give it a thought. If you change your mind, all you have to do is show up at my studio in Boston. I even have a friend of mine who works for a top modeling agency, and I'll ask her to take a look at them. What've you got to lose?"

What I had to lose was my faith in a good man, if he pulled anything—as well as my husband who wouldn't like the idea of me going to Boston one bit. But I thanked him again for his interest and finished my shift. It was the end of my workweek and I had a couple of days off. I looked forward to spending them with Dick and the kids once I had a good night's sleep.

The shift had been a relatively calm one, and with my conversation with George Resnik erasing my anger from the night before, I left work in a far better mood than I'd had when I started the day. The next day was Saturday, and though I worked every other weekend, this one I had off. I looked forward to finally spending some time with my kids. The day was hectic, and began with Dick taking off on his motorcycle, little Shelley clinging to his legs, pleading with him not to go.

Shaking her off as if she were a yapping dog, he left without a glance toward his daughter, but I took the kids to a park by the Winnipesaukee Lake, and we had a great time playing together and even had a small picnic. It was warming up after a long, cold winter, and it felt wonderful just getting out of the house, not having to work, and being a regular family playing by the riverside. Well, regular minus their dad.

We got back about mid-afternoon and it wasn't long after that that I heard Dick's motorcycle pulling in the drive.

"What in the world does he have with him?" I said out loud, drawing the kids' attention. I have no idea how he'd done it, but he managed to bring a little boy's Schwinn bike back on that motorcycle.

"Daddy!!" Michael cried out as he saw the shiny bike. "Is that for me!?"

"Of course, it's for you," Dick answered, untying it from the straps he'd jerry-rigged on the back of the seat, "You don't think I'm going to ride the damn thing, do you?"

Just then, a terrible clatter sounded as the bike fell onto the ground and Dick screamed bloody hell, cursing up a storm.

"God dammit! Jesus Christ, just look at what that damn thing did to my bike!" I hurried to see what the problem was, but all I could see was a small nick on the chrome, nothing that anyone would notice.

Little Michael was so eager to ride his new bike, but as he drew closer, Dick's rage pushed him back and I ached to see my little boy so happy one second and so frightened the next. Doing my best to calm Dick down, I said, "I think it looks fine, honey, and look how happy you've made Michael."

"It isn't fucking fine, Darlene! For Christ's sake, you're such a fucking idiot! It's fucked up my bike and probably cost hundreds."

"What are you talking about?" I asked him, bewildered.

"My fucking bike was worth hundreds more before this fucking piece of junk fell on it!" He tossed the new bike across the lawn and Michael burst into tears. As I went to get the bike off the grass, Dick grabbed me and flung me aside with the same force he'd flung the bike. Then he marched into the house, slammed the door, and in moments, was heading back out the door again, dressed in his police uniform.

"I'm going to work. Someone in this family has to serve the community to pay for all this fucking shit!" And with that, he got in the car, slammed the door and took off.

I got Michael onto his new bike as Shelley and I watched him ride up and down on the sidewalk, each of us stunned into a performance of joy.

Determined to enjoy what little time I had left of my weekend off, I invited Deborah to spend the evening with me and the kids.

We must have talked for hours, swapping stories, drinking wine and carrying on like the girls we once were before we'd married. And before life had become just a series of nonstop arguments or efforts to avoid those nonstop arguments.

"I don't know, Deborah," I said after my second glass of wine, "I knew marriage was going to be tough, but I never thought there would be so much fighting. We never fought like this before we got married; now we can't even choose a movie to watch without a fight. How do you and Pete manage to be so happy all the time? It seems like you never disagree. What's your secret?"

Deborah laughed. "You want to know our secret?"

"Prayer?"

"Well, yes, there's that!" she agreed. "But we found something that works even better. Years ago, when we first got married, we made a promise to each other that if the argument ever became too heated up, one of us would strip nude."

"How would that change the situation?" I asked her, utterly confused.

"Have you ever seen two fat people trying to have an argument while one of them is naked?" Deborah answered.

We howled in laughter at that one, as I imagined her trying to fight with a naked fat man. Imagining fighting with my naked husband was even more impossible, given how good he looked when he was naked, and how scary he looked when he was mad. We agreed that naked either way, fat or thin, it was an entertaining way to keep the marriage alive.

By the time she was ready to leave, I'd put the afternoon's incident behind me and was looking forward to seeing Dick when he got home and sharing my good mood with him.

As I hugged Deborah goodbye and stood in the doorway watching her get into her car, a bat flew into the house, like Dracula come to visit. I quickly got little Shelley out of the way and went to the phone. I wasn't prepared for battling a bat, but since Dick was on patrol, I knew he wasn't far. I'd give him a call and ask him to drive by the house and get rid of the bat.

But when I called the police station, I was told he wasn't scheduled for duty that night.

If he wasn't on duty, then where was he? It finally dawned on me that all those nights he was out "working," he was really out with another woman. What else could it be?

Boy, did I feel like a fool. He might be putting on his uniform to serve the community, as he said, but the only servicing he was providing anyone was from the waist down. An image of that "milk stain" on the front of his pants flashed through my mind. How naïve I was! A milk stain! I walked over to Michael's room, grabbed a baseball bat and went back into the living room. I would have to come to my own rescue and get that bat out of the house myself.

My happy mood had turned to such fury so fast that the poor bat didn't stand a chance. Boom! It was history. Then I took the baseball bat and another glass of wine and sat on the front porch, waiting for Dick to come home.

As I waited in the hot summer night for my philandering husband to come home, the same old thoughts kept running through my head. *Didn't Dick say he would always take care of me? Didn't he promise to love and honor me? Didn't he respect me when I told him I didn't want an open relationship?* Apparently, he hadn't; he hadn't done any of those things. He left me alone to take care of the kids while he was out screwing around.

As my cheating husband pulled into the driveway, I watched him get out of the car and started giving him hell. I told him I'd called him at work and he wasn't even working that night.

"What crazy goddamned ideas did you put into your head this time?" he yelled, storming up the front steps. "I *wasn't scheduled* to work the main office tonight. I had to chaperone a dance club!"

"A dance club?" I shouted back, not caring if I woke the neighbors.

"Yeah, a dance club! The Outer Limits! That's why I'm late so often. They don't let me patrol, because I'm only part-time. So instead they send me out there to work with all the drunks and I can't come home till after closing. You think that's what I wanna be doing?"

I followed my husband back into the house and shut the door.

And started stripping off my clothes.

Chapter 4

Heartbeats

When I was in high school, my dad and I fought constantly. He didn't think I was his daughter, because I looked nothing like him, or like anyone else in the family for that matter. That may have had something to do with the fact that my mother had been married to another man when she got pregnant with me.

The way the story goes, my mother confessed to her husband Jimmy that she was having an affair and was pregnant with her lover's child. Jimmy forgave her, however, and vowed to raise the child as his own. But my mother couldn't get my father out of her mind. He was a handsome World War II war hero who danced like Fred Astaire and had swept her off her own Ginger Roger's feet. They were hopelessly in love.

She did her best to forget my dad and be a good wife to Jimmy. Then one day during her pregnancy, she was riding in the car with Jimmy when they both spotted my dad in his car. Jimmy told my mother to get out of the car and tell my dad to stay away because she and Jimmy were going to make their marriage work.

She obediently got out of the car, walked around to the passenger's side of my dad's car, and sat in the front seat to tell him it was over.

A few minutes later, as Jimmy waited for her to return, they drove off together and my mother never went back to poor Jimmy.

It was a touching love story, aside from the heartbreak of Jimmy, but the fact that my mother had been married when she got pregnant had always colored my relationship with my father. He was convinced I wasn't his, and his "proof" was that all the other kids looked like him, but I looked just like my mother.

It wasn't until I finally had Michael, who looked so much like my dad that there was no mistaking I was his child, that he finally accepted I was his. Until then, however, my dad was so convinced I wasn't his daughter that he did nothing to conceal his rage at my existence. When I was in high school and it had been time for me to start thinking about college, even though I had the grades, my father wouldn't consider it. College was no place for girls, he said. His only interest was in seeing my little brother Danny continue his education—but that plan had been shattered when my dad promised to take Danny fishing, but spent the day drinking instead. Waiting outside the American Legion Hall for my dad to come out and head to the lake, Danny grew bored and jumped on his bicycle. Minutes later, he lost control of his bike and slammed into a car and at the age of 15, my sweet little brother would never walk again without assistance. His spine and pelvis were crushed.

Colleges weren't exactly accessible to the disabled back in the early seventies, so Danny never did get that education my dad had planned for him. As for me, I had dropped out of high school, figuring there was no point in getting a high school diploma if I couldn't get into college. Instead, I married the handsome lumberjack I'd been dating and had my babies. By the time I started working at the hotel, I knew nothing about the real world.

But that was about to change. Working the tables became my higher education.

I was exposed to professional women who took their careers as seriously as any man—if not more so. I overheard conversations about the Vietnam War, what was wrong with it and why we needed to get out. Boys just out of high school were being drafted right after graduation and sent to a foreign land to die for something no one was really sure of—at least Danny would be spared that experience. The deaths in Vietnam were mounting daily. It sure wasn't the war my father had fought in, when they knew what they were giving their lives for.

Instead of listening to housewives talk about Hamburger Helper, I listened to professional women talking about serious issues, about the law or journalism or politics. Politicians were discussing campaigns and how to win them, and by January 1971, George McGovern had announced he was running for president and running for president meant focusing on the New Hampshire primary. And the New Hampshire primary meant getting together at the best hotel in town. Serving tables was the next best thing to sitting in on college classrooms—it was opening my eyes to all kinds of issues all over the world and I was loving every minute of it.

It was just as my tableside education was gaining ground and my eyes were opening to the problems our country and our world were facing that an Italian television crew arrived to cover the primary. Unlike so many groups of men, these men were refined and polite, but still a lot of fun to be with. I'd serve them their meals or drinks and they'd tell me about the stories they'd covered throughout the world, especially here in the States. I soon realized that they had probably seen more of my country than I had, and knew more about it, as well. Talking to them, I realized that there was a whole other world outside New Hampshire— a world I'd never really considered, having spent my whole life in one of the smallest states in the country, caring for my husband and children, and now helping out with my disabled little brother. Dreams of this foreign land that was my country began to take hold, and with each veal scallopini I served to the crew, and with each cheap Chianti I set before them, I fantasized about all the cultures and adventures I was missing out on.

One Saturday afternoon, as I was shopping for Carole King's new album, *Tapestry*, I ran into one of the Italians, Angelo. Angelo was a news cameraman who looked like the pop star Ricky Nelson; he was kind and gentle and with his dark eyes and sexy smile, he was easy to look at, as well. We got to chatting, and he asked if I knew a good place for him and the crew to unwind later in the evening.

"I know just the place," I told him, thinking about the dance club where Dick worked. "It's called The Outer Limits; my husband works security there and he says it's real popular."

"Alright then, that's where we'll go. And will we see you there, *bella dona?*"

I blushed. The first time one of the crew called me *bella dona*, I heard *belladonna* and thought they were saying I was poison! But I learned it just mean beautiful woman and hearing the words from Angelo's mouth completely charmed me.

"No, I can't. I have kids and—" Angelo cut me off before I could continue.

"You can find a babysitter, can't you?"

I hesitated only a moment before I thought, why not? I could ask one of my sisters to watch the kids, and lord knows I hadn't been out in ages. I could even take Danny—he'd been mastering his braces and crutches like a champ and loved to dance, leaning on one crutch and swinging the other to the rhythm of the music. Girls loved dancing with him. And wouldn't that surprise Dick for us to show up while he was working. He'd been complaining lately about how many hours he had to work and said the reason he wasn't able to give me any attention was because he was working so hard. Instead of staying home complaining about being neglected, I could surprise my husband and spend some time with him while he chaperoned at the dance club. I'd never even seen the place he worked, so it was high time I paid him and his work a bit of attention.

I promised Angelo I'd get a sitter and see him at the club, but I kept my plans a secret from Dick. After all, the *Cosmo* magazine was always reminding women that we had to keep some mystery and surprise in our marriages if we wanted them to work. As soon as Dick left for work that evening, I put on a sexy dress, took the kids to Julie's, picked up Danny and headed to the Outer Limits. I kept imagining how surprised Dick would be to see us—he adored Danny almost as much as I did.

Well the surprise was on me the moment we passed through the door. My husband was not checking ID's in the doorway or, for that matter, anywhere on the dance floor. I looked everywhere but couldn't find him.

"Don't worry, Darlene," Danny said, "he'll show up. Let's dance!"

Spotting Angelo on the other side of the dark club, gesturing for us to join them, I figured Danny had the right attitude. We'd come to dance, so we would dance. Besides, Dick would show up soon enough. After greeting Angelo and sharing a drink with him and the crew, Danny and I headed onto the dance floor and we started dancing to the beat of Diana Ross & the Supremes.

I've always loved to dance. That was one thing that I got from my father that I treasured—his love of dancing. I'd watch the way he and my mom would spin around dancing and dipping while Glenn Miller played on the record player, and I knew they were in love.

I was having a ball when I saw my husband. But there was no look of joyous surprise in his eyes. He was enraged.

"Go home, now, Darlene!" he shouted at me through the loud music and heavy percussion of the dance floor.

"No, we just got here!" I screamed back at him, still dancing, as he reached for my arm and grabbed it, nearly knocking me over.

"Let go of me! I came here to have a good time!" I shouted.

"Get the hell off this dance floor, *now*, Darlene!"

I was utterly humiliated and confused, wondering why he was so furious, when my eyes focused on a lone girl standing a few feet away on the dance floor, watching us. The dance floor lights illuminated the tears falling across her cheeks, and it was obvious for anyone to see—including my little brother and Angelo—that she was crying to see her man with another woman—and that other woman was me, his wife.

I realized in that moment, that I recognized her. I'd been running errands with the kids one day when I ran into Dick. He was talking to her and introduced her as Sheila. I asked who she was and he just said someone whose power lines he'd repaired and he was just giving her directions. Now I realized that he'd been seeing her for months.

I nodded to Danny and we left the dance floor, and in moments, we were outside.

"Come on, Danny, let's just get out of here," I said, hurrying my brother to the car. I couldn't get out of there fast enough

"Slow down, Darlene!" I heard him yelling behind me, but I was so devastated, his cries just didn't register. Then I heard an unmistakable *thwack!* I spun around and *bam!* I fell flat on my butt, and there was my little brother, crutches akimbo. We'd both slipped on the ice and landed in a snowbank.

After a moment, I began to laugh. "Come on, Danny, my ass is getting cold!"

"I wish I could feel it," he said. Though it was said in good humor, his words thrust through me like a knife. Dick's infidelity was a terrible pain. But helping my little brother get to his feet, feet he could no longer feel, was humbling. He couldn't even feel his own ass, and all I could think of was I was married to one.

"Come on, Danny, let's go home," I said again, this time in a different tone. This time gently, humbly. As I helped him to the car, his words still haunted me. If he couldn't feel his own ass, he couldn't feel his own penis. Here I was furious at Dick for using his, while my poor little brother would never know that feeling. We each had our own wounds to bear, and while mine was tearing me up, I knew my pain wouldn't last a lifetime. Danny would never feel any pain at all below his waist. He'd never feel anything at all.

As for confronting Dick with the scene I'd witnessed on the dance floor, I knew it would do no good. He'd just deny it. He'd tell me I was crazy and jealous and imagining the whole thing.

But I needed to know the truth.

The next morning, after putting the kids down for a nap, I went up to Dick and asked him to lie down with me. It had been a long time since we had made love and I wanted him to be as relaxed as possible before putting my plan to work.

I had no problem getting him to follow me into the bedroom. He'd been in a happy mood all day, no doubt because he was convinced he'd gotten away with his little affair even though I'd caught him red-handed the night before.

And I had no problem enjoying the feel of his muscular body beneath my hands, against my own soft body. I loved that man's body as much as I was growing to hate the man inside it.

After we made love and lay beside each other on the bed, I placed my hand on his heart as tenderly as I could. He was practically purring, he was so relaxed.

And that's when I said it.

"Sheila."

Just one word, and he froze. But he couldn't stop his heart—his heart started beating so fast that I thought it would shoot right through his chest.

There was no denying it now. He knew I was onto his affair.

He'd been betrayed by his own heart.

How fitting.

Of course, he tried to blame it all on me. He claimed that my refusal to have an open marriage had forced him into it. He even said he was using Sheila as his "wife" at the Outer Limits, because it turned out that this dance club was for swingers! I sure hadn't known that when I suggested Angelo—and especially my little brother, Danny—go there!

As for Angelo, I didn't see him for a while after that, which was just as well, since he'd seen the whole thing and I was so embarrassed. As the weeks went on, our household returned to some shade of normalcy, but I knew I would have to find the courage to move on, one way or another. It was also clear to me that the job of supporting my children and providing them a healthy home and environment would fall on me. I had to figure a way out of this unhappy marriage, because I sure as hell couldn't trust my husband anymore, and it was clear that neither of us believed in our marriage, much less our vows.

After a few weeks, Angelo dropped in at the hotel and asked if I'd like to talk sometime. I could tell by the gentle look in his eyes that he was referring to that painful night. By that point I had held my emotions in check and my mouth shut for so long that I hadn't even dared mention it to a soul. The pain was becoming unbearable, but maybe talking with a stranger like Angelo would help. So I said yes.

We met for drinks after work, and he ordered me a "Sambuca with flies." I had never had hard liquor before and couldn't imagine drinking what he'd just ordered.

"They're coffee beans," he said when the drinks arrived, three dark brown spots like little pebbles resting in the drink. "One is for prosperity, one is for health, and one is for your happiness." He lifted his glass in a toast, his face luminous with a playful mystery.

I took a sip, and it wasn't so bad. It tasted like licorice.

"Is good?" he asked.

"Oh, yes, yes, it's good," I assured him. I took another sip, and another, and soon my own face felt luminous and I relaxed. Telling this sexy man my private thoughts was feeling as easy as this sweet drink.

As we drank our Sambucas and ordered another, I told Angelo all about what was going on at home, and he listened with the patience of a therapist and the wisdom of a priest. This stranger from a strange land was slowly becoming a friend. But our friendship would have to wait because the next day he and the film crew were leaving, returning to their offices in New York City.

As I drove home that evening, I felt a strange mix of guilt and comfort. I may have been a faithful, married woman, but I was going to miss talking to this Italian gentleman with his long brown hair and thick mustache; he was a man who listened to me. None of the men in my life had ever listened to me, certainly not my father, who raged against me. Danny was so much younger, and he had his own concerns to deal with, so I certainly didn't pour out my heart to him, and he knew better than to ask. And my husband never even gave me credit for having a valid thought. The simple fact that someone seemed to care about me was a sign of hope.

But how would I support my children? Where would I go? As hard as I worked, my tips would never support a family of three, and a woman couldn't even get a mortgage without her husband's signature.

When I got home I went straight to my desk where I rummaged through the drawer until I found what I was looking for.

George Resnik's business card.

Chapter 5

Shoot Me

Iremember ordering escargot. I'd never before eaten a snail, but George assured me they were delicious. When the snails came, the aroma of garlic and butter irresistible, I had no idea how to eat them. George showed me how to hold the shell in the silver tongs the waiter had served them with, and as I tried to grab hold of one of the butter-soaked shells, it flew into the air and fell straight down onto my lap, staining my brand-new pantsuit.

We both burst out laughing. It had been an amazing afternoon, and I still couldn't believe all that had happened. The snail in my lap was the only real mishap of an otherwise remarkable day.

"I'm telling you, Darlene, you can make more in a day than you'd make all week waiting tables." George seemed as enthusiastic as I was about me launching a new career. So much had happened that my head was spinning.

"Are you sure they'll call?" I asked him. "Some of those girls at the agency were gorgeous. Why in the world would they want *me?*"

"Darlene, don't sell yourself short. You're a knockout, and this business is about how hard you're willing to work, how much crap you're willing to put up with, and who you know. You sure have mastered the first two by working your ass off serving jerks like that guy at the liquor control board."

"Well, you're right about that. But I don't know anyone in the modeling business."

"You know me," he said with a wink, setting his napkin on the table. "And if you'll excuse me, I have to make a trip to the john."

George went to the restroom and hadn't been gone more than an instant when a well-dressed, middle-aged woman approached my table.

"Excuse me," she said in a tone that automatically put me on guard, "I couldn't help seeing you dining with Mr. Resnik. How do you know him?"

I was so startled I could barely reply, but after a second of bewilderment, I looked her straight in the eye and said, "He's a professional fashion photographer and I'm a professional model. How do *you* know him?"

"Oh, everyone knows George Resnik," she said and, after gushing some false flattery about how she had thought she recognized me and I certainly was lovely, she departed. I watched her return to her table and lean closer to her dinner companion—another well-dressed, middle-aged woman—and share the juicy gossip her investigation had revealed.

I'd no sooner taken a sip of my wine when another woman approached me, this one dressed in a short turquoise dress with dangling earrings and fingernails painted bright orange. Her legs were so thin I wondered if they might break in half by the weight of her mascara.

"Are you modeling for Mr. Resnik?" she inquired.

By this point I was wondering if George had set me up for a prank, but the eager look on her face made it clear that she, too, wanted to know who I was.

"Yes, as a matter of fact, I am," I replied. "Now if you'll excuse me, I'd like to finish my dinner."

By the time George had returned, I had gone from waitress with some headshots to a full-fledged professional model who was making every tongue in the restaurant wag.

"What'd I miss?" he asked when he returned. "You look like you just discovered a pearl in the escargot. Your eyes are practically electric."

"I just discovered you're a very popular man, Mr. Resnik. And how to eat escargot." And with that, I very elegantly plopped a slimy slug into my mouth and smiled ever so imperceptibly. For the first time in years, I saw myself as something other than a wife and mother and waitress. I saw myself as just what the headshots said I was. Darlene Young. Model.

After George walked me to the bus station and said goodbye, I rode back up to New Hampshire with my head flooded with thoughts. So much had happened from the moment I'd gotten off that bus and found myself walking up to George's studio just two weeks earlier. I'd never been in such a big city as Boston before. Everything seemed to be moving so fast—the cars, the people, the sounds. Even the pigeons seemed to be in a hurry. I felt thrilled and awed and overwhelmed all at once. There really was a life outside of rural New Hampshire.

When I'd called George and told him I wanted to take him up on his offer of free headshots, he was true to his word. From the minute I walked into his studio it was all work. He posed me in all kinds of positions, most of which didn't feel normal at all, but he assured me would look good in a photo.

"Lean in, but keep your shoulders low," he'd say, pushing a shoulder down, pulling my chin forward. "Tip your head down, yes, like that, now look up, good, good, a little to the left, a little to the right, higher, lower, shoulders, turn your waist, hips straight ahead, head on your hands, softer, relax, smile, look up, look down, smile, no, not like that, like you mean it . . ."

Getting me to smile a natural looking smile was proving to be a challenge. Every effort I made either came out as a grimace or a ridiculous laugh. Finally, George taught me a trick.

"Don't look into the camera, look away. I'm going to count one, two, three, and as soon as I say three, turn around and smile. That will look more natural."

I tried it, and sure enough, it worked. Somehow that little trick caught my smile more instantly, before I had a chance to freeze it into place like a mentally unbalanced nitwit.

As nervous as I'd been when I first got there, he put me right at ease as he bent me this way and that, all the while click, click, clicking the camera, taking photo after photo after photo. But at first, to get me to relax, he'd given me a glass of wine, which he cautioned was something he didn't normally do.

"I know you're real nervous, so just this once, the wine might help relax you. But in the future, never have a drink, not even a glass of wine, before a shoot."

"Oh, George, don't be ridiculous," I told him. "I can handle a glass of wine and not be falling over."

"Oh, I know, it's not that. The wine makes your eyes look glassy. So for future shoots, no drinking. Got it?"

"Got it!" And to this day, I never have a drink before a shoot, no matter how festive the atmosphere may be.

I returned home on the bus at the end of the day, but now two weeks later, after he'd developed the film, I returned—for the big meeting he'd arranged with the Gloria Nash Agency. It was all happening so fast I didn't have time to even consider if I was making good decisions—it was as if the universe had just swept me up and plopped me down in an entirely different life in Boston.

When I got to the agency offices, nervously clutching my new portfolio that George had put together for me, I greeted the receptionist, introduced myself and was promptly escorted to Gloria's office. On the way, I passed several rooms. One had a stage and a makeshift runway, where someone was teaching some young girls how to walk, pivot and smile before a make-believe audience. I might become one of those girls myself, I thought, and I giggled inside just thinking of how silly I would feel to be preening like that.

Another office had a sign that said, "Drama Coach," and I asked the receptionist what that was for.

"Oh, that's where you'll learn how to land a commercial," she said. "All the girls want those!"

A commercial? I couldn't imagine myself in a commercial. And then I pictured myself dancing through a swanky apartment in heels and pearls, spraying Lemon Pledge on all the furniture with a look of pure bliss, and thought, sure, why not?

Another office was marked Makeup Room, and the receptionist explained that that was where we'd learn how to apply stage makeup.

"You'll need to learn," she said, looking my face up and down.

It was all so much more than just standing in front of a camera being told how to pose. I'd had no idea modeling entailed so much. Or that instead of feeling beautiful, the prospect of modeling would leave me feeling so plain.

Looking around at all the girls I soon realized that they were not like me. They were young and beautiful, and I was already a housewife with two kids and bills to pay and probably heading for a divorce. Just one look at them and I knew they had been told from infancy how special they were and how their looks could get them anywhere. I was told that my looks would only get me into trouble. I was told that my looks would only get me a husband. I was told my looks made it clear I didn't belong in my own family. I was never coddled or told I was special. And it sure never crossed my mind that my looks could land me on magazine covers, much less commercials. I'd dreamed of becoming a veterinarian and saving the lives of puppies. I dreamed of dressing in denim and rubber boots and going fishing. I didn't even like the feel of lipstick. To get me to wear lipstick, my mom would kiss me on the lips as I headed out the door, then pat my face and say, "There, that looks better." The minute the door closed behind me I'd wipe her lipstick off my lips. I hated it.

I just wanted to turn around and walk back out the door as fast as I could. But George had gone to a lot of trouble to set up this interview for me, and I didn't want to disappoint him. Still, I felt like I didn't belong there. Not just because I couldn't possibly compete with such beautiful girls, but because I was so far from home—what if my kids needed me? My sister was going to pick them up after school and watch them until I got home, but what if something happened? How could I get back to them in time? It would take nearly two hours to get back home on the bus. What was I thinking by going to Boston to become a model? It was ludicrous.

I felt so alone. But I also knew that if I turned around and walked back down the hall past all those rooms, the other models would wonder why I'd left. They'd think I wasn't good enough to get a contract, that Gloria Nash had sent me home. Of course, I probably *wasn't* good enough to get a contract, I figured, and Gloria probably would send me home, but I couldn't bolt out the door without giving it a shot. I had to at least go through the motions, and once I did that, I could go home and back to my ordinary, but familiar, life.

That short walk from the receptionist's office to Gloria Nash's office had seemed to take a lifetime, so many thoughts ran through my head. But once I made it to her office, my nerves seemed to vanish. She was old enough to be my mother, but she couldn't have been more different from my mom—who showed fear all the time. This woman sitting behind the desk with flaming red hair and striking good looks radiated power. And kindness. A rare combination, but one that immediately put me at ease and inspired me at the same time.

"Miss Young," she said, rising to shake my hand. I was used to shaking the hands of powerful men, but never before had a powerful, professional woman stuck out her hand to shake mine. "It's so nice to meet you. I was just looking over your portfolio and I see you're a Gemini, just like me."

That sealed the deal, and we hadn't even started discussing the contract. I already felt as if I'd found my own Gemini twin, this one so unlike who I was, but so like who I suddenly wanted to become. She looked like a woman who had just stepped off the cover of *Cosmo* magazine, and onto the cover of the brand-new *Ms.* magazine.

The script that had been forming in my head, of babbling out all the reasons I couldn't model—my kids, my age—I was already 23, practically ancient in the modeling world, even back then—my lack of poise and polish, my husband—none of those were things I could tell her. It would be way too much for her to handle and she wouldn't want to offer me a contract. The contract that just moments before had seemed so out of reach and so frightening, now seemed to be something I desperately wanted. I didn't want to leave that office with a rejection. I wanted Gloria Nash to like me, to like me well enough to sign me to her agency and turn me from a waitress into a model. My future was in her hands. And I could tell in just the softness of her face and the warmth of her words that she really understood how it felt to sit across the desk from someone who wanted to be a model.

"Delia, bring Miss Young a glass of water, will you?" she asked her assistant. Her tone was not at all commanding, but clearly designed to ease my obvious discomfort. Then she turned back to me. "How has your day been, Darlene?"

I stammered out something about how busy I'd been and how exciting it was to be in Boston, and how thankful I was that she was taking the time to see me, when she interrupted me.

"I'm the one who should be thanking you for giving our agency a shot," she said. "George told me you were a natural, and from the looks of these photos, and now seeing you in person, I see that he's right. Of course, he usually is."

I remained baffled, wondering how a woman of her position could possibly find someone as ordinary as me the least bit impressive. But as she spoke, my confidence began to blossom, and I kept thinking she was the kindest, wisest, most graceful lady I had ever met. Yet aside from all the kindness and grace, she had the power to make things happen—she had the power to change my life. I trusted her, almost instantly. I knew she wouldn't take advantage of me, like a man might have done if he'd been sitting behind her desk. Of course, I had no real reason to trust her other than George's endorsement and her friendly first impression. But as naïve as I was, growing up with an abusive, alcoholic father, and being married to an abusive husband, my instincts had been sharpened. And in this brief meeting, my instincts were telling me that I was safe.

And that I was going to walk out of that office with a contract signed by both of us.

And that's exactly what I did.

"Come on, I'll introduce you to the staff," Gloria said, rising from her seat, our business discussed, agreed upon and signed and notarized. "You'll get to know them pretty well because you're going to be taking classes here for awhile before we send you out on interviews."

"Classes? You mean like the makeup classes?" About the only thing I knew about makeup was to brush a little blue powder on my lids and peach blush on my cheeks for nights on the town.

"Yes, stage makeup, runway, posing. And of course, we'll teach you how to carry yourself, how to dress, how to smile. You look so somber, Darlene. You will need to learn to smile."

"I can smile," I said, smiling.

"You can pretend to smile," she said, "but you aren't really smiling. You're cautious, and that's understandable. But you don't really show your own joy. But don't worry, we'll bring it out of you; by the time we're done with you, you'll be smiling all the way to the bank!"

I genuinely smiled at that thought.

"And we'll work on your accent."

I didn't even know I had an accent.

"Don't worry. You're going to be brilliant! You have a natural beauty; that's what they're looking for these days. Monica, I'd like to introduce you to Darlene Young. She's one of our new models . . ."

As she introduced me around the office and showed me all the classrooms where I'd be training, my thoughts were swept away by all the things I'd have to learn. How would I be able to do it all? I still needed the steady income of my waitressing job, and I still needed to take care of the kids. What would Dick think when I told him what I'd done? I imagined he'd be furious. How would I learn to get rid of an accent I didn't even know I had? How would I learn to smile when I thought I'd known how to smile all my life and just chose not to do it? What was wrong with my posture?

But as I met one woman after another, I realized that I did want to learn to be as poised and elegant as they were. I did want to learn how to be as savvy as Gloria Nash. And I did want to succeed as a professional model, and not wait tables all my life.

By the time the day ended and I found myself eating escargot with George, my entire life had been upended and I was filled with fear, doubt and most of all, excitement.

Now I was heading home on the bus to face the music—I'd have to tell Dick what I'd done and figure out a way to get back and forth to Boston, work my shifts at the hotel, and be the wife and mother I was supposed to be. And learn to smile and lose my accent.

Chapter 6

Flour Child

The next couple of weeks passed more slowly than those snails had before they became escargots as I waited to hear from Gloria whether anyone wanted to hire me. But I was kept busy. I had to take classes on how to walk, pivot and stand, how to model in a showroom and a runway, hold products (and smile!), apply makeup and be charming, all the while waiting tables, taking care of my kids, house and husband, and staying beautiful and sensual, as *Cosmo* assured me I could and should do if I wanted to be happy.

I wondered whether, if the founder and editor of *Cosmo*, Helen Gurley Brown, had had children, her magazine would be so preoccupied with driving men wild in bed. Just once I would have liked to have read an article on "What to Say When Your Preschooler Catches You Giving Your Husband a Blowjob," "How to Have Mind-Blowing Climaxes While Trying to Write the Grocery List in Your Head," or "What a Dominatrix Can Teach You to Help Keep the Kids in Line." Somehow all the liberating advice that *Cosmo* had to offer presumed that children were what other people had. Still, I read those articles as fast as they were published, ravenous for life tips that would keep my marriage together while at the same time helping me to escape it.

As for Dick, instead of being furious as I'd expected, he took the news of me signing with the agency and going through training as calmly as if I'd told him I'd signed up to sell door-to-door cosmetics.

"Great, now you can make some decent money," was about all he said. "Just be sure you don't fall behind on dinner and the kids. I didn't marry you just to have you spending your time on getting your picture taken!" Then he'd wrap his arm around my waist and whisk me off to the bedroom. I soon got the message—here's the sexy payoff for being a career woman, but there's a price to be paid for your liberation. In other words, Dick wasn't about to clean the house, cook the meals, do the shopping or take care of the kids, but he was happy to have me making money. And as for that extra money my tips brought in, it appeared to be going to the new Harley he brought home. Just keep your mouth shut, Darlene, I told myself, just keep your mouth shut and keep the battles at bay.

The training was a crash course in becoming someone different. I so rarely wore makeup that I had to learn everything from scratch. It wasn't that I'd never wanted to wear makeup. In fact, when I turned sixteen and was finally allowed to wear it, I was so excited I went straight to J. J. Newberry, the five and dime in Tilton, and bought my first Cover Girl foundation. I was so excited to show my friends in high school that when we were all gathered in the bathroom, I fumbled as I pulled it out of my purse and it dropped in the bathroom sink, shattering it—and shattering me. I felt so terrible, and I knew my parents wouldn't give me the money to buy any more. So I did something that taught me a big lesson, a lesson that haunted me when I so much as thought about wearing makeup again.

After school was over, I went back to J. J. Newberry and stole a bottle of makeup. I had never stolen anything before and my heart was beating so fast that it's a wonder I got away with it. By the time I got home it bothered me so badly to think I had done such a thing that I had to confess to somebody. I wanted to tell my mom, but I didn't want her to be disappointed in me, so I couldn't tell her. But what I could do was tell my dad because he didn't like me anyway, so I figured it wouldn't change his opinion of me.

I sat at the kitchen table, hating myself for what I'd done, and waiting for my dad to come through the door. The minute he did, I had a change of heart. His big body filled the whole doorway and suddenly I was scared. Stealing was a serious offense and I knew he'd be very upset with me, whether he loved me or not. But I gathered up my courage and said, "Dad, there's something important that I have to tell you."

He looked at me with a face of utter shock. "Oh, my God, you're pregnant." There wasn't a spark of compassion in his expression as the disgust swept across his features in a flash.

"No," I said, my heart sinking, "I'm not pregnant. In fact, I'm still a virgin."

"Then what is it?" he asked, still void of any compassion, and not much interest either.

"Never mind," I said and went to my room. That was the last time I ever tried to talk to him again about anything important to me. Stealing a bottle of makeup suddenly seemed so minor compared to what he thought I really did, that I never did tell him.

And I never stole anything ever again.

Now here I was, seven years later and surrounded by bottles and palettes and tubes of makeup, more makeup than I'd ever had before me in my life. I learned how to match my foundation color to my skin tone, apply this "pancake" makeup as if my face was in need of a thick coating of batter, contour the hollows of my cheeks with a darker tint, set the whole thing with powder pressed into my skin with tissue, apply rouge to the apples of my cheekbones, highlight those with an even lighter color, paint my eyelids not just light blue, but with a deeper color on the corners and the crease, and then paint a thick band of eyeliner on my lash line with a chunk of mascara and some spit.

Back then there was really only one mascara and eyeliner available and that was Maybelline. It was a long waxy rectangle of black that came in a little red plastic case. You slid the top off and there was the skinny black rectangle and a tiny little brush that looked like a miniature toothbrush. You spit in the wax and used the little paintbrush to mix it in, then painted on a thick line that had to be expertly curved upward at the outer edge of the eye and perfectly tapered into a dramatic wingtip, for that sensual cat's eye look.

Then the little toothbrush was dipped into the waxy rectangle and brushed on the eyelashes. After that, we brushed Johnson's Baby Powder onto our lashes, and then another coat of mascara. But even though the other girls had no problem with it, the talcum powder burned my eyes. So I was told to use flour. Yes, that's right. Pillsbury All Purpose Bleached Flour was brushed onto my eyelashes every day. It was all-purpose alright, but I sure hoped I didn't go out in the sun on a hot day and start smelling like a piece of toast. But it worked, and since I had thick, dark lashes anyway, once the mascara was on, my eyelashes looked like a couple of spiders had settled on my lids and spread their legs wide open, which was exactly the look they were after.

Makeup wasn't all I had to learn. I'd never had a manicure or pedicure in my life, and now I had to keep my hands and feet in perfect condition at all times, in case I was ever called for a shoot at the last minute. If a nail broke, it was patched with tissue paper or covered completely with cheap plastic nails that were glued on. They were nothing like the acrylic or silk nails we have today. These things looked like guitar picks and were so fake looking that I feared if I so much as scratched an itch I'd break off a guitar pick. Whenever I washed dishes, I had to put lotion on my hands and wear rubber gloves. At night, after the kids were asleep, and I was so dog-tired all I wanted to do was crawl into bed and lapse into a coma, I had to put baby oil on my cuticles and push them back with a wooden orange stick, then slip my hands into white cotton gloves. Which made it hard to turn the pages of *Cosmo.*

Then there was the hair. I'd always worn my thick, dark brown hair in the style of the times—natural. I kept it washed and conditioned and woke up every morning and brushed it, maybe tying it back with a hair clip, scarf or some such thing. That was all there was to it, and I always received compliments on how beautiful my hair was.

Apparently, it was not beautiful enough for photos. I had to make my thick hair look thicker. So I was taught to lean over, put my head between my legs, brush my hair vigorously, then spray a shitload of

Aqua Net hairspray all along the back and along the roots. When I returned to an upright position, it would look like I had an even bigger head of hair, which would be curled into a flip or styled into a high-rise coiffure straight out of James Bond.

There was one woman in the training group who had hair like Farrah Fawcett, though this was a few years before Farrah Fawcett's hair was famous. She smelled real sweet and it made me realize I didn't even own a bottle of perfume and probably smelled more like fried chicken and baby shampoo. I felt so out of place. Everyone was so young and excited and every class was filled with chatter about sex and boyfriends and parents and the future. All I could think about was the past, even though I was only a few years older than they were, but those years had left their mark. While the Farrah girl gushed about how sweet her dad was all the time, all I could think of was the looks my dad gave me and the cruel things he'd say to cut me down. Everyone smiled so naturally and readily, but I could only smile on command. It never came naturally to me. The truth was, I'd never really had a youth, going straight from my father's home to my husband's home and having babies right away. It was killing me to be away from them so much, but I knew that one day of work would pay for a whole week of waiting tables, so I kept my mouth shut, didn't talk about guys or babies, and just did as I was told by the staff at Gloria Nash's. I was learning fast, but there wasn't a day of that training that I didn't wonder what in the world I was doing trying to be a model. How could I possibly make it when these young, single, childless girls who smelled like honeysuckle and roses were my competition?

Then there was the runway. I may have been a klutz at smiling and applying makeup, but when it came to the runway, I was practically a ballerina. Maybe it was all those years of learning how to duck, dive or spin full circle and get away fast when I sensed a man's temper was about to explode, but walking the runway, pivoting and turning came naturally to me.

The room we trained in wasn't all that big, but it had a makeshift runway set up, complete with a stage and some steps so we could learn how to walk up and down them with elegance and grace. We were taught to walk with our knees bent, our chin parallel to the floor, our arms swinging gracefully back and forth, and our bodies held at a certain angle so that the camera never caught our bodies head on. That way, we looked thinner, and in the wake of the Twiggy era, we could never be thin enough.

We were never to look down or from side to side, but always toward the camera, our eyebrows raised so that we looked interested, but not animated, our smiles pleasant and pleasing, but not grinning. And we were to come to a stop with our front leg bent provocatively, as if gently stepping on a naughty suitor.

Next came the Dior pivot. The Dior pivot was especially good for bridal gowns, which were so heavy and had so much fabric that almost all the models tripped over them when they turned, because the fabric wrapped around their ankles. But I took to it easily, learning to put my right foot in front of the left, make a complete 360-degree turn without taking a step, then continue down the runway, having revealed the entire dress, front and back, before even reaching the end of the walk. The trick was to hold the gown about a half inch off the floor as you made the turn so that no one could see you doing it, all the while looking straight into the camera.

Learning the runway was a blast—it was the most fun I had during training. But I also had to learn to pose for the camera, and once again I had problems. I had a habit of what they called "beating the flash." I instinctively blinked, making every photo come out as if my eyes were closed. I had to work really hard to train myself not to blink but instead, look directly into the camera every time—these were the days when every photo was expected to look like it came off the cover of Vogue, so I did my best not to blink, despite my lashes being heavy with flour and mascara.

Still, I couldn't get smiling down, so Gloria wanted to train me for other things. She thought I might be good with my hands, so I was taught how to hold a champagne glass without ever exposing the back of my hands, only my newly manicured nails, and how to hold cans of peas, cleaning supplies and the occasional invisible product to be spliced in at a later date.

And then I'd get back on the bus for the two-hour bus ride back to Concord, change into my uniform, wait tables all evening, then head back home, pick up the sleeping kids from my sister's, get home, tuck them into bed, take off all the makeup, and fall fast asleep in seconds. I wouldn't even hear Dick come home and climb into bed, unless he woke me for some pleasure, which he very often did do. But pleasure for me those days had nothing to do with anything I read in *Cosmo*. Pleasure meant going back to sleep, because the whole thing would start all over again by five in the morning. And still I didn't know if it would turn into anything. Gloria still hadn't sent me out on any shoots. The whole thing could turn out to be a spectacular waste of time, but at least I'd walk away knowing how to pivot in place while holding a glass of champagne and almost smiling. And how to apply flour to my lashes without blinking.

Chapter 7

The Babysitter

Each day that passed without a call from Gloria was another day I spent telling myself that no one wanted such an old model, one nearly pushing 25 with a couple of kids to boot. One day I'd be telling myself my future was secure, I was going to be a model! The next day I'd be kicking myself for thinking any such thing, convinced that I'd fallen for a pipe dream; no one wanted a near-quarter-century-old mom who couldn't even smile.

My marriage wasn't getting better, but it wasn't getting worse, since we only saw each other in bed or passing in the hallway. Sheila was history, as were Dick's days at the Outer Limits, and he spent most of his time working his two jobs, as a lineman and a part-time police officer. His hours on the force were picking up, and in the evenings and on weekends when he wasn't on duty at the mall he was at the police station. It seemed he had no time for affairs. And not much time for me or the kids, but at least he was staying out of trouble—and we were both too exhausted to fight.

All the while, however, in the faraway recesses of my mind I was hoping that Angelo would return so I would have someone to tell of my excitement about becoming a model. My mom had taken on a full-time job to help cover the costs of Danny's care since his accident. Between her caring for him and fighting with my father, there seemed no point in telling her about my adventures in Boston and the new career I hoped would happen. It had become hard to even visit her because she was aging daily and had grown so terribly depressed. The joyful, dancing mother of my childhood, the mother who swooned in my father's arms and danced with him like Ginger Rogers, so happy and in love, was long gone. And the woman who'd replaced her was increasingly a stranger. Those Friday Night Fights had turned into nightly fights as the years wore on, and now she was drinking right alongside my father, washing her life away with every sip as if that was all that could keep them together.

As for my sisters, they had lives of their own and we were so unalike that we never really had been close. They still watched my kids when I worked, but I didn't want to bring up the modeling because I feared it would only lead to resentment, and if I dared mention I was considering divorcing Dick, it would be just another topic of gossip. As for Deborah, she was just too damned religious to encourage any woman to model for a living. That would be like telling her I wanted to be a hooker. So I kept my plans to myself.

I did want to tell my dad, however. Oh, how I wanted to rub it in as revenge for all the cruelty he'd made me suffer on account of my looks. He always considered my looks evidence that I was another man's child, that I didn't belong in the family. And he always considered my looks something that would just lead to trouble. Now that my looks might actually bring me money, I wanted nothing more than to tell him. But, ever since that shoplifting confession I'd attempted, I knew better, so I said nothing.

I wished instead that Angelo would call, and the more I thought about telling him my good news, the more I thought about how much I'd like to see him. Somehow, rather than feel guilty for daydreaming about a sexy guy I barely knew when I had my own sexy husband to think of, the only guilt I felt was guilty pleasure. I wasn't ready for an open marriage much less a secret affair, but I hadn't been ready for Sheila or the milk stain, either. On the other hand, I sure was ready for fantasizing about a dreamy Italian who I hoped to see again someday.

Then one day, the call from Gloria came.

"Igotta gocy forya," she said.

She might as well have been speaking Martian.

"Can you say that again?" I asked, not wanting to sound unaware, but I was completely unaware.

"A go-see. I send you to the client, and you go see if they want you."

"Oh . . . I see. Okay, who's the client?"

"It's an aspirin company," Gloria said, dashing my dreams of selling Lemon Pledge in pearls and high heels. Also dashed were my dreams of selling something glamorous, like the pearls themselves, or that glass of champagne that would highlight my new beautifully manicured hands. Instead, I got aspirin.

"This will be an easy interview for you, since you never smile. If you need to look like you're in pain, just think of something sad and the pain will show on your face. That's what they're looking for. You've got the face for that."

I had the face for pain. Well, there was no arguing that. So I lined up my first interview for a modeling job, and sure enough, when they asked me to smile, not even George's one-two-three trick did the trick. Finally, I just thought of my brother Danny's horrible accident, of seeing him on the Stryker frame, the doctors telling us he'd be a paraplegic for life, and the tears started trickling down my cheeks. That was enough for the aspirin company to sign me on. I did such a good job feigning a headache, a hangover and a backache that the agency started using me more often for several small jobs.

And though the jobs were small, the pay was not. Just as George Resnik had predicted, the money I was making was exceeding anything I'd expected. I could finally afford to hire a babysitter to give my sisters a break. And they sure needed it. They were the ones who were pitching in for my mom with Danny's care, because I just didn't have a spare minute. I loved Danny with all my heart, but between waitressing, being a mom, and now modeling, I couldn't give him the care and attention he needed.

Not that he wanted me to. Danny was growing increasingly independent and wanted nothing more than to move out on his own. He didn't want us taking care of him—he wanted to take care of himself.

"No, Darlene, let me do it myself!" he would say every time I tried doing something for him, like getting him something I thought would be too difficult for him to get or helping him secure his braces. I could see that all the attention the family was giving him was no longer helping but hurting. He might not be able to walk unassisted, but like any young man, he needed to learn to take care of himself—and he needed to get out of his parents' home.

"I can't take it much longer," he told me one day when I was taking him on a trip to the mall. "I need to find some kind of job and get out and get my own place. They're fighting constantly, and I'm afraid Dad's gonna kill Mom. And I can't protect her anymore."

"Oh, Danny," I said, my heart breaking, "it's not up to you to protect our mother. She needs to protect herself and get out of there, and she's just never going to do that."

Danny sighed in exasperation. He knew it was true. Our mother had even gone so far as to divorce my dad one time, but no sooner was the divorce finalized than she went right back to him, convinced that he had changed. But he hadn't. After the honeymoon phase had ended, he went right back to treating her like his sweetheart all week long, then beating the shit out of her come Friday night. We all feared our father really might go too far one day and kill our mother—if she didn't kill him first. We'd tried talking her into leaving him for good, but she just wasn't going to do that.

The more I thought about my mother spending her life with a man who beat the crap out of her, the more I thought about not following in her footsteps. I had to get away from Dick. I just needed to muster up the courage.

But like my mother, that courage seemed to elude me. I thought about divorcing him every day and told myself that was why I was working. But divorce was failure. And divorce in a town the size of a schoolyard was scandal. And divorce was being on my own, with two small children to take care of—during a time when unmarried women couldn't even get contraception or credit cards. So, like my mother, I told myself it would get better. But it never did.

Now I had to tell Dick that it was time to hire a babysitter. He wasn't likely to take that well. He seemed to take my modeling in stride, but babysitters cost money, money that didn't go to him. I could just hear the argument. He'd forget that he'd had no problem with me working. Instead, he'd remind me I should be home with the kids, he'd remind me that I wasn't turning out to be the wife he'd expected me to be, he'd remind me that I had to make more money before spending it on a sitter. There was no way to win such an argument, but there sure were a lot of ways to lose it.

"Hey, that's great, babe!" he said when I proposed we hire someone to watch the kids. Like my fear of telling him about the modeling, the fight I'd anticipated over the babysitter had been all in my head. I needed to give Dick more credit than I gave him. Maybe the problem wasn't him as much as it was me assuming the worst of him. Maybe if I treated him better, he'd treat me better.

"You're not upset?" I asked him, seductively pressing against him in an effort to maintain his good mood.

"No, I think it's great you're making more money, and as for the babysitter, we can find a girl to watch the kids. Hey, I even know someone who might be interested!"

"You do? Who?"

"Her name's Brenda. Her mom had a car accident a few months ago and they brought her into the station. We tried to save her, but it was too late, she died. I had to take care of the paperwork and I've checked in on them a few times. Her dad's been having a rough time with her ever since."

I felt a pang of sympathy for a poor girl who'd lost her mother, and admiration for my husband whose part-time job with the police had him saving lives on occasion—even if this one couldn't be saved. "Oh, that's so sad. How old is she?"

"Old enough. I'll check with her dad and see if it's okay with him. Is that cool?"

"Sure," I said, thrilled that everything was going so smoothly. "You're sure she's mature? I don't want to leave the kids with some wild kid."

"Oh, she's quite mature," he assured me. "Maybe a bit too much. Her dad says she's been acting like a tramp lately. Maybe you could talk to her. She could use an older woman's guidance."

So I was an older woman, even in my husband's eyes. Well, at least he trusted me to provide some guidance to a teenager.

"You can teach her how to be a lady, that'd probably help a lot. She's a good kid, she just needs someone to set an example. And watching the kids might be good for her, get her out of the house, you know."

I couldn't imagine losing a mother at such a young age and thought Dick's idea sounded like a good one. I could help her, and she could help us. Delighted the babysitter issue had gone so smoothly, I agreed to meet Brenda and talk with her, and if all went well, she could babysit.

When I met her, I could see what Dick meant. She was very pretty, blonde with blue eyes and large breasts that would certainly attract the boys. And I could see in no time that she had quite the rebel streak in her. Without a mom to keep an eye on her, it would be no surprise if she was sneaking out every chance she got.

But she seemed sweet enough and was great around the kids, so I talked with her awhile and made it clear that she couldn't have any boys coming over when she was watching the kids.

"Oh, no, you don't have to worry about that," she assured me, "I get what you're saying, and I promise you, I won't have any boys over."

And that's a promise Brenda kept.

Unfortunately, as I was to discover.

With Brenda available to watch the kids through the summer, things were looking better and better. I'd be able to pay Brenda with the extra money I was making, and if the jobs kept coming in, I'd stop working at the hotel and put my focus on my modeling career.

I couldn't believe it. I was really becoming a model.

All thanks to the pain that showed on my face. That and a decent figure.

I began getting regular work with trade shows, modeling for Best Buy, the PGA golf tournaments, audio shows and that sort of thing. I even got work playing a patient for medical students. I'd lie in an icy cold room—apparently surgeries are performed in cold rooms so the surgeons don't drip sweat onto the patients—and lie there like I was getting my organs removed. When Gloria got me a show modeling bras, I was so embarrassed (and naïve) that I asked if I could wear a sweater over them! She said no, while casting me a withering look, and I learned to model bras as calmly as if I were modeling a swimsuit.

Eventually, Gloria landed me a shoot with a beer company and even better—I was about to become a poster girl! Just the thought of it made me laugh. I would be photographed for beer posters that would be distributed to colleges throughout the northeast. *Marilyn Monroe, move aside*, I thought! *This old mother of two is going to put you to shame!*

The shoot was a busy one and I had a wonderful time. I had to remove my wedding ring, because poster girls weren't supposed to be married, so for a whole day, I pretended to be single again. After a full day of shooting, I had to head straight to Concord, where I had another shift waiting tables before heading home. I thought it would be exhausting, but no sooner had I put on my uniform and hit the floor than who do I see sitting alone at a table but Angelo. No crew, just him, with a look on his face that was unmistakable. He was there to see me.

I was so happy to see him, and after flirting a bit with him and telling him about my day shooting for a beer poster, his joy at my success was just the shot of support I needed. The shift flew by I was in such high spirits. By the time my shift ended and Angelo had finished dinner, we were talking so happily that I found myself walking alongside him all the way to his room. I was feeling a powerful attraction to him, and every time he'd say anything in that thick Italian accent, I was attracted even more. And I could feel that he cared for me, genuinely. He had an unmistakable warmth and concern that I hadn't felt before from a man.

As we reached his door, I allowed him to give me a goodnight kiss and I was surprised at my reaction. I really enjoyed that kiss, and immediately felt like a female again. For so long I had felt anything but attractive to Dick. Though we still had sex, I felt more like his possession than a woman he wanted. I'd even stopped being aware of it—until that kiss from Angelo reminded me of what a kiss could do to a girl!

It wasn't long before the beer company was so pleased with the posters we'd made that they wanted me to go on a tour of campuses in Maine to promote their beer. I was told that the students were excited to meet the poster girl who was already hanging on the walls of their dorm rooms. I'd be going with one of the executives for the company, a short, chubby guy named Stu, who would chaperone me through the trip. Stu assured me I'd have my own room throughout the trip and all our expenses would be picked up by the beer company.

Dick didn't mind once I'd told him the daily salary I'd receive—which was more than I had ever dreamed—and Brenda could watch the kids while he worked.

The trip was a blast and I felt like a celebrity meeting all the young college boys who swooned the minute they saw me, like soldiers meeting Jayne Mansfield. I had to keep my wedding band off, of course, because I wasn't supposed to be married, and I had to pretend to be their age, but I don't think they really had their mind on my age. The cameras clicked, the boys rejoiced, the beer poured, and we had a marvelous time.

And through it all, I found myself talking on the phone every evening with Angelo, as he enchanted me with stories of his work. He worked for a television network based in the same building that housed the Metro-Goldwyn-Mayer Studios, which brought him into daily contact with all sorts of movie stars and producers. And his work had him meeting all sorts of politicians, New York celebrities, and practically anyone who was in the news. For a girl who'd grown up in the tiny town of Tilton, New Hampshire, listening to his stories was like listening to fairy tales—fairy tales made all the more magical told in an Italian accent.

But Stu, on the other hand, was turning out to be less the chaperone and more the letch. Halfway through the trip, I began to feel uncomfortable with him. He was becoming a lot friendlier and it was obvious he wanted more from me than just my smiling face. Despite being twice my age and thrice my size, he seemed to think I'd want him. Hopefully, I was misreading him.

When I shared my concerns with Angelo, hoping he'd reassure me it was all in my head, he did just the opposite. When I told him about the way Stu would stare at my breasts when he spoke to me, wink whenever he made a joke, or stand so close I could smell his sweaty armpits, Angelo confirmed my fears.

"He's trouble, Darlene," Angelo said, "He wants to get you into bed, and if he doesn't, he could cause you problems with the modeling agency. You need to be careful."

Though his words were intended to help, they hurt deeply. All my self-confidence seemed to dissolve just hearing those words, and my pride at my work took a nose dive. I had been feeling so good about myself, so confident in my emerging profession as a model, and had been so trusting of Stu as he escorted me from campus to campus, but now my trust in him, and in myself, was gone. One day I had been over the moon with joy and pride, and now I felt as if I'd been dropped *off* the moon. I just wanted to go home.

But I had a job to finish, so I prayed that I was mistaken about my employer's intentions and Stu did respect me. Just in case, however, I began to keep my distance.

The next couple of days went by rather fast and I loved meeting the college students and being on a college campus. I wished them all well in their studies and sincerely meant it. I saw my little brother Danny in each of these boys and wanted them all to succeed. And the more young men I met who loved meeting me, the poster girl, the more my doubts about Stu faded into oblivion and I felt as if I, too, were succeeding.

With the trip coming to an end and one more college to visit, Stu and I met in his hotel room late in the afternoon to prepare for the next and final day. As we were going over logistics, Stu abruptly shifted the topic and suggested we go out to dinner to a very expensive restaurant.

"To celebrate! You've done a great job and I want to reward you for all your hard work!" Again, the wink.

"Oh, thanks, Stu, but I didn't pack anything for a place like that. It's much too fancy. Let's just grab something nearby here. I'm pretty tired."

"I've already taken care of it," he said, his face glowing with pride. He walked over to the dresser, where a large rectangular box rested, the kind that comes from department stores. He brought the box over to me.

"Go ahead, open it," he said, nodding toward the box.

A red light started flashing in my head. I did not want to open that box. But I obediently complied, and after removing the top, I peeled away the tissue paper, to find a sheer, clingy, red dress with a neckline so low it was unmistakable what was on his mind.

"Go on, try it on," he said, urging me to slip into it for his own delight.

The red light that was flashing like a strobe light in my head was matched by a blinking yellow one urging caution. What was I going to do? He could ruin my career before it had even begun.

I was so frightened, I started to shake. He knew I was a married woman, but he also knew I was probably heading for a divorce because we'd talked about it on the two-hour drive to Maine. Oh, how I wished I hadn't said a word to him! Telling him I was unhappy in my marriage was like telling him I was up for grabs. His grabs—which I sure didn't want.

He also knew I needed the money and had to keep my job, so he felt he could do or say anything he wanted, and I wouldn't say a word to Gloria Nash or my husband. *This can't be happening*, I kept thinking over and over as my head swirled with fear. All I wanted was to go home.

As I held the dress in my hands, the shaking stopped, and my fear left me. In its place was anger. I was so tired of taking crap from men. First my father who put me down endlessly because he didn't like the way I looked. Then my husband, who thought that since I was his wife I had to do as I was told and devote my life to pleasing him—or get a shotgun in the back or a fist in the face. And now someone I had trusted, someone I thought respected me on a professional level— someone I was making money for, god dammit—thought all he had to do was buy me a slinky dress and I had to put it on to please him. I had no idea I had it in me, but somewhere from the depths of all that pain and fear I'd felt in the face of men who treated me like crap, came a voice like a bellows.

"I have your home address and your home number," I screamed, throwing the dress in his face. "And if you don't take me home *tonight,* I'll call your wife!"

"Bu-bu-but what are you talking about?" he said, the dress lying at his feet like a puddle of crimson blood. "Are you crazy? All I did was buy you a nice gift, so I could take you out to dinner. Jesus Christ, what's your problem? The only thing I've ever done is be nice to you!"

"Oh, yeah?" I answered right back. I'd heard Dick play that game so many times I knew it by heart. *I* was the crazy one. *I* was the one making a big deal out of nothing. *I* was the one who had misunderstood. No, I hadn't misunderstood a thing. I knew that man's look, and I knew that man's game. And I was having no part of it.

"You think that's what your wife will think when I tell her you bought me a red cocktail dress? When I tell her how you've been looking at me like you plan to have *me* for dinner?"

I didn't need to say anything more. He kept his mouth shut all the way home. But I'd found my voice. I'd learned not to keep my own mouth shut, not when I had something that needed to be said.

It was a long, silent drive back to New Hampshire, and it wasn't until we turned on to my street that I was sure he was taking me home. I was still trembling as I got out of the car and I was so eager to be home that I ran to my front door. I was safe. It must have been past midnight, and the house was dark, but I don't think I'd ever been so happy to walk through my own front door before. Dick wasn't expecting me until the next day, and I knew he'd be sleeping, but I hoped when I woke him up that he'd listen to me and show some compassion once I told him what I'd just been through. I tiptoed through the dark house to the bedroom, careful not to wake the children by turning on any lights. I slowly opened the bedroom door, and there, sleeping soundly in our bed was my naked husband, the soft light of the streetlights illuminating him. His arms were curled around our babysitter.

I didn't rant, I didn't rave. I didn't throw a fit and toss them out. I simply said out loud, in the silence and the dark, "Thank you, Brenda."

The two sat bolt upright in bed, as startled as if I'd fired a gun in the air.

"You just showed me what I had for a husband."

I shut the door, turned, and walked down the hallway to my baby girl's room. Crawling into bed with little Shelley, I hugged her close. I needed to feel her beside me.

Exhausted from the two ordeals that had struck me one right after the other, I drifted off to sleep, listening to my husband start the car. He was gone.

Chapter 8

Mother's Little Helper

When I woke up the next morning, Dick still gone, it hit me. My marriage was over. I knew he wouldn't be back, and I knew I sure as hell didn't want him back. But as the day progressed, I realized a looming divorce wasn't nearly the liberation I'd imagined it would be. I was 24, with two kids, and would be branded a "divorcee"—a brand that in those days only seared the reputations of women, not of men who gained status as "eligible bachelors."

The only thing I was eligible for was welfare, or so it seemed. I did still have an income from waiting tables, and I did have a promising modeling career that had brought me in a bit of money, but the modeling was still sporadic, and now I couldn't possibly give up my waitressing job without Dick's income. Worst of all—now I had no babysitter!

I panicked. I was flooded with emotions. I was furious. I was enraged. I was humiliated. I was shocked. I didn't believe what I'd seen with my own eyes—and what they both admitted to. I felt like a fool. Why hadn't I seen it coming? No wonder he was so happy for me to be gone such long hours, no wonder he immediately knew of a babysitter and didn't care that she'd be watching our children, rather than me. No wonder we weren't fighting so much—he was happy! And all the while

I'd been hustling tables to earn some tips to pay the babysitter, taking long bus rides to Boston to pose for cameras so we could pay for Dick's Harley or whatever else it was he felt we needed to look like a proper middle-class couple, while in reality, he just wanted to look like some young stud free to come and go as he pleased. All the while I'd been batting away letches and creeps who made passes, like Stu, my "chaperone," and all the while I'd been dreaming of a romantic Italian man but sleeping beside a no-good cheating louse who was dreaming of fucking a teenager.

And the payoff? I would probably end up with the divorce I'd been hoping for, and along with it, poverty, stigma, and sole responsibility for my kids who'd lose their daddy—except for every other weekend. I had no idea how I'd make it. My father had been right. I didn't deserve an education. I didn't deserve the same privileges as a man. I didn't even deserve a man. I was just a pretty face and figure, and I got what I deserved.

I spent the entire weekend in a state of rage and panic and self-pity; I was enraged at Dick for cheating on me, I was panicked about losing him and ending up divorced, and I was convinced that my life was the most pathetic one there ever was. I don't even recall how I took care of my kids; I think I sent them back to my sister's. The more I thought about how badly I'd been betrayed, the more enraged I became. I never wanted to see that SOB again. The more I thought about how I'd never be able to afford the house on my own, the more I panicked. I didn't want to get divorced. And the more I thought about my kids losing their daddy—and me losing what little help Dick had provided in caring for them—the more I collapsed. I was already working constantly. I was already taking on so much more than I could possibly handle. And now I had to do more? With less? I just couldn't do it!

By Sunday, I had worked myself up into such a state that I thought my heart would explode. That's when I remembered Barbara's pills. I rummaged around until I found where I'd hidden them—so that the kids would never find them—and took one. Then I called Barbara and sobbed into the phone.

"Dick left me! I caught him screwing the babysitter and now I'm scared my marriage might be over!" I blubbered some more incomprehensible laments into the phone until she interrupted me.

"Stay right there. I'm on my way!"

And sure enough, in fifteen minutes, her broad arms were encircling me as I cried inconsolably.

"Come on, Darlene, let's sit down and talk." She took me by the hand and set me down, then listened to my incoherent sobs as I rambled on about what a disaster my life had become.

"Honey, your life is far from over and pretty soon you're going to forget all about that loser. Any guy who'd rather bang the babysitter than a beautiful woman like you isn't worth the time it takes to spit in his beer. Here's what you're gonna do. You're gonna get a good night's rest and in the morning, you're going to go back to work with a smile on your face and you're going to meet a dozen handsome young guys who'll make you forget all about him and maybe even one of them will ask you out."

I looked at Barbara and sobbed even louder. The last thing I wanted at that moment was another man to deal with.

"I don't ever want to talk to another man again!" I wailed, which only managed to invite Jesus into the conversation. "I just want my husband to love me!"

"Now don't talk like that, Darlene," she said, "I know you're not very religious, but you do know that the Good Lord loves you and He wants you to be happy, honey. You've just got to open your heart to him and once you do, Dick is going to come around and be the husband I know he can be. And if he can't be, then the Lord is just going to send a better man to take care of you and love you and treat you real special."

I cried some more, cursed up a storm and finally, she reached into her purse and offered me one of her pills.

"Here, honey, take one of these, they'll calm you right down. Trust me."

I obediently took the little pill she'd offered, not even thinking that I'd already taken one barely a half hour before.

We sat at the table and I cried and screamed and cried some more, all the while Barbara listened patiently, occasionally assuring me that if I'd only pray, all my problems would be solved. After a while, I started feeling sleepy, and leaned my arm on the table, my head propped on my hand to hold it up. It wasn't long before my elbow started slipping off the table and I couldn't hold myself upright.

"Oh, my goodness, Darlene! You're passing out! I only gave you one pill, it shouldn't have knocked you out like that!"

Barbara rushed to the bathroom and came back with a cold, wet washcloth and started blotting my face and neck, anxious to wake me up, panic rising by the second as I slipped into deep sleep. "You didn't take anything before I came, did you?"

I nodded, mumbling something about the ones she'd given me.

The next thing I remember, I was being put into an ambulance, as I overheard Barbara tell the medics, "An overdose. Her husband left her."

As they snaked a tube down my throat I heard from what seemed far away in the distance, "suicide attempt."

I woke up the next morning and had no idea where I was or what was happening. As I began to realize I was in a hospital, a tall shadow moved toward me. It was Dick. He came to a stop by my bedside, the tubes running in and out of me, a painful needle thrust into my arm. His face showed no comfort or compassion, only repulsion.

"Darlene," he said in the firm voice I'd come to know meant he was about to make a command. "I want a divorce." Then he walked out of the room, without another word.

I felt like a wounded animal, abandoned to die, with no one to love, appreciate or understand me. A scream rose from the back of my throat, as if it were somebody else's throat, as if my body were no longer my own. *"Noooooooooooooooo!!!!!"*

My scream brought the nurses running. They gave me a shot to once again tranquilize me, then stayed with me until I fell asleep. Sleep brought silence, to blot out the nightmare of my life.

The next morning I was discharged, as if the whole thing had never happened. My youngest sister Sherry lived nearby, so I went to her house, where I could rest without dealing with Dick. But as soon as I called to speak to Michael and Shelley, he announced, "I'm taking the kids."

"Over my dead body!" I screamed.

"Yeah, well you couldn't even do *that* right!" he screamed back. "And now thanks to your suicide attempt, you can't be trusted to take care of your own kids. You really blew it this time, Darlene!"

"It was no suicide attempt!" I shot back through the phone, "It was an accident. I'm perfectly fine and perfectly capable to taking care of my own children."

"Well, apparently, you aren't!" and with that, he slammed the phone down.

If I'd been panicked the night before, now I was absolutely traumatized. I had never felt so enraged, so frightened, and so helpless in my life. I had to get my kids back, and by God, that's exactly what I'd do. But first, I had to get my thoughts together. My mind was racing with worry and rage, my emotions completely out of control. All I wanted was for my kids to be back with me, for my husband to be gone forever, and to know that I'd be alright. And none of those things could happen until I could calm down and think clearly.

I called into work sick and poured out my sorrows to Sherry. I knew my sister wouldn't turn on me, she wouldn't betray me, she wouldn't panic and send me to the hospital just because I took a couple of tranquilizers. She'd take care of me.

"You just get some rest, Darlene, and don't worry about anything," she said, urging me to lie down. "Just get some sleep. You'll get the kids back, don't worry."

She tucked me into bed with the tenderness of our mother, and when I woke up, she made a hot cup of coffee for me and we sat outside on the porch, enjoying the late afternoon sun and talking in that special intimate way that sisters do, completely comfortable with each other's company, no matter what differences and battles life has brought between them as they grew from little girls into young women.

And that's when I saw them. Michael and Shelley, playing across the street, laughing and utterly happy.

Because in a town as small as Tilton, you can't cross the street without running into family or foe. Right across the street from Sherry's house was the house of my in-laws. Naturally, Dick took them there. The alternative was taking care of his own kids himself. I felt a terrible sense of dread seeing them over there. One of his sisters was a friend of mine, in fact, she was the one who introduced me to Dick. But his other sister, Karen, was anything but a friend. She was nasty and spiteful, and she never had liked me. It wouldn't be long before she'd be cheering Dick on, encouraging him to keep me away from my own kids. Far worse, she'd do to me what she tried to do to another woman we knew—Karen couldn't have children herself, so she'd tried to prove the woman was an unfit mother and adopt the child herself. Her plan didn't work, but I felt it in my bones that she'd pull the same stunt on me.

And sure enough, as Sherry and I sat on the porch, watching Shelley and Michael run around in their grandma and grandpa's yard, Karen walked out the door, glared at us from across the street and with her face still on us, hustled the children indoors.

My misery grew darker, my spirit sank lower, and I crawled back into bed and cried.

After a few days, I went back home and a few days after that, my children were returned to me. I felt a tremendous relief. Sherry had been right. My children had been returned to me.

But as I was putting little Shelley to bed, she said, "I'm going to miss you, Mommy."

"What!?" I asked, "Why would you say such a thing, honey? Mommy's not going anywhere."

"No, but I am. I'm going to live with Aunt Karen and Michael's going to live with Daddy."

"That's not true! You're staying right here with me. Who told you such things?"

"Daddy and Aunt Karen told me," she said.

I froze in horror. How could they tell my children such things? What were they up to? Whatever it was, I had to nip it in the bud right then and there.

No one was taking my children. I would fight them tooth and nail, but they were not taking my children! And Shelley would not be raised in Karen's filthy home, and I sure wasn't going to see my children only when I was allowed to.

I went straight to the phone and called Karen and told her what Shelley had just told me and asked if it was true.

"Yes," she said, "You're not fit to take care of those kids and I'm going to take Shelley and raise her properly."

"How can you possibly say that? You know I'm a good mother to those children!" I don't think I'd ever been so angry, and I had to force myself not to march right over to her house and ring her fat neck. How dare she try to take my kids?

"Look, Darlene," she said, "you're too busy working to even be a mother. And you've got some mental problems, or you wouldn't have tried to commit suicide."

"I did *not* try to commit suicide," I spat out, "it was an accident. And you will *never* take my daughter!" I hung up the phone, and spent the rest of the night shaking with rage. My entire life was coming unraveled and the only thing I had any control over was raising my own children. No one was going to take them.

A few days later, Child Protection Services knocked on my door—to question me about my drug use and suicide attempt—even though I never used drugs (not even marijuana, which everyone was smoking back then), and I sure as hell hadn't tried to kill myself.

While Michael and Shelley played on the floor, I answered a slew of questions in which I insisted I never used drugs, hadn't tried to kill myself, and would never do anything to hurt or neglect my children. Then I watched as the stranger with his clipboard walked through my house, scrutinizing each room, picking up my *Cosmo* magazines, staring a bit too long at my makeup in the bathroom, going through my medicine cabinet. He even opened up the closet doors, as if he was looking for a naked man or stash of drugs. I held Shelley and Michael close in case he tried to snatch them away right then and there.

As I watched, my heart paralyzed, my thoughts raced to the beer poster, the modeling, my commuting to two jobs and working all night. What better evidence would he need to prove I was an unfit mother? With my thoughts racing around my head faster than I could control them, I felt panic begin to rise inside me in a way it never had before. Then he walked into the kitchen, opened up my refrigerator, nodded, then closed it again.

"Okay, everything looks good," he said, and smiled like some realtor who I'd invited to come list my home. I cautiously began to relax. "You've got a clean house, clothes for the kids, food in the fridge. They're clean and well dressed, seem to be happy. I don't see anything to worry about here." After writing some notes in his file, he left as suddenly as he'd arrived.

I needed an attorney. I had never needed an attorney before, and I didn't know where to turn. But even if this man or another one like him never returned again, it was clear that Dick would do anything to hurt me. We'd already agreed to get a divorce. Now I needed someone to be sure I didn't get screwed in the process.

"Why don't you ask Mom?" Sherry suggested. "Remember when she and Dad got divorced? She had to find a divorce lawyer."

I'd forgotten all about that. When your parents live together, you just don't think about them being divorced, but Sherry had a point, so I called my mom.

"Oh, yes, I remember him," she said, trying to recall the man of many years before. "He was a real nice man. He really helped me out. You should call him."

And so I did, and after I'd explained to him what was going on, he agreed to take my case. I felt so relieved to finally have someone on my side. Having satisfied Child Protection Services that I was a good mother, I had another battle to wage. I couldn't let Karen or Dick take my kids.

But that was exactly what they wanted, and in the weeks that followed they launched a character assassination on me as an unfit mother for no better reason than they claimed—falsely—that I'd tried to kill myself and far worse, that I was not just a working woman, but a model—they might as well have accused me of being an escort. It didn't seem to matter that I was working to give my children a better life, that I hated being away from them but until the modeling became more steady I had to work two jobs, and that Dick also worked two jobs and was never home.

But what did seem to matter was that Dick was continuing to see Brenda, and she was still in high school. Just like me, when he started dating me. That was my trump card, but it didn't mean that the battle would be easy. It was a very small town, Dick was an officer of the law, and now they were spreading a rumor I was suicidal.

I had no choice. I had to be home in the evenings with my children. My sisters could help out during the day, but not the long hours at night when I was scheduled to wait tables. And my mother could no longer watch them because she was caring for my brother Danny around the clock, and she needed help even more than I did. Ever since his accident, she'd had to go to work to help with the costs of his care and all the special equipment he needed, and on top of it all, she was effectively a round-the-clock nurse.

It was right around that time that the catheter disaster happened. Because he no longer had any sensation below his waist, Danny couldn't feel when he had to empty his bladder, and needed a catheter at all times. But one day, the drugstore ran out of catheters, so he inserted his penis into a small bottle to pee. Not being able to feel the bottle, he also didn't feel when he leaned over it with all his weight—and broke it.

His penis was horribly sliced up, and though he couldn't feel any pain, it became terribly infected. Getting him back and forth to the doctors, dressing his wounds, getting the antibiotics and making sure he took them—these were each one-in-a-million crises that my mother was having to deal with as she cared for a paraplegic son and put up with an alcoholic abusive husband. I could hardly expect to burden my mother any further with my own woes—she needed me as much as I needed her.

It was time to face facts. I no longer had a babysitter or father to watch my children in the evenings, and the tips didn't pay enough to cover any babysitter and still have enough for groceries. My brother needed my help, and the longer I worked nights at the hotel, the more likely Dick and Karen could win in their efforts to take the kids away from me. So I quit my job at the Concord Hotel, and when Dick wouldn't contribute enough for us to live on, I found myself on welfare.

As for modeling, the only way they'd call me for more shots was if I smiled more. So my only chance at making something of my life was learning how to smile.

Then dammit, that's what I'd do. Even if all I really wanted to do was curl up in a ball and cry until my eyes fell right out of my head. Instead, I'd learn to smile.

Chapter 9

Wet T-Shirt

I was already running late. After the nearly two-hour commute to Boston, a traffic jam kept me trapped in the bus for an extra half hour. By the time I reached my stop, I was so worried I'd miss any shoots that came along that day that I dashed across the street, weaving around parked and moving cars, their horns honking, drivers cursing, when *wham!* One of them hit me. It wasn't enough to even knock me down, but it was enough to hurt like hell and I knew I was going to have one heck of a bruise on my leg. That would mean no shoots that showed any leg until the bruise was gone—and since most shoots required showing some leg, it was probably going to cost me money— money I couldn't afford to lose.

I limped to the curb and hurried to the building where Gloria's agency was, then ran up the stairs, worried not only about missing any work, but gaining a reputation as someone who couldn't be counted on. By the time I got to the top of the stairs, I must have looked a mess, soaking in sweat, my long hair splattered across my face, and my nerves practically flying out of my skin I was so worked up.

I found the other models all sitting around finishing their lunches packed in little brown paper bags. No doubt their moms made their lunches, I thought, wishing I'd had time to pack something for myself. I was in such a rush to get the kids off to my sister's that I'd just grabbed an apple and a banana, and both became my breakfast on the long ride to the city. Now I was hungry already, but more hungry for work than for food. I hated being on welfare; it was a personal shame I didn't dare share with the other models. The training phase completed, we now met up every afternoon to see if any calls came in, whether a "go-see" for a future shoot or a last-minute call for a model—or half a dozen models—to hurry to a set for whatever ad campaign might need us.

"Hey, Darlene, you're just in time. We were just leaving," one of the models said as she got up and threw her lunch bag in the trash. "Boy, don't you look a wreck." She looked me up and down as if I'd failed her exam and she couldn't be more delighted.

"We figured you weren't going to make it today, but here you are," said the Farrah-haired girl. "You know, my daddy's like that. He's always running late. This morning I thought I'd never make it to work because he had to go take my car in and get it washed and fill up the tank. He's so afraid of me running out of gas or some silly thing." She laughed like it was the funniest thing in the world, to have someone helping her like that. "And then when he finally made it back, he brought me a whole bag of little cinnamon rolls, and I had to remind him I couldn't eat things like that!"

Farrah really did mean well. She just needed some age. She picked at the last of her salad with her little plastic fork, and I thought about how much I'd give to bite into a nice warm cinnamon roll. I didn't understand all these salad eaters. The only time I'd ever had to watch my weight was after my babies were born, but other than that, I could eat anything and never seemed to gain a pound. No doubt because I never had two minutes to sit down. I was constantly on the run.

I couldn't imagine living on the diet sodas and iceberg lettuce that these girls swore by. Some only drank a strawberry or chocolate drink made with an instant powder called "Slender," which was pretty much just Carnation's instant breakfast served at lunch. Others ate nothing but grapefruit and a few too many didn't seem to eat at all, replacing food with diet pills that were clearly just amphetamines that kept them slim but in a constant state of activity and psychosis. And then there was the "sexy pineapple diet," which was some fad from Denmark where they'd eat nothing but pineapple for two days, and then anything they wanted. I'm not sure what was so sexy about it, but it seemed just that word alone was enough to make the girls eager to try it. Once, at least. Not many went for another 48-hour round of nothing but pineapple.

Farrah pulled a crayon out of her bag and began writing something down on her empty brown paper bag. "Here," she said, passing the bag to me. "We got a call for a wet T-shirt shoot! This is the address. You should come, Darlene, your breasts are perfect for it!"

"Thanks . . ." I said, the hesitation in my voice betraying my caution.

"Oh, it'll be fun!" she said, "Besides, you're getting a divorce, you don't have to worry about what your husband will say."

And with that, a chorus of young voices began chiming in about what their boyfriends might think of them posing in wet T-shirts, the consensus coming down to they'll hate it and love it and let's go for it!

But for me, the concern was something else entirely. If I posed in a wet T-shirt, I could lose my children.

"You should do it," Gloria said after I'd explained to her my problem. Gloria was becoming not just a mentor and agent, but a friend, as well. She had listened compassionately when I told her I was getting a divorce, she was understandable about my children, and she really did seem to be trying to get me work—even though I still couldn't smile worth a damn. But now she wanted me to pose in a wet T-shirt.

"I don't have a problem with it being a wet T-shirt shoot," I explained, "but if my husband or in-laws or someone from the State sees it, I could lose my kids."

"No one will see it. I'll make sure it's published somewhere here in Boston, where no one from New Hampshire will ever come across it. You need to build up your portfolio and this is a good opportunity. Just go, have fun, and I'll make sure the only people who see it are the people who need to see it." She got up from her chair, walked around her desk and gave me a big hug. I knew she understood, and that was enough for me. I went on the shoot.

It was a blast, and though there remained a niggling worry that someone might see the photos, once I got drenched with water and focused on my work, I set those worries aside. Getting hosed down in a sexy romp with a bunch of squealing girls posing for the camera was just the break I needed from the anxiety and gloom that had become my home life. I felt just like one of my kids, playing in the backyard with a garden hose and not having a care in the world.

Once I got back home, however, it was back to cold, stark reality. There was a stack of bills in the mailbox, including another one from my attorney. With a paltry welfare check of just a couple hundred dollars a month, I was barely getting by. And now I had legal bills to pay. How in the world was I going to be able to make it on my own if everything I made went straight to my lawyer? I gave him a call and asked him to please be patient and not drop me as a client.

"Don't worry, Darlene," he assured me, "I've got you covered. You'll be fine."

"I hope you're right," I told him, not as sure as he was. "I can't keep living on welfare and modeling isn't paying enough to get by. And I need a car and I'll have to pay the mortgage. Oh my God, the mortgage! What if he gets the house?"

"He's not going to get the house, Darlene, you're the mother. You'll get it, along with alimony and child support."

"But the house is in his name. The bank wouldn't let me put my name on it. I wasn't even 18 when we got married." The truth was, even if I had been 18, the bank wouldn't have let me put my name on it back then. Mortgages—and the property that went with them—went to men. Women couldn't even buy cars on credit, much less houses.

"That won't matter," my lawyer said, "just leave it to me. I'll take care of you. You have nothing to worry about. That's my job. Your job is to take care of your children and get your career off the ground."

That was exactly what I needed to hear, so that was exactly what I did. I took care of my kids, worked as hard as I could, and let my attorney defend me from Dick's unrelenting attacks.

But sometimes, the stress of the divorce was more than I could take. Sometimes it felt like he'd stopped knocking me down physically, just so he could knock me down in other ways.

Living in a town with a population of 2,500 is both wonderful and awful. It was wonderful because I knew everybody, my family all lived in walking distance, and I felt safe. It was dreadful because everyone knew everybody, you could never escape your family, and when it came to rumors and scandal, nobody was safe. Especially women. While the scandal about Dick and the babysitter didn't help him any, it didn't seem to hurt him, either. He did lose his job with the police force once they learned about it, but he quickly found another job in law enforcement in the next town over. He did have to move out of our house, but he moved into his mother's house, and continued to see Brenda—who lived right across from Michael's school. When I'd go to pick him up, I'd sometimes see her sitting out front or at her window, watching my son, and the fear and rage inside me just shot through the roof. I felt as if she were a predator, waiting to steal my son—and the fact that she was still sleeping with my soon-to-be ex-husband who wanted that son didn't help any.

The scandal, it seemed, stuck to *me*. I was the one rumored to have attempted suicide. I was the one running off to Boston to be a model. I was the one who couldn't hang on to her husband.

And when that husband rented an apartment with the babysitter, I was the one who hadn't stayed home to watch her children, leaving them in the care of a horny teenager. And I was the one who'd been investigated by Child Protection Services, not him.

The stress became unbearable, as I counted every penny, took care of the kids and house and tried to land more modeling gigs, and saw the glances and turned backs whenever I went to the grocery store or Michael's school or took him and Shelley to the playground. I was feeling like an outsider in my own hometown, the town I'd grown up in. I spent as much time as I could with my family, because they helped me to feel like less of a cast off and more like a member of my own community, but still, each day was a more unbearable struggle than the day before. And on top of it all, the welfare office told me that I had to get a GED in order to continue getting checks, so with everything else I was juggling, I was spending every evening studying for my high school diploma. And every day eating macaroni and cheese.

"I'm sorry, Donna, but this is all I've got." I put the macaroni and cheese, cooked from a box, on the table. I didn't even bother to put it into a serving dish, I just offered up the orange glop straight from the pan. I'd made burgers for the kids—mine and Donna's two—but couldn't afford enough hamburger for all of us, so Donna and I would have to eat the instant macaroni and cheese, which at four for a dollar, had been pretty much all we'd been eating for weeks. "I'm sorry, Donna, but this is all I've got." I was so embarrassed to not even be able to offer my sister a hamburger.

"That's fine, Darlene, I've had those spells myself. It won't be forever." Donna went to the fridge and got some milk for the kids while I started dishing up their burgers.

The dinner was rather chaotic, as dinners with four kids usually are, and after they were done and had run off to play, Donna and I started clearing the table.

As I washed up the dishes, the tears started to fall. Giving my children hamburgers was a luxury—one I couldn't even afford to extend to my sister.

I felt her arms around me and turned and sobbed onto her shoulder. "I'm sorry, Donna, I'm just so embarrassed that you have to see us like this. Just a few months ago I was serving you leg of lamb, and now all I have to offer you is a damn box of macaroni and cheese! I hate living like this!"

She pushed me at arm's length, so she could see my face. Holding my hands in hers, she said, "That was the first time I ever had lamb, Darlene, and the last! It tasted like deer meat and I hate deer meat. I'd rather eat macaroni and cheese anytime!"

That was true. Donna wasn't much for what she called "exotic" foods. She didn't care for the lamb at all.

"You know what I remember most about that meal?" she asked.

"What?" I asked, wiping my tears away with a dishtowel.

"I remember you working all day making that dinner, and when Dick took his first bite he started yelling at you and insulting you because you hadn't made it the way he wanted. He yelled that you were a terrible cook, a terrible wife and a terrible mother."

I'd forgotten all about that. It was another one of those horrible times that I just pushed out of my head. But Donna's reminder triggered another torrent of tears. Then she shook some sense into me.

"Darlene! I didn't remind you about that dinner to make you feel bad. I reminded you about that dinner to remind you of how awful he was to you. You're much better off without him and if that means you have to eat macaroni and cheese for a while, isn't it worth it?"

Yes. It was worth it.

"And no more ironing the sheets!" she added, and I finally let myself smile. Dick had always insisted that the sheets had to be ironed, so no matter how much work I had to get done, there was always a laundry basket filled with cotton sheets that I had to painstakingly iron. I thought all housewives had to do that. It wasn't until my sisters pointed out that ironing sheets was not something most housewives had to do that it occurred to me that Dick was being a dick.

Donna's reminders about the awful things Dick had said to me and the ridiculous expectation that his sheets be ironed brought a wave of relief. She was right. If I had to eat nothing but macaroni and cheese for the rest of my life, it was a small price to pay to be rid of him.

But poverty still wore me down. As relieved as I was to be divorcing him, the poverty, constant work to take care of the kids, getting a GED while launching a modeling career, along with the social scorn for doing so, compounded my daily stress until it felt as if there wasn't a moment in the day when I didn't feel the world collapsing on me. And on top of it all, Dick still screamed at me, insulted me, threatened me, and reminded me of what a disappointment I had been and how it was all my fault he left me for our babysitter.

Finally, one day, he went too far.

In addition to Cinnamon, Michael's dog, we'd acquired a cat, Marlo. And Marlo was having kittens. It was the last thing I was ready for. Where in the hell would I find homes for all those kittens—and how in the world would I be able to live among so many animals until I found them homes? I thought it would be the final straw to send me over the edge and straight to the asylum.

Then they were born. And they were adorable. All those teeny tiny little newborn kittens squeaking and crawling and climbing reminded me of how much I'd dreamed of being a veterinarian when I was a child. I loved animals, and I loved those kittens. But I couldn't keep half a dozen kittens who would turn into half a dozen cats, and I finally appealed to Dick to help me find them homes.

"Alright, Darlene, I'll take care of them," he said, without much enthusiasm, but without much anger, either. He had come by to drop off the kids after his weekend visitation, and as I was getting them unpacked and settled back into their rooms, I heard the gun shots. One right after another, until I'd counted six altogether.

Then he left, leaving the kittens dead in the backyard, unburied. Shelley and Michael came running into the backyard, and I couldn't turn them away in time. They saw them.

If there had been any shred of love or respect for Dick left inside me, it was gone, right then and there. Even worse, what he had done to those kittens, and to our children who had to see them, as horrible as it was, could have been done to me.

"Take that son of a bitch to the cleaners," I told my attorney, "I don't care if he can't afford a cup of coffee when you're through with him."

"Don't worry, Darlene, I will," he assured me. "He won't know what hit him."

In the meantime, my sister Sherry grew so concerned for me that without my knowledge, she made a phone call.

"If you care about Darlene," she said into the phone, "then you'd better get up here and talk to her."

The next weekend, Angelo was knocking on my door. I hadn't spoken to him in weeks, but that visit from Angelo was just the wake-up call I needed. It got me thinking about how to move forward, and though at first I was mad at Sherry for interfering in my personal life, the truth was, I was immensely grateful. There are few things more healing for a woman going through a divorce than a sexy, handsome Italian who treats her like a queen. As overwhelmed with the chaos of my life as I was, as Angelo started coming up each weekend when Dick took off with the kids, I was growing smitten with his attentions.

Like me, he was constantly working, and while I lived in a small town in New Hampshire, he lived in Yonkers, New York, and worked in the city. When we did get together, I had his full attention and he had mine—not only was he so dreamy to be with, but he had an absolutely fascinating job. He was constantly sharing stories of the news he was covering or the stars he was meeting, and for a small-town girl in New Hampshire, nothing could be more exciting. Soon we became best friends, and then lovers, and it wasn't long before I was head-over-heels. But I had to be careful, because while a man could run off with the teenage babysitter, for a woman to date a grown man before the divorce was finalized, well that was another thing altogether. I was already branded as the town trollop by some just for modeling; I couldn't afford to destroy my reputation altogether.

If the divorce wasn't enough to ruin my reputation, I worried that my work would. One of the very first jobs that Gloria got me was for a boat show. The stress of my divorce had caused me to lose so much weight that I'd shrunk to the size of a kid, which in that line of work, was considered a good thing. They wanted someone small to make their boats look bigger.

At any rate, the man who hired me told me I'd need to wear a gown for the shoot, something a little sexy, and when I told him I didn't own a gown like that, he told me not to worry.

"I'll take care of that," he said. He was from out of town so rather than go to his office, the interview took place at the modeling agency, and everything seemed professional. "If you come by my hotel the day before the shoot, I'll give you a gown you can wear."

This was my first shoot in a gown and I was quite excited, so when the day came to pick up the gown, I called his hotel to confirm he'd found a gown and we arranged a time for me to come by. When I got there and I had the hotel staff call his room, I thought he'd come down to the lobby with the gown, but instead they told me I was to go up to his room. So I took the elevator up to the 18th floor, went to his room and knocked on the door. When he opened it, he was wearing nothing but a towel and a grin and asked me to step inside.

Instead, I turned around, went straight back to the lobby shaking and in near tears, and called Gloria.

That was the end of the boat show.

I was afraid my career was over, and thankful the divorce was almost over. All I had to do was appear in court one last time, and the divorce would be granted, the house would be deeded over to me, and I would be a free woman. Or at least I hoped so.

"Darlene, trust me. I have your back," my attorney assured me. "Everything will be settled on Monday. Relax."

"I know, but I'm still worried. What if I don't get any alimony? How can I pay the mortgage on my salary? I barely make enough in tips and the modeling money is good when I get it, but it's still not enough to support two kids and a house."

"He's going to be paying you child support and alimony and he'll have to pay you a hefty settlement, as well. That will be more than enough to pay the mortgage."

"I hope you're right, but I just won't relax until it's over," I said, knowing that I was working myself up over nothing. "At least I've got the kids this weekend, so I won't have much time to think about it."

"Darlene," he said, patting me on the back, "you're just nervous. That's normal. I'll tell you what. I've got a weekend place up at Lake Winnipesaukee. Why don't you come by tomorrow and relax? Come around lunch time and bring a bathing suit. A day by the lake will do you good."

He was right. It was my weekend with the kids and what could be a better way to spend it than relaxing by a lake, swimming and enjoying the summer sun.

The kids were overjoyed to hear we were going to a lake so the next morning we gathered up bathing suits and towels and suntan lotion (we didn't know a thing about sunblock back then) and water toys and drove north to the lawyer's lake house.

No sooner had we reached his house and climbed out of the car, all of us thrilled for a break—when he walked out the door and the instant I saw his face, I knew I'd made a huge mistake. He hadn't expected the kids.

The visit turned out to be brief, especially when we went out back to the patio and I saw the table set for two, with china and crystal and the champagne chilling in a bucket. The entire set up was designed for seduction. Well, at least there wasn't any slinky red dress I was expected to put on. Then again, he did tell me to bring my bathing suit.

It was such an awkward encounter, but I just made the best of it and let the kids play for awhile in the water, but I was moving them along very fast, telling them it was time to go home shortly after.

"But we just got here!"

"Yeah, Mom, we're still playing!"

"I know but it's time to go home. We can't leave Cinnamon alone much longer. Let's get going!"

I apologized for bringing the kids and hurried them into the car and we were gone. For the whole hour's drive back, I listened to the kids pout and argue and to the thoughts in my head as I scolded myself for being so naïve and foolish, and my attorney for being so presumptuous. I got on the phone and called my mom, spilling out the whole entire embarrassing story.

"He did the same thing to me, Darlene," she said, in the same tone she'd complain about my dad ignoring us. "But it was years ago, when I was getting a divorce."

"Then why the hell did you refer me to him?" I asked, but that only made her mad, and I was in no position to alienate any more people, so I let the issue go. I didn't know what bothered me more after that phone call. The thought of him doing that to my mom, or the thought of her not warning me. Whatever it was, it was just too much for me to figure out. I needed to stay calm for the next two days because I had a court date pending.

But I couldn't shut off my thoughts. I was so angry with myself and with my lawyer and with the world and with Dick who made it all happen. I was only 24 and already two days from being a divorcee. Branded. Up for grabs. No one to trust around your husband. No one to trust to keep a husband. I fell into bed sobbing. My father had been right. My looks just got me into trouble. My looks invited my attorney's desire. My looks proved to my dad that I didn't belong in my own family. I just didn't belong.

When my attorney called me the next day to talk about the final hearing Monday morning, I was still a wreck. The emotions of the last few months all came rushing at me. The betrayal. The humiliation. The letdowns. The put-downs. The arguments. The kittens. Oh, God, the kittens. The highlight of my career was getting shot in a wet T-shirt. I was so overwhelmed. I never had a free moment to myself, and the one weekend that promised to give me a break turned out to be the break.

"Darlene, you looked really stressed when you were out yesterday," my lawyer said. "You don't need to put yourself through seeing Dick in court tomorrow. I'll take care of everything. You just stay home and let me handle it. How's that sound?"

It sounded like I was being pushed aside, yet again. But he was probably right. Why did I need to be there? Why go to court and have to see that man who did so much to hurt me? Besides, wasn't that what I was paying my attorney to do, represent me?

"Okay," I said, "Promise you'll do a good job? You'll get me a good settlement and stick it to him with the alimony?"

"Of course," he said, "I'll take care of you. Trust me."

Never trust a person who says trust me. They'll screw you every time. I didn't get a settlement. I didn't get any alimony. My child support for two children was $70 a week. And Dick got the house.

"I know, Darlene, but there was nothing I could do," the rat bastard lawyer said. I could tell by his tone that he didn't care, that he hadn't even tried, that he was just trying to dismiss me from his life as fast as he could. "But you can stay there for another thirty days. That should give you enough time to find another place."

"How in the hell am I going to find another place with no money?" I screamed into the phone. But it was like screaming into the toilet bowl. All I heard were my own words echoing back to me. I was no longer his problem. Just as long as I paid my bill.

I did pay my bill—at five dollars a month. As long as I paid him that little bit, he couldn't send the creditors after me. In the meantime, I called Gloria and begged her for work. The welfare payments were coming to an end, and I couldn't possibly find another place to live on such a paltry income. She did line up a few small jobs, but they didn't pay much. That was all she said she could do for me seeing as I had not yet made a name for myself in the modeling world.

Not long after, she called me back. "I've got some good news for you, Darlene," she said.

"Good. Because I've had enough bad news!"

"You remember the wet T-shirt shoot?"

"It's not the sort of thing I'd forget!" I told her, laughing.

Well it turned out that the photos had been developed and one shot of me that pretty much looked like I was sniffing my armpit was chosen to be published in a newspaper in Boston. When I saw it, I thought it looked ridiculous, but I suppose it wasn't my armpit the guys would be looking at. True to her word, however, Gloria put it where no one ever saw it, except the ones who needed to see it. I started getting more calls, and more calls meant more money. One of the best gigs she got me was a booking on the weekends at a liquor store promoting different types of wine. Though I wasn't much of a drinker, the money was okay, and Gloria was right—I needed to make a name for myself in the modeling world.

As the work started coming in I told Gloria that I was willing to work hard if she could get my name out there so that when her clients called, they'd ask for me. But she still wasn't sure. She wanted to help me, I had no doubt about that, but between having to take care of my kids, never smiling, and living so far away, I just kept falling off the radar.

"I'll tell you what," she finally said. "I'll enter your name in an upcoming Model of the Year Contest. You aren't the only model I'll enter, I've got several others in mind, but at least this will give you a shot."

"Thanks, Gloria, that's all I'm asking for," I said. I hung up the phone and rejoiced. All I needed was a stroke of luck, and even if I only made runner up, at least it would be a boost.

But I didn't make runner up. I took first place. Just like Miss America, I heard my name called as the first place winner and found myself walking down the runway to the song "Shaft," by Isaac Hayes. Damn, that song seemed so appropriate after all that I had been through. I might have gotten the shaft from my husband and my lawyer, but I became the victor in the end.

The calls started coming in and by the end of the year, Gloria made me the cover girl for her top modeling catalogue.

As for Dick, now happily divorced, he announced that he and the babysitter were getting married. As soon as I packed all our things and got out.

Chapter 10

Leaving Home

I was in the basement when my heart stopped beating. Angelo had been visiting from New York when Dick came by to pick up the kids for the weekend.

"Hey, Angelo, mind if I speak to you alone?" Dick asked.

I couldn't imagine what he was going to say. Tell him the worst possible things about me? Threaten to beat him up? Whatever it was, I excused myself and headed to the basement, where I knew I'd be able to hear every word through the ventilation.

After a flustered Angelo flashed me a sexy, imploring look, as if to ask my permission, I grabbed a laundry basket and headed down the stairs, like the obedient ex-wife that I was.

That's when I heard what Dick wanted from him.

"Yeah, Angelo, you know, if you're going to be seeing Darlene all the time like it looks you are, it seems to me that I shouldn't have to pay so much every month for the kids, it's just not fair to me. I can't afford to shell out so much money every month, and I just got a lot going on, so why don't you take Darlene and the kids down to Yonkers with you and start your own family? I mean, it's not like she's got anyplace else to go anyway, and you two being together and all, well, it just seems to me that if you like Darlene so much, you might as well take care of her and the kids. What do you say?"

Whatever it was that Angelo had to say, I didn't hear it. Dick had already kicked me out of my home. Now he was kicking me out of my own home town. I rushed up the stairs and flung myself at his feet, wrapping my arms around his legs just like little Shelley did when she didn't want her daddy to leave.

"No, Dick!" I sobbed, blubbering like a little girl. "Please don't do that, please don't make us go!"

I was already in a state of shock having to move out, and I couldn't bear the thought of leaving the only community I'd ever known. I felt as if I was being driven out of town with flaming torches, sent away from my parents, my sisters, and worst of all, my little brother, Danny, who needed so much help. I had lost all control over my life and my children. I had no home for them, and now I was being cast out completely. Worse, my children were being kicked out of the only home they knew, and now Dick wanted them to leave their grandparents and aunts and uncles and all their friends. And on top of it all, he was threatening to stop paying child support. I had no idea how I'd make it—I still wasn't making enough on modeling to support a family, but I was making just enough for welfare to cut me off. And if I went to New York with Angelo, I'd be too far from Boston. I'd have to give up my modeling career. Maybe I couldn't even go to New York. Surely Angelo would leave me, now that he was being told to take on my whole family. If that happened, I'd have nowhere to go.

I wailed and wailed, pitifully, but all Dick did was kick me away, just as he would do with Shelley when she wrapped her arms around her daddy's legs and begged him not to go.

"Oh, for Chrissakes, Darlene, you can't even handle yourself, much less the kids. Come on, kids! Let's get going, Daddy's leaving *now!*"

He clapped his hands loudly and rounded up the kids while Angelo pulled me off the floor and hugged me close, kissing my hair and whispering into my ear that everything would be all right. I wiped off my tears and gave the kids hugs goodbye, but the minute the door was closed I collapsed in sobs once again. Angelo just kept hugging me tightly, kissing my tears and assuring me everything would be fine.

"Let's do it, Darlene," he said, "let's just get out of here and you can start over. Come on, *vita mia*, my darling. Let me take care of you and your children. No one is going to take them away from you. I love you. Let's just go."

Here was a man who really did seem to love me. A man who wanted to give me a home and take care of me and my family. He never complained about the long drive he made every weekend from New York to come see me. He listened to me when I had something to say and he shared his own thoughts and daily experiences with me. But the thought of leaving my family behind—especially Danny—tore me up. At the same time, the thought of remaining in Tilton, eating macaroni and cheese, and running into my ex-husband and the babysitter whenever I left the house tore me up even more.

Angelo was right. It was time to go. Michael was seven and Shelley would be starting first grade; there was no better time to move them, before they became rooted to their school and friends. I wanted freedom from chaos, freedom from poverty, freedom from drama. Now was the time to start our new life. No one would come into my home to try to take my kids away ever again. No one would whisper behind my back when I went to buy groceries ever again. And no one would shoot my children's kittens ever again.

"Okay," I said, kissing Angelo's warm, eager mouth. "We'll move to New York."

We didn't move to New York. "I don't understand," I said, "Why can't we move to Yonkers? It's in New York, you've already got a place there, and it's so much closer to the city. I don't see why we need to spend more money to find another place. There's plenty of space at your place."

"Because it's too close to my mother," he said. "Besides, you'll like it in Bloomfield."

"But I don't mind living near your mother," I said. "I want to live near family, especially now that I have to leave mine."

But Angelo wouldn't listen. He was dead set on us living in New Jersey. Finally, after I nagged him endlessly, he told me the truth.

"Because you're divorced."

The words hit me like a fist.

Angelo sighed, then took my hands in his and looking into my eyes, he said, "My mother doesn't approve of me dating a woman who's divorced, especially one with children. I'm sorry, *bella*, but she's from the old country, and that's just how these Italian mothers are. I'm sure she'll come around." He tried romancing me with kisses, but my heart felt as if he'd crumpled it. I didn't know how much more rejection I could take.

But I had been raised to believe that men were in charge of these decisions, so we moved to Bloomfield and settled down, and I set out to win the approval of Angelo's mother, one way or another.

The move to Bloomfield was just what I'd needed, and to make it even better, Angelo took me to Italy to see his country and meet his large, extended family. I'd never even been outside New England, so a trip to Europe was the most exotic experience of my life. He took me to Rome, Venice, and even Pompeii, and I loved every minute of it.

In the space of a few months, I had gone from welfare and a diet of macaroni and cheese with no future in sight, to being the model of the year, taking a trip to Italy, and living in a beautiful home in New Jersey with a gorgeous Italian who adored me and my children. I'd even passed my GED! All those tears of self-pity and woe had been wasted—it was if a divine hand had reached down and plucked me out of my dark hole of despair and deposited me into heaven.

As I settled into a happy domestic life in Bloomfield, however, I had to put modeling behind me. I had enough to do just taking care of the kids and Angelo's career was well paying. I'd enrolled the kids in school and they were happy and fast making friends, and I was learning to speak Italian. I was determined to have a happy home, and Angelo was proving to be a dream. He treated me like a queen, something I'd never before experienced with a man. First my father, then Dick, had treated me with such contempt and control that I'd had no idea what it was like to be respected by a man. Angelo was totally different. He adored me and my children just as much as if they'd been his own. The only problem was his mother. And mine.

Angelo's mother, Lucia, was very suspicious of me. She spoke a heavily accented broken English and was convinced her son had taken up with a harlot. Determined to win her over, I got an Italian cookbook and began to teach myself to cook. I'd never had eggplant parmigiana before, but it sounded exotic and just the thing to impress her. It was a complete mess to cook and must have dirtied up every pan in the house, but in the end, it was worth it because she loved it. After that, she started teaching me to cook, and she taught me how to make meatballs and homemade tomato sauce, how to bake bread, how to properly cook pasta, salting the water but never, ever adding oil to it the way all the housewives I knew did. She taught me to cook vegetables by adding just a touch of garlic and red pepper and not letting them turn khaki green. For years I'd eaten vegetables so overcooked they didn't even require teeth to chew them. My mother's idea of cooking was to open up a can—my dad said if the can opener ever broke, we'd all starve. Now the vegetables I cooked were flavorful and bright green and perfectly done and the only thing that came from a can were the tomatoes.

She taught me how to properly roast a leg of lamb with lots of rosemary and red wine, and if it wasn't perfect, well, I never knew, because Angelo always praised it. And she taught me how to make the most delicious desserts—my favorite was *zeppole*, a cross between a cream puff and a deep-fried donut. One evening when she was coming to visit, I spent the whole day in the kitchen making them. I had an orange and a lemon on hand, so I decided to get creative and grated the rind of both into the dough. It was a hit—she was so impressed that to this day I think it was orange and lemon rind that won her heart. Whatever it was, the food we were eating was fantastic, and as I learned to cook, I grew more confident. But it was not without its mishaps.

One day early on, just as Lucia was getting to like me, she gave me a few jars of her homemade tomato sauce, which she'd packed in Mason jars. It wasn't thick like I was used to, but much thinner, so I thought it was tomato juice. Well, what was I going to do with all that tomato juice? There was only one thing I could think of—I served my guests Bloody Mary's made with Lucia's tomato sauce! I don't know what they thought of them, but at least no one complained!

As Angelo's mother warmed up to me, my own mother was much slower to thaw when it came to getting to know my new boyfriend. The first time I took him to meet her, just after my divorce had been finalized, Angelo was dressed in a white shirt with white lace and wearing a gold chain. I thought he looked gorgeous and incredibly stylish.

Well, we hadn't been there more than ten minutes or so when my mom pulled me into the bathroom.

"Darlene," she said in a loud whisper, "there's something you should know about your new boyfriend."

"What, Mom?" I asked, utterly puzzled as to what she could know about him that I didn't.

"Some are called *homosexuals*. They don't like women, they like men. That's why they dress like girls."

I couldn't stop laughing. A shirt with lace and a gold chain was all it took for my mom to conclude he was gay!

No matter how hard he tried to charm her, however, my mother was certain that Angelo was no good, and she was not going to be fooled by him.

"Watch, I'm going to make her melt," he said with a sexy brown-eyed wink.

My mother sat down on her chintz-covered couch, and Angelo sat close beside her. She inched away. He inched closer. She moved to the far end of the couch. He moved closer. Annoyed, she got up and moved to another chair.

The next time we came by, the scene was repeated.

"I can't stand the way he does that," she told me. "Doesn't he know that's annoying?"

"He's just trying to get you to like him, Mom."

"Well that's not the way to do it. Tell him to stop it!"

Instead of stopping, he began putting his arm around her when he'd sit down. She'd stiffen up.

Then one day, he stopped. He sat on the far end of the sofa, as if she wasn't even there.

She inched closer, as slow as a clock, thinking no one was noticing. After nearly an hour, she had finally reached the end where Angelo was sitting. Then she began to wiggle her body against his until at last, he put his arm around her.

He'd won her heart.

Life in Bloomfield was everything I'd ever wanted—peaceful, loving, and happy. But as time went on, Angelo's career covering the news was becoming more demanding. Watergate was in its infancy, and it was clear that this unfolding story about the President's re-election campaign was going to be taking up some time. The days and nights began to get lonely.

"You should get back into modeling," Angelo suggested. "You really enjoyed doing that."

"I did, but Boston's too far away," I told him.

"You could model in New York."

"Are you crazy? I'm just a country girl. I can't just go up against those New York City models! I'd never stand a chance."

"They'll never stand a chance," he told me, brushing my hair from my face and kissing me. "You're beautiful. And you're good at it. Why not try?"

Why not try? Because I was enjoying our domestic life and knew that if I started getting rejected again and again—which was what would happen if I went out on calls up against the pros—then I'd start losing the confidence I'd been gaining in the months since I moved in with Angelo. I didn't want to return to a life of rejection and put-downs, which was what the competitive world of modeling would mean.

But I did want to return to modeling. I had really enjoyed it. Well, I could at least give it a shot, I figured, and when it didn't work out, I could tell Angelo that at least I'd tried. But every time I thought about it, I would get this lump in my throat. I was so afraid of facing that rejection.

"Feel the fear and do it anyway," I read somewhere, probably *Cosmo*. I couldn't argue with that. I'd tried once before, thinking nothing would come of it, and I ended up Model of the Year. Might as well pick up the phone.

So I picked up the phone, and called my old boss, Gloria. She got back to me the very next day and was happy to hear from me. When I asked if she could help me find a new agent, she didn't hesitate.

"I know just the one," she said. "I have a friend who runs an agency in the heart of Times Square and I'll be happy to refer you. I'll let her know that you got every booking I ever sent you out on, and while I can't guarantee she'll sign you, I'm sure she'll at least agree to meet you."

Just hearing those words from Gloria's mouth gave me the self-confidence I needed. She made the call and I was all set to go with an appointment with a Miss Newman with Model Service Agency in New York City.

After giving me the address, Gloria had some advice. "Be sure to smile. I don't want her thinking I'm sending you for a funeral commercial."

I smiled. I was going to miss Gloria.

"And wear pantyhose," she added. That really did make me smile— it was not wearing pantyhose that got me into modeling in the first place. It had been nearly two years since I'd met George Resnik at the hotel when that letch of a customer pinched my legs and threatened to tell my boss I wasn't wearing pantyhose. If that incident had never happened, George might not have shown any interest in helping me. I hadn't seen him more than a couple of times since then, but I would be forever grateful for his help.

"I promise, Gloria, I'll wear pantyhose."

"Good. And don't worry. You'll be fine." Like a mother sending her oldest off to school, Gloria was watching out for me. She had mentored me, befriended me, and helped me when I needed help the most. I knew I didn't want to let her down. I had to do a good job on this interview. If I blew the interview, my career in modeling would be over at the age of 24.

A week later I put on my best smile and took the bus to the Port Authority in New York City, an hour away.

If I thought Boston was a big city, New York was something else entirely. I felt completely swallowed up by all the buildings, and the traffic was absolutely insane. The horns honked nonstop, drivers cursed, shopkeepers called out in a melody of languages, trying to sell their fruits, vegetables, flowers, scarves, trinkets, souvenirs, you name it, they were selling it. I could hardly breathe from all the car exhaust, and the sidewalks were even more crowded than the streets. As for my smile, it wore off quickly and I swear I didn't see another smile in all the thousands of faces that I passed. It sure was a far cry from Tilton.

As I was heading toward the agency to meet Miss Newman, I saw this small, old woman pulling her bags in a makeshift wagon. I'd never seen such a sight before, and I approached her.

"May I help you carry your bags?" I asked her, wanting to be of some help.

She looked at me with a rage, and I noticed her rotten teeth and filthy fingers. Then like a madwoman she began yelling at me, spitting out the worst swear words I'd ever heard in my life. I was flabbergasted.

I mustered up the best mom voice I had and said, "How did a little old lady like you learn to swear like that?" It was a rhetorical answer. I didn't wait for a reply, because I knew it would come with more cussing. Instead, I turned away and hurried to my destination.

As I walked into the offices of the Model Service Agency, I remembered how nervous I had been when I first went up to Gloria's offices. Now, in some ways, I felt like a seasoned pro, even if my career was still in its infancy. But it didn't feel so new at the time. By that point I'd been in front of cameras more times than I could remember. I'd learned to smile when the flash went off, how to pose and how to dress. I'd learned how to wear makeup and how to walk and pivot. I may not have gone to college, but I'd sure gained an education in the last couple of years. Still, I was nervous. I wondered if this new agent would be able to see the scars that life had dished out to me. Well, if she did, at least I could fall back on Angelo who'd support me financially and emotionally. He'd become my comfort zone, even though I didn't know what a comfort zone was at the time. All I knew was that for the first time in my life I felt safe and protected and loved.

Now I just had to hope Miss Newman would love me. I walked into the building, nervous, but hungry—hungry for the excitement of the city and for the chance to return to my modeling career, where I earned my own money, and felt valued by a world that to this small town girl seemed glamorous. By the time I reached the receptionist area, I knew I desperately wanted to get back to work. I wasn't going to leave without a contract.

I was greeted by a young woman named Lynette, who offered me some water and chatted pleasantly as I waited. There were lots of models going in and out, far more than there'd been at Gloria's busy agency. This was the real deal, and Gloria had assured me that they had an excellent reputation.

When I was finally ushered into Miss Newman's office, I instantly felt at ease. She was a small, older Jewish woman, her dark hair nearly turned to silver. She was dressed in a skirt and blouse and adorned in heavy, expensive jewelry. The rings on her hands looked so heavy it was a wonder she could lift her hand to shake mine. She reminded me of an older version of Gloria—confident, gracious, and all business. I liked her right away, but it wasn't long into the interview that I could tell she wasn't as impressed with me.

"I don't know about that accent," she said, shaking her head at my New England accent. "You won't be able to do commercials. Maybe I could use you for live shows, but I'm not making any promises."

"I can lose my accent," I assured her, "and until then, I'll take anything you've got. I've done a lot of camera work, and I'll work hard."

"You're too short. You'll need to get some shoes with three-inch heels."

"Okay, I can do that." At 5'6", I didn't consider myself short, but in the modeling business, height was everything and I was the next best thing to a midget.

"Well, you do have a good figure." She looked me up and down. "But you don't have any butt. You won't be able to model any pants. Your backside is as flat as an ironing board."

"I won a Model of the Year contest," I offered. "I took first place."

"Yes, I saw that," she said, turning her gaze from my body to my portfolio.

"I'll go on any go-see you can line up, all I need is a chance."

"It doesn't look like you've done many showrooms." She sighed. "Have you ever done a bridal show?"

"Yes, I've done a few," I lied. I hadn't done any, but I had the Dior pivot down, and how hard could they be?

After a terribly uncomfortable silence, she finally said, "I suppose I could send you to Bridal Creations. They're looking for some models for one of their shows that's coming up."

"Oh, thank you!" I said, "I won't let you down, I promise. I'll do a good job."

"I expect you to do a great job," she said, and for the first time I saw a glint of confidence in her face. "But you're going to need to smile. And keep wearing pantyhose."

It was pretty clear that Gloria had filled her in.

"I've got an extra pair of L'eggs right here," I said, reaching into my bag and pulling out a giant white plastic egg stuffed with pantyhose. That was how they came back then, and that was how I bought them.

She approved. We shook hands, I left, and the next day I was at Bridal Creations, lying through my teeth about my experience. I knew I'd eventually have to tell them the truth because I had no idea how to do a bridal show, but if I could just charm them until right before the show, I stood a chance of them keeping me on, if for no other reason than they were running out of time and all the other models would be booked. It was a huge gamble, but the alternative was no shot at all. If it worked, I'd have three weeks of work and a chance at a contract with Model Service Agency. If it didn't, I'd go home to my sexy Italian paramour and spend the rest of my life cooking pasta, which I figured wasn't such a bad way to spend a life.

The interview went well and they agreed to book me. Then, two days before the show, I confessed to my lie. I told them I'd never done a bridal show before and wasn't sure how to do one, but I could do the

Dior pivot. Were they annoyed? Yes. But they were also impressed with my honesty, and my pivot, so I got a crash course in how to show a bridal gown in a crowded showroom. I learned how to put on a bridal gown in less than a minute, how to lift the hem and how to glow like I was walking down the aisle. The only bridal gown I'd ever worn was a knee-length dress I bought at the Princess Shop in Concord when Dick and I got married. I had thought it was the most beautiful dress at the time, even though it probably didn't cost more than twenty dollars—which was a fair amount of money back then. Now I was wearing twenty-pound dresses that cost more than a mortgage and I felt like a royal bride every time I put one on.

The opening of the show finally came, and the very first bridal gown I wore was so heavy with beadwork that as I made the Dior pivot, I let the gown fall on the foot of one of the women buyers—who promptly let out a cry letting it be known that I'd offended her innocent toes and messed up spectacularly.

I was certain that I'd blown it. But the event was so busy and the gowns changed so constantly that it wasn't long before my mishap was forgotten, and I smiled and pivoted my way through bridal gown after bridal gown until I felt as if I'd married every buyer in the place. And they loved me.

They loved me so much, in fact, that I was hired to do a special shoot. Because it was quite expensive for buyers to come to New York all the time, and since every town had a bridal store that sold bridal gowns, prom dresses, and mother-of-the-bride dresses, it was standard practice to produce a book of photographs of the many designs and send the book to the buyers of these bridal stores.

One of the vendors, a man I'll call Pete, had become a familiar face, so when he asked if I could come to his home to model for a shoot of the new bridal line, I accepted. While it may have been unconventional, it wasn't uncommon for a photographer to have a small studio setup at his home and do shoots out of there occasionally—after all, that was how I got my start, when George Resnik took my first headshots and got me into the business. Besides, Pete assured me that his wife would be assisting me, so I was happy to do the shoot.

When I got to his home we began the shoot. There was a screen which I ducked behind for my changings, and Pete's wife helped me in and out of the heavy, fragile gowns. I was already growing accustomed to strangers seeing me in my underwear, so I felt comfortable with her helping me. In fact, I needed her helping me to get in and out of those gowns quickly, because some of them had layers and layers of stiff crinoline to give the skirts a puffy bell shape, and navigating those skirts could be a challenge. The skirts also gave the bridal gowns a nineteenth century antebellum feel, made all the more fun by a sheer, transparent parasol Pete sometimes had me hold. We laughed through the whole shoot and I couldn't believe I was actually being paid to play dress up!

As we reached the end of the shoot, as I was undressing behind the screen, Pete called for me to come out for one more shot. I put on my robe, and stepped out from behind the screen.

"We like to give the salesmen a little something to smile about when they're on the road," he said, his wife standing by my side. "Can you just pick up the parasol and stand behind it, then untie your robe?"

I looked to his wife, and she was smiling a mischievous smile.

"It's just a little something all the girls do," he added.

While I knew he could be saying that just to get me to do the shot, I also knew that the other models probably did do it. And if I didn't do it, this photographer wouldn't hire me anymore—and all the photographers hung out together, so it could have a ripple effect. He might even say something bad about me to Miss Newman. If I did do it, however, I'd be essentially doing a pinup shot.

Having kids to feed and bills to pay, however, and his wife right there in the room, I dropped my robe, twirled that parasol, and laughed like Bettie Page.

It was during this time that I began to learn something about the fashion world. Up until then, I'd mostly been learning about being in front of the camera. I did learn about makeup and hair and gained some sense of style, but I hadn't learned anything much about the world of high fashion and clothes. But at the bridal show I learned about buying. The buyers would buy the dresses they liked—if they liked any at all—and it was up to us to convince them that the dresses were worth buying. A buyer who was "open to buying," was OTB, and those were the ones we courted. It was our goal to get them to go from OTB to "leaving paper," which meant leaving an order to buy. I'd thought my job was looking good in the clothes, but I was learning that my job was also about making a sale.

If the showrooms were where the sales were made, it was in the backrooms where everything happened. There was a room in the back where the patternmaker was busy measuring and cutting fabrics, making alterations, adding beadwork and lace and pinning the designs to a clothes dummy.

There was one particular patternmaker I came to know fairly well because the changing room was behind his work area. His name was Fabio, and like Angelo, he was from Italy. Fabio instantly liked me, the minute I said my first word in Italian.

"You have *la bella figura!*" he said, looking my body up and down with a swath of white silk draped over his arm and a measuring tape draped around his neck. He made a gesture for me to turn around, and I complied.

"*Bella, bella!*" He wrapped the silk around me, stepped back as he held it in place, then removed it. "I make *you* my model. Not *this.*" He gestured with scorn to the adjustable women's dress form he'd been using to pin his patterns.

And so it was that in between showing the bridal gowns, my breaks were spent having the muslin they used for samples pinned to my body.

After three weeks of doing the bridal shows, and getting pinned in the backroom in between, I walked back to Miss Newman's agency and signed my contract with MSA.

But not without spotting the same old woman, resting in a doorway, her wagon piled high with her bags. This time, I walked right past her.

I was learning to harden my heart, and wasn't sure I liked it.

Chapter 11

Coat Hanger with a Mouth

As the months passed, Miss Newman kept me steadily employed. She was fair and honest and made sure that her models were well taken care of. She knew I was pretty naïve, but that didn't dissuade her from sending me out on calls. Instead, she kept an eye out on me so no one took advantage of me, and always made sure I didn't get stuck working after five because she knew I had a family to take care of.

But I still had to prove myself. She was not going to send me out if I didn't maintain the agency's reputation. As long as I worked hard and impressed the clients, she gave me plenty of work.

She started me in the showrooms. Showroom modeling didn't require a lot of experience, and though I'd gotten some experience with Gloria, New York City was a whole new ball game. I was a new face. I was starting from scratch.

One good thing about the showrooms was that it was pretty much a nine-to-five job, Monday through Friday. That gave me time to be with Angelo and the kids, but the work was hectic. And it tended to be seasonal. By the time I'd finished up with the bridal show it was early fall, which was fur season. I went from warehouse to warehouse where old brick buildings were converted into what we now call lofts, with high ceilings, big windows and lots of space. The space was filled with tables and chairs—each buyer had their own table—and racks and racks of clothes. The racks would be moved when it was time for a show so we had room to walk around, strutting in luxurious furs, opening them to show off the satin lining and exquisite stitching, closing the coats once again, and doing a pivot so they could see the coats from the back, then strutting over to the next table and the next and the next, hoping the buyers from the top department stores and most exclusive boutiques wouldn't leave without buying.

I learned to fluff up the fur to make it look as thick and luxurious as possible, but on cheap furs, little bits of fur would be flying all over the place when I fluffed it. I winced to think that any animal gave its life to be converted into one of those wretched coats. Others were fabulous, worth tens of thousands of dollars, and I felt like a movie star putting them on. But luxurious or cheap as rat's hide, I treated each coat as if it was the most magnificent coat ever made.

In February and September it was Fashion Week. That was when all the top designers showed their new lines to buyers, the press and the public. If I thought I was meeting VIPs at the Concord Hotel, Fashion Week was a veritable spectacle of wealth, fame and conceit. Everyone was beautiful. Everyone was beautifully dressed and adorned. And everyone was dripping with money as they gaped and gazed and occasionally snickered or sneered at the endless array of outfits we'd parade before them.

Fashion Week was frantic, but it was also glamorous. I especially loved it when they set up tents in Bryant Park in Midtown Manhattan. Inside the tents the music never stopped playing and the champagne and the egos flowed. There were so many celebrities wandering around that I felt as if I was one of them.

The buyers were worshipped—the vendors would do anything to make the sale, showering them with so many gifts—from copious champagne to some over-the-top gifts such as home renovations or expense-paid vacations—that they felt entitled to everything—including the models. It was playtime for them and many took models back to their hotel rooms, which only made it harder for the rest of us who had to tell them no without losing the sale.

It was the showrooms, however, that were a real education. It was far different from the work I'd done with Gloria. There are rarely cameras in the showrooms, but there are designers, their design team, and buyers from all the top department stores eager to see the new lines. It was my job to impress the designers by wearing their designs so perfectly that they'd want me back again. More importantly, it was my job to impress the buyers by looking so beautiful and moving so elegantly in those designs that whether they were OTB or not, they'd end up leaving paper—ordering enough of those designs that the designers would call me back. Everything became focused on getting the call back, because that's what would impress Miss Newman and get me paid. And getting the call back meant learning the tricks of the trade, such as taking our bras off several hours before a show so there wouldn't be any bra lines showing on our flesh when we wore a strapless gown or something else that showed our skin. Well let me tell you, it could be damn cold in some of those showrooms so in order to keep my freezing cold nipples from showing, I'd cover them with Band-Aids—only to have the Band-Aids pop off occasionally, right in the middle of a show!

I was learning a lot, and it wasn't just about dressing and undressing. I quickly discovered that the buyers, virtually all men, weren't just interested in the garments. Many of them were from out of town, and a trip to New York City to watch beautiful women strutting around them was the next best thing to a bachelor party. Some couldn't control their hands, others couldn't control their mouths, and it was up to me to turn them down without losing the sale, which wasn't always easy. I increasingly wanted out of the showrooms and into the backrooms, where hands still groped occasionally, but far less often.

When I had first started working for Miss Newman, word had gotten out that I could do fittings after my little fittings with Fabio during the breaks at the bridal show. The fittings were in the backrooms of the garment district where the patternmakers, cutters, and sample hands—the men and women who sew the cut pieces together—all worked, and it wasn't long before I was spending more time in these backrooms than I was in front of buyers, because my measurements were almost exactly the same as their dressmaker dummies. In fact, some places even had their dummies made to my measurements, so if I was unavailable for a fitting, they could pin the patterns to the dummies until I returned. After the first dummy was made to my measurements, I started paying close attention to my posture and learned to hold myself as straight as a dummy—if I slouched, the clothes wouldn't fit.

"I'm getting quite a few calls for you to do fit modeling for the designers," Miss Newman said not long after I'd signed with her. "It seems you're making quite an impression as a coat hanger."

"Coat hanger" was the term for fit models, the models they pin their patterns to, and though I hadn't even heard the term before I started working in New York, I was learning fast. My job was to stand still and not say a word, as they pinned their clothes onto me like a dressmaker's dummy, jabbing me with their scissors and pins as if I were indeed that dummy. But I'd been a dummy far too long in my life. I'd kept my mouth shut when my dad would get drunk and knock me around. I had kept my mouth shut when Dick would tell me how worthless, disappointing or stupid I was. And I had kept my mouth shut when guy after guy had come on to me for no better reason than I'd been friendly to them.

Now that I was working, just as I was learning to walk past the bag ladies and beggars I passed each day, I was learning to say no when I meant it. Just as I had told that "chaperone" on the beer shoot to take me home when he offered me a sexy red dress, I was learning that speaking up got me what I wanted. I had been so timid at first, so afraid that what I thought and felt and wanted simply didn't matter. But it did matter. Maybe it was all that waitressing, maybe it was all that abuse from Dick, but whatever it was, when they were pinning those clothes to me, I couldn't help but share my opinions.

"No woman is going to want to wear a dress like that," I'd say. "It isn't something she can move in. You need to make it looser."

"No, it's too loose. It won't show her curves. Cinch in the waist a bit. Women want to feel sexy."

"These pants ride up too high. They're fine for standing, but not for sitting."

"That's just what I need," one client sarcastically retorted. "A coat hanger with mouth."

From that day on, that's what they began calling me—a term Miss Newman liked so much she even began putting it on my promotional materials.

"Darlene Young, The Coat Hanger with the Mouth."

I was coming to feel good about that mouth. I was learning that I didn't need to stay silent and obedient, even with our best clients. My thoughts mattered. Women's thoughts mattered. And as it dawned on me that my thoughts mattered, something else dawned on me as well. I could make myself indispensable with my mouth, just by telling the designers what they needed to know about the way their clothes were being made. But designers weren't the only ones I had to please. I'd stumbled into an entirely new world where everyone wanted to be pleased and not everyone could ever be pleased. As for my agent, Miss Newman, she was pleased as long as I got the callbacks, and as long as I didn't gain or lose a single inch on any part of my body.

Miss Newman or one of her staff measured me every week. They measured my chest, my waist, my hips and my thighs. They measured my shoulders, my arms, my neck, and my ankles. It was just a fluke of nature that I was able to still eat all that delicious Italian pasta and pastry and not gain any weight. No doubt it was because I was constantly on the run, and never had a chance to sit down. There was one small problem, however. I was out of proportion. My small butt didn't match my big boobs. But I'd figured out how to solve that problem early on. In one of my first go-sees, for a line of pants, I was afraid the client would reach the same conclusion as Miss Newman had when we first met— that I had no butt. Knowing they'd be measuring my hips, right before the interview I had an idea. I pulled the shoulder pads out of my coat and slid them under my underpants. Not only did it pad my ass, but it gave a nice, smooth clean line that would impress them.

"A perfect figure! And such a nice derriere," the client pronounced. I got the job and from that day on, I kept my derriere padded—being sure to lean against a wall whenever Miss Newman measured me, so she couldn't feel it and discover my secret!

When there was no work in the showrooms, Miss Newman put me on the runways where I could show off my Dior pivot. Between the showrooms, the runways, and the fittings, I was constantly working, often up to eight shows a day and at different sites, which meant running from block to block, if not across the city. By the end of every night, when I went home and took off my three-inch high heels, my feet were bleeding.

One thing I was learning was that when it comes to the fashion world, there are a lot of different players involved, and each one has their own self-interest in mind. For the designers, it's getting their name known. And they do that by designing the dresses and other garments that women want, and more importantly, by broadcasting their name and line as if they're the most original designs to ever walk the runway. They aren't always as original as the public might think, however. It wasn't uncommon for designers to send someone to the department stores over the weekends to see what was on the racks, and then have them return again on Monday to see what sold off the racks. The clever staff who got these gigs learned early on to make friends with the sales staff who would tell them what had sold. Once they knew what was coming off the racks, they'd buy a few pieces, take them to the patternmakers, have them take the clothes apart, and make patterns out of them. Then the sample hands would sew them into "new" designs.

But they couldn't use just any fabric. As my career in the garment district was flourishing, so was my Italian. Between Angelo and his mother and my own efforts to learn some of their language—along with what I overheard in those backrooms where the Italian patternmakers were chattering back and forth—I started to get pretty good at learning the language. The better I got, the more they talked to me.

I hadn't been there very long when I discovered what probably everyone who works in the garment district already knows, but to this small town girl was a big revelation. And that was that the Gambino family was in charge of pretty much everything that was bought and sold in the garment district. They determined what fabrics would be used by the manufacturers, which were not always the same fabrics that the designers wanted their clothes to be made of. It led to some heated arguments, but no one questioned the power of the cartels to dictate women's fashion.

And neither did I. As far as I was concerned, they were just another player in the chain of production, and I was just a small link in that chain. But as I learned about fabrics and weaves, threads and stitches, cuts and collars, I also learned that there was cheating at every level. What one vendor said he was selling might be far lower quality than he stated, or what one manufacturer was producing might be a far cry from what the designer had ordered. These "shortcuts" almost always led to the clothes not selling or ending up on the sales racks and costing money.

I quickly learned that the average hanger is 17" wide. Anything I had to tug to get off the hanger was not going to go over my head very easily. And since I was changing clothes faster than a quick-change artist, getting that sweater on and off quickly was important. It wasn't just important to me—it was important to any woman who wanted to get that sweater over her head.

If I was trying on a pullover sweater, it would have to have a head opening of at least 22" in order to come off that hanger—and over my head. If it was any smaller, it would flatten any woman's hairdo and her makeup would be smeared all over the sweater. She wouldn't want to buy it. It also meant that it was under the spec measurement. The spec measurement would be the measurements the designer had given the patternmaker. Most of the sample hands who made the clothes knew what they were doing, but there were some houses where they liked to cut corners and they used inexperienced sample hands to cut the clothes and inferior materials, like cheap thread.

Cotton thread doesn't have any give. But it's cheaper than polyester thread or poly-wrap cotton thread, so a lot of vendors would cheat and use cotton—which not only makes it harder to put on, but keeps popping out at the seams—a hallmark of cheap manufacturing.

I had to take as many garments off and on as I possibly could in an hour because I was usually booked back to back. So the minute I struggled to get one on over my head, I knew the vendor had used cotton thread. If it was a cheap house, selling discount clothes, that was to be expected. But many of the vendors were selling to upscale department stores at a high price, claiming their clothes were well made when they weren't. When I'd point out to a vendor he was using cotton thread and he argued that he was using a poly-wrapped thread, I would pull a piece of the thread out of the seam in his garment, take a match and set fire to the thread. If it was cotton, it would burn fast. If it was poly thread, it would make a little ball at the end of the thread and burn more slowly.

Tricks like that might not have earned me many points with the vendors, but they did catch the attention of the manufacturers, who started calling me because it would cost them a lot more money in the end to fix a garment or to discount it.

As a result, I was finding myself doing more and more fittings, standing still for hours as they draped and pinned their fabrics over my body, telling them what they needed to do to make the garments something women would wear. I was becoming so good at it that designers were requesting me by name—or asking for the "coat hanger with the mouth." The vendors asked for me, as well. They found that I could help them fix the problems in their clothes before they were sent to the stores, which saved them a great deal of time and money.

The work was coming in so fast that I'd find myself with a stack of paychecks from Miss Newman, each representing a different vendor or designer, with her commission deducted. I'd come home and hand them straight to Angelo, since I'd been raised not to think about managing my money. Money was something men took charge of. My job was to work and keep the house running.

Then one day, Angelo said to me, "You know, you're making more than I am!"

I was flabbergasted. Angelo made good money. I was so convinced that my income was just something "extra" that I'd paid no attention to it. It had never occurred to me that it was adding up. But it was. Just one year before I'd been making ninety cents an hour. Now I was making a hundred and fifty to two hundred an hour, which in the early seventies was astronomical for a college-educated man, let alone a woman who'd dropped out of high school.

Yet I was still that young girl who'd dropped out of high school. I still lived in a world where men were in charge of the important things, like life decisions and money. I continued to hand over my paychecks, not thinking twice about where that money would be going. Now that I knew it was coming in, my focus was on making more. My career was taking off.

The only problem was, I wasn't always enjoying it. I didn't like the showrooms and the runways that left me feeling like a spectacle to gawk at. It triggered that same feeling I'd had all my life—that my only value was in my looks. And standing still for hours, not even free to go pee, could be excruciating. Yet through it all, my home life couldn't have been better. Angelo had a busy career, as well, but we always found time for each other. He adored Shelley and Michael, and me more than ever. We laughed, shared long kisses and long conversations, and ate the best food in the world. Still, there was something missing. As happy as I was, sometimes it felt as if my entire life was spent rushing from show-room to runway to backroom to home to school to pick up the kids then back home to fix dinner and clean up the house and then doing it all over again. I missed my family, and I missed something special they had given me—a sense that I was a part of something greater.

Maybe it was Danny's accident and paralysis that had triggered this need inside me. Seeing his life cut short like that, and his struggle to live despite his injuries and limitations, or maybe it was watching my father struggling with his rage and shame as his life took him from war hero to war wounded, a man reduced to his spiritual pain and his own self-loathing. Whatever it was, I knew that my own life needed a greater meaning. Just as Danny had learned to find that meaning when he could no longer walk, I had to find that meaning now that I finally could walk—not just on the runway, but on my own two feet, increasingly confident and self-reliant.

And that's how I gave up all my power, and let a group of men I barely knew make all my decisions for me.

Chapter 12

Witness Protection

As any parent discovers, especially working parents, we just can't do it alone. We need a community of parents who help out when we need it. And since I often found myself running late from a booking in the city, it was a great relief and comfort to know that Michael and Shelley could always go to the home of their new friends just up the street. Their parents, Joe and Lela, were also from Italy, and not only did we fall in love with their five kids, we fell in love with them. They were warm and funny and delightful and always watched Michael and Shelley when neither of us could get home in time. We became fast friends, and there wasn't anything we wouldn't do for them in return.

There was just one drawback. Michael began coming home after visiting with them, talking about the Bible. Of course, like most Americans, I'd grown up with respect for the Bible, but like so many, particularly in the seventies, I'd grown to distrust the religious teachings of my childhood. I wondered if there was a God, since I'd felt abandoned so many times. I wondered about the church, since it taught that I was a sinner, for divorcing and living "in sin." Far worse, although neither Dick nor I had been Catholic, I was stunned to receive a letter from a bishop of the Catholic Church, informing me that Dick had had our marriage annulled!

It seems the babysitter was Catholic, and in order to marry her, he'd converted to Catholicism and erased the fact that he'd ever been married to me in the eyes of God—despite the children that we'd borne.

Given my estrangement from the church, when Michael started talking about the Bible, I immediately grew concerned. What was he being told? How was he being misled? What dangers were before him?

My fears about the Bible and religion were inextricably linked to a memory so deeply painful that even though it had happened years before, it still left me feeling a cold, penetrating dread that I could only shake by turning away from the church altogether.

It was the summer of '69. I had just put away the groceries and was watching my two little ones playing on the front lawn while Dick mowed the grass when we heard the ambulance go by. Our house had been just off Route 93, and being so close to the highway, we were used to hearing sirens.

"This happens all the time," I said, shaking my head and looking out toward the busy street. "When will people slow down on this road?" I moved protectively toward my children. Michael was already three and a half and Shelley had just started walking. It wouldn't be long before they might be running into the street; we would have to find another place pretty soon, *a place further from the road,* I thought. Of course, I'd had no way of knowing back then that the other place would never come, at least not for me and Dick. But at the time, my mind was on keeping my children safe, and imagining a brighter future with my new family.

I don't know why I even noticed the ambulance that day, but the sound of its siren lingered in my mind like a heartbreaking song, until the telephone rang.

It was my sister, Julie. She was sobbing. "Danny's been in an accident, on his bike," she said, her words hard to make out through her cries.

My mind froze. The image of my little brother on his bicycle, the fear I felt, it all hung suspended in midair. I'd just run into him outside the American Legion Hall, waiting for my dad to come outside and take him fishing. I knew my father was inside drinking, and would never take Danny fishing.

I'd urged Danny to leave, to get on his bike and have fun. And that's what he did. He started riding his bike and didn't see the car illegally parked at the bottom of the hill until he rode straight into it.

"He can't move the lower half of his body," she said. "He's at Franklin Hospital. Hurry!"

I hung up the phone and sat right down and sobbed. I could do nothing else. It had been Danny in that ambulance we'd heard. And in that moment, I knew what my little brother was facing. The horror, the broken bones, the agony and fear, all the terrible suffering he was going through was just the beginning of a lifetime ordeal.

I picked up the phone and made a call before rushing out the door. I called the church rectory and asked that they pray for Danny. In that terrible moment, I made a confession—I confessed to the woman who answered the phone that I was scared my prayers would not be heard.

"Oh, that's not true at all," she said. "If you've been a good girl, God will hear your prayers and your brother will be fine."

Her words stopped me cold. Those words scared me even more than my own doubts did. Now the burden of my brother's recovery had been placed on me. I thought back to all the things I'd done in the sight of God and I gasped in horror.

Oh no, I thought, *Danny is in so much trouble and it's all my fault!*

That was when Dick had been pressuring me for an open marriage. That was when I'd briefly considered going along. Thinking that way, I felt guilty. An open marriage wasn't something a newly married woman should ever consider. But I was getting to the point where I'd try anything. Yet the fact that I was considering it, even if only in a desperate effort to please my husband, had filled me with guilt. Thinking God would never listen to someone with guilt like mine, I stopped praying. That's why I couldn't pray anymore. I knew in my gut that an open marriage was wrong, and I felt ashamed for even considering it.

In that hideous moment, a moment that haunted me for years, pure panic for my brother hit me like a bullet in the chest, followed instantly by self-loathing. Cold fear, creeping guilt, shame and self-blame—all the emotions and fears that had been inspired by the church for as long as I could remember—washed over me as if to drown me.

I muttered a thank you into the phone and hung up.

All through my childhood and into my teens I had tried to be a good girl, but I'd dropped out of school to get married, fantasized about other men, had lost faith in my husband. I had failed, and now this woman from the rectory was telling me that God surely wouldn't listen to my prayers now. I had not been a good girl.

In that moment, holding the telephone receiver in my hand, I had felt a chill so cold and damp that it was as if a ghost had embraced me. My world became dark, black as a coffin. I moved as if both dead and desperate, hanging up the receiver, grabbing my keys, and rushing to the door, when the phone rang again.

It was my mother. She wasn't crying, but speaking in a tone I'd never before heard. Every syllable was serious, efficient, intentional. A long, deliberate breath separated every sentence.

"They're taking Danny to Hanover," she said, referring to the nearest big-city hospital many miles away. "Franklin wouldn't admit him. They can't help him. He's in bad shape, Darlene. His back is broken, and his pelvis is shattered. Their doctors aren't trained for this kind of orthopedic trauma. He'll get better care in Hanover."

She was relaying the information she'd received as if every line would somehow bring greater clarity and control over the situation. I knew she was in terrible pain and felt so helpless to undo all the damage. And I dared not reveal to her my sins before God, the sins that may have caused Danny's punishment.

I felt as much a little girl as I had ever been, a child concealing her shame before her mother, as if her bad behavior had broken her brother's favorite toy. Only it wasn't his toy that had been broken. It was his body. I had not been a good girl. And Danny was paying the price.

"We've found a new way of being led into faith," Lela one day confided. Like Angelo, she and Joe had grown distrustful of the Catholic Church. "We've become Jehovah's Witnesses," she said. "You should check it out. Come with us to the Kingdom Hall this Sunday. You'll like it. And Michael has shown a real interest."

I couldn't have been more surprised if she'd announced she and Joe had decided to become Chinese. Jehovah's Witnesses? I knew nothing about them and I was just as distrustful of this new way of being led into faith as I'd come to feel about the Catholic Church. And my son wanted to join them? I didn't like that one bit—I immediately feared losing him in some way to what I imagined was some kind of cult.

Still, I felt that my children had a right to choose what they wanted to believe. Michael had been so lost since we'd moved to New Jersey. His dad hardly ever saw him or Shelley, except when I took him to New Hampshire for the summers.

"It seems so unfair," Brenda said to me, already pregnant with the first of their children, "we give the kids all the candy, and you have to take them to the dentist." She was speaking metaphorically, and she sure did hit the nail on the head. They saw Michael and Shelley so rarely that when they did see them it was like one big, happy vacation. When they came back to me, there were house rules and bedtimes and all the other responsibilities of daily living. In between those "vacations," there weren't many phone calls or any visits from Daddy or Brenda. Michael's father had so little to do with him. And Michael was growing older; he needed something more than I alone could give him. Was that something going to end up being the Jehovah's Witnesses? Was I wrong to be afraid? Could this "new faith" help him?

Angelo seemed receptive, as well. He was an adult; clearly, he had a right to believe anything he wanted. Just because the church had given me bad advice so many years before didn't mean that Angelo and Michael might not find some truth and fulfillment for themselves. The only thing I could do, I reasoned, was have an open mind.

Besides, Lela was so loving and gentle, and not at all foolish. Surely, she had thought this through. I was overreacting. She wouldn't just join some crazy cult. As for Angelo, he seemed eager to learn more, and he certainly wasn't foolish. I had to learn for myself what this "new faith" was all about. So I went to the library and read up on the Jehovah's Witnesses. Rather than alleviate my worries, however, it only made them worse. I didn't like at all what I read. I learned that if Angelo and my children did join the Witnesses they would be forbidden from speaking to me unless I joined, too. That didn't sit right with me, not at all. In fact, it sounded downright awful.

I also learned that the men controlled their wives and children, telling them what to believe and how to behave and even what shows they could watch on TV. If you failed to believe or behave, you would lose your family. The more I read, and the more I listened to Joe and Lela, the more I heard, "conform, become one of us because everyone else on the face of the planet will not make it into the New Kingdom, so you'd better do as we say, think as we think, and pay your price of admission."

Red flags went up for me all over the place. Yet I closed my eyes to those red flags as I began to meet some of these Jehovah's Witnesses that Joe and Lela introduced us to. Everyone I met seemed so loving. They had such a strong commitment to family and it seemed that the men really loved their wives more than they loved themselves. It was also great not getting hit on by them. I had grown so accustomed to being cautious around men—whether single, married, vendors, buyers, designers or "chaperones"—that not getting hit on felt incredibly free-ing. I liked that feeling.

They were also making a difference in the world. They didn't believe in war and if my son did join them and the draft—which Nixon had only recently ended—was resumed, I wouldn't be losing him to war, as my mother said of my father. In fact, she felt so strongly that the war had destroyed my father that when we were told Danny would be a paraplegic, the first words she uttered were, "Well, at least we won't be losing him to war."

Those words had shattered me then, and now as I watched my own little boy grow older, I began to fear the same. I'd seen what the war had done to my father. It was war that drove the violence into him, my mother had said. Before World War II, he'd been a different man. But he came home damaged beyond repair with a chest full of medals he wore on his Eisenhower jacket like a proud but broken general.

My father's name was Clyde, but everyone knew him as "Lucky." It was a name he had certainly earned. He'd been in a Sherman tank when it blew up and couldn't get medical attention right away. By the time they got to him, all they could do was put a tourniquet on his leg while he kept slipping in and out of consciousness. They didn't even have morphine to give him. They put his knee back together with steel and sent him back into battle.

A short time later he was in a tank that got firebombed. It was engulfed in flames but he managed to escape, only to be shot in the stomach five times. When they found him, parts of his intestines were lying on the ground along with a part of his scalp. All his hair had burned off. After they finally got him back to a hospital, they pulled jagged pieces of steel out of him, and put another back in—a steel plate they screwed into his head.

But not all his war stories ended badly for him. He loved telling the story of how one time he was outside relieving himself when the enemy tried to kill him but he grabbed the man's own sword and killed him first, then finished his business and pulled his pants back up. He brought that sword home with him like a trophy. A trophy that had come at a cost, because though he'd killed in self-defense, killing takes a toll on any man's soul.

The sixth bullet in his stomach he gave to himself after a fight with my mom when she'd tried to leave him.

Naturally, she came back. She always did, no matter how dark and ugly their marriage became.

I'd lived my life under the weight of that Eisenhower jacket, each heavy metal a testament to my father's wounds as much as his victories. I'd lived my life under the fear of his temper; the temper the war had sent him home with. I'd lived my life under the dark shadows of his drinking, the drinking that had kept him inside the American Legion

Hall that afternoon, as Danny waited outside for him to take him fishing, the last day he'd ever walk.

I couldn't imagine sending my son to war if it meant he might return as damaged as my father had been. I was a proud patriot, but my own childhood had been a casualty of warfare. I didn't want that for my child. I didn't want it for any child.

As a Jehovah's Witness, Michael could probably be considered a conscientious objector. The more I thought about their commitment to peace, the less I thought about the red flags, and the more I focused on the good things that I was coming to love about the Witnesses. The kids didn't do drugs, honesty was very important to them, and the men were monogamous. Impressed by these values, we began to go to the Kingdom Hall with Joe and Lela, and soon we were regulars. It wasn't long before I found myself not just going to the services but reading the Bible cover to cover to learn as much as I could. Maybe through this new faith I would find God and fill that spiritual vacuum that had seemed to be growing inside me ever since Danny's accident and my divorce.

I just wanted to believe so much that I had found the perfect life for my children and Angelo. Still, in my gut, I remained cautious. So I did what I always do when I feel trapped or uncertain—I kept myself busy. My work was a great distraction and keeping me so occupied that I didn't have time to give much thought to the Witnesses. They were, for a time, just a source of great comfort and community, and that seemed to be enough.

It was certainly a relief to walk into a place of worship and feel accepted and loved. As we came to live by the rules of the Witnesses, we adapted our lives to the religion, and the more we adapted to our new faith, the more safe and protected I felt. So when the elders told us we needed to be married, we got married.

It didn't feel so much like an order at the time. In fact, it felt quite romantic. The whole day had been magical—Angelo and I had spent it buying a house together. This time, my name was on it, right alongside Angelo's. I'd been hearing for some time from the elders, as well as from Joe and Lela, that having a different surname from Angelo's didn't look right. Even Michael had started bothering me about it. But having different names wasn't on my mind that day. All that was on my mind was that I finally had everything I'd ever wanted—a loving partner, two precious children, a well-paying career that kept me busy, and now, a home of my own. The only one who wanted something more was Angelo. He felt that being legally married would be best for the kids—how could we keep going to the Kingdom Hall when we had to explain to everyone we met that we weren't husband and wife?

The more people mentioned it, the more I began to feel that I was being selfish by not wanting to ever be dependent on a man again. Angelo had done so much for us and I did love him. Besides, I reasoned, nothing would change if we married. It was just a piece of paper, after all. I'd still have my own income. So when he surprised me at the end of that wonderful romantic day with an even more romantic proposal—telling me he loved me and wanted to spend the rest of his life with me—I said yes and we hurried home to tell the kids. The next day, we told Joe and Lela, and then the elders.

Everyone was thrilled, even Angelo's mom, who had grown to adore me. She had only one request of me, which she made right after we'd said our vows.

"Darlene," she said, "you do me one favor. You no wear heels for wedding picture."

I was taller than Angelo when I wore my heels, and she didn't want me to be taller than her son in the wedding picture. I looked at my new mom and said, "Angelo is not a tall man in height, but his strength and wisdom make him tower over every man I know." Then I walked over to my new husband and got ready to take the family wedding shot. By this time, I'd had enough photos taken to have my timing down. Standing tall next to Angelo, I looked over to my new mother-in-law, smiled and kicked off my shoes, just as the photo was taken.

She beamed. She knew that I loved her and her request had been honored.

I just wondered how she was going to feel about not having any grandchildren of her own. Surely, she wanted them. After all, she was

Italian and all Italians loved family. Angelo did, as well, but he had assured me that my two children were all he needed, because I sure didn't want any more. I just couldn't imagine taking care of another, the two kept me so busy as it was.

"I love you, Darlene," Angelo had said when he proposed, "and your kids are my kids. I don't need kids of my own."

That had been what sealed the deal. He knew that as much as I loved the two I had, I didn't have it in me for any more.

And there was another reason I didn't want to have any more babies. A big reason. Miss Newman still measured me every week. If I gained so much as an inch, I lost a lot of money. If I became pregnant, my career wasn't just put on hold for nine months. It was over.

"You're making a name for yourself, Darlene," she had said, impressed with my rising demand. "Just be sure your measurements never change. Those numbers are what are bringing you in all that money."

Getting pregnant was not an option.

But I didn't give it much thought. If anything, I was taking my success for granted. I was so happy with my life, that I didn't worry about much of anything at all. I would just smile as I walked into the Model Service Agency from a new booking interview and see the eyes all turn on me. This time, the eyes weren't looking me up and down like I was some hopeless old lady. This time, I'd hear, "We might as well just go home, now that Darlene is here."

I was becoming one of the top fit models in the agency, the first one they asked for. My career just kept getting bigger and bigger. I still did the runways and showrooms, and from my initial debut bluffing my way into bridal shows, I had become a seasoned pro showing bridal gowns. While I had married Angelo in a white cotton peasant dress, by the time I'd said, "I do," I'd probably worn more elegant bridal gowns than any woman in New York.

One of my best clients was Ron LoVece, one of the top designers of bridal gowns. Ron was an attractive silver-haired gay man who dressed impeccably in pinstripe suits. His gowns were the dream of every Manhattan bride. They were magnificent; romantic dresses with the most exquisite lacework and beading imaginable. Every one of them looked like something a princess would wear, and just putting one on transformed me from small town girl to royalty. Ron loved the way I looked in his dresses because I was chesty and my large bosom would hold up the intricate beadwork for all the clients to see. But there was one thing he didn't like—my long, black hair.

"Cut it off!" he commanded. "The buyers are all staring at your hair, not my dresses!"

The thought of cutting off my thick, luxurious dark hair was unthinkable. It was my hallmark—I couldn't imagine myself without it. I was wearing it in the Farrah Fawcett style of the times and being told to cut it off felt like a horrible punishment.

But he made it clear that if I didn't cut it off, he wasn't going to use me as his model anymore—and that wouldn't go over well with Miss Newman, or with other clients who would soon catch wind of it and they, too, would decide my hair had to go. There was no getting out of it—my hair would have to come off.

"Yes sir," I told him, "but not until after my wedding."

He agreed, so after the wedding, when Angelo and I were honeymooning in Italy, I went to a salon and had them whack it off. Unfortunately, my Italian wasn't good enough to express what I wanted, and the hair stylist didn't speak a word of English. I did my best to mime what I wanted and to embellish the mime with the rudimentary Italian I knew.

The results were terrible. The woman hacked away at my hair, then blew it dry with no style whatsoever. I was able to get it into shape myself, but the experience was so upsetting that weeks later, changing in the back during a show, I shared the upsetting experience with one of the other models.

"It was the worst blow job ever!" I told her, telling the story of the horrible cut and blow dry.

Moments later, Ron stormed into the backroom. He was livid. "The buyers can hear you!" he loudly whispered, "If you're going to have such a fowl mouth, you're out of here!"

I laughed like I'd never laughed before. It had never occurred to me that what I'd said had another meaning. I explained to Ron that I was talking about my hair styling, and his fury quickly changed. By the time I returned to show off one of his new designs, a stunning off-white strapless gown with a long and provocative veil, the room was all smiles. He'd informed the buyers of the true meaning of my terrible *blowjob!*

Besides modeling and fitting gorgeous fashions, I had a steady stream of business fitting uniforms, like the kind workers for fast food restaurants had to wear. We didn't have a strong overseas market at the time, so to avoid paying decent wages to the skilled laborers in New York, they often employed prisoners who were paid a fraction of the ninety cents an hour I'd been making as a waitress. The work for me, however, paid well, and I felt valued because my own experience waiting tables helped to make the uniforms better. I reminded the patternmakers that many of the women who worked in these places were heavier and so they needed to increase the measurements in the hips, bustline and waist. And because there's so much bending and reaching, they had to make the skirts longer.

I got one job working for a major airline that was fitting a new line of uniforms for the flight attendants (called stewardesses back then). Most of my work was in the garment district, but this meeting would be on the east side, a much classier side of town. I was really excited; I saw myself finally making it in the city.

I took the subway across town, found the building and took the elevator up to main offices, where a meeting was scheduled to discuss the new uniforms. I stepped off the elevator and a strikingly attractive woman sitting behind a beautiful oak desk greeted me and walked me to the conference room. As I walked down the hallway, I kept looking at the beautiful oak walls adorned with vintage photos of all the different jets they'd flown. It looked more like a successful clubhouse at a prestigious golf course than a corporate office. I was quite impressed.

When I walked into the conference room, there must have been over a dozen people sitting there and they all stood up to greet me. I felt so important, standing there at the end of a long mahogany table where everyone was gathered to listen to what I had to say.

The new uniform they were designing was a sharp one, quite nice looking, and it had a white tie, which gave it a distinguished, tailored look. It was definitely a beautiful design. There was just one problem, which I had to share with them. When I started to speak, I saw I had their full attention.

"The problem is," I began, "women aren't used to tying ties. And when we do tie them, they're on our husbands—we have learned to tie them backward. So if you put a hidden button under the collar, the stewardesses could just attach them easily."

"Like a clip-on tie," one gentleman remarked.

"Yes, exactly," I said, "but classier!"

They could see I knew what I was talking about, and life would be much easier for the stewardesses if they had to get dressed in a hurry.

"And one more thing," I added, "you want your brand to be consistent. Nobody ties a tie exactly the same way. I see twelve different angles and knots in this room right now."

I watched as each man felt the knot in his tie.

"This way, every tie will be identical."

My presentation was a hit, and they agreed to change the design of the ties. At the end of the meeting, one of the gentlemen stood up and walked me to the elevator. It felt great to be working and respected in such a prestigious atmosphere. I felt an enormous pride in what I'd just presented. As I waited for the elevator, pleasantly chatting with this man, he put his arm around my waist and pulled me in tight for a hug goodbye, slipping his phone number into my hand as his hand ran down my butt, just as the elevator door was opening up.

I stepped into the elevator, my spirits deflated as I realized that no matter where you worked in the city, uptown or downtown, east side or west, a scumbag was a scumbag.

But a butt is not a butt. I got the last laugh because all he grabbed was the padded derriere I wore to round out my ass!

As successfully as my career was going, however, my focus just wasn't on my career. My focus was on my perfect newly married life. When I wasn't working, I was so busy putting down new roots in our new home, making a life safe and happy for my kids, helping them with their homework, fixing dinner, spending time with Angelo, and going to meetings at the Kingdom Hall that my career seemed to be taking care of itself.

We even started taking trips up to New Hampshire to see my family, especially my brother Danny who had moved out of my parents' home and was living independently. I was so thrilled to see him enjoying life, living on his own. He'd even gotten a job trimming the grass around the tombstones in the cemetery, and bought himself a specially equipped truck to haul the equipment. He'd pull himself from tombstone to tombstone, dragging his body across the grass, where he'd lie alongside the dead and manicure their graves. I'd watched him once without his ever knowing I was there, sitting in my car parked at a distance, and though it broke my heart to watch him dragging himself like that, I was incredibly proud. There was a tenderness to his work that came from the tenderness in his heart. He never complained and he never sought pity. He saw himself as a servant of God, and he was serving God's call like Jesus washing the feet of the poor. Nothing was holding my baby brother back, not even paralysis.

These were the happiest years of my life. Since leaving Dick and New Hampshire, my heart had gone from stone to clay, and my family had been the sculptors who had pushed all the broken pieces of it back together again.

I'd made a safe, loving and structured life for me and my children with my marriage to Angelo. And he was as happy as I was.

What I didn't see coming was the slow, progressive suffocation that would come of "just a piece of paper." As we settled into our new and perfect life as husband and wife in our new and perfect home, little by little my husband's needs became our family's priorities. Little by little, Angelo became the master of the house, as befits a Jehovah's Witness.

Like watching my own children growing, I didn't notice the changes as they happened. I began to accept the increasing control they had over our lives as if it were completely natural. I began to accept my place as a wife. I began to accept my role as a Witness. And as I did, I began to fear breaking the rules. I began to fear being disfellowshipped, my friends and family forbidden from speaking to me. Just as I'd learned to adapt to my alcoholic father's moods, I began to conform to what was expected of me by the Witnesses just to keep the consequences of displeasing them at bay.

At the same time, I began to conceal the reality of my life from the elders, and even my friends, Joe and Lela, in order to maintain the illusion that I was safe and protected. And that reality that I was learning to conceal was my career, a career the Witnesses clearly didn't approve of, but one I wasn't about to give up, not even for the elders. I didn't lie about it, but just as I didn't discuss the Witnesses at work, I didn't dare discuss my work when I was with the Witnesses. I learned to live a double life and tell myself that it was normal.

Chapter 13

It's a Wrap

I held the dress up, wondering how in the world it would look good. The fabric was ghastly—a bright green jersey knit with a haphazard stick-print design. I'd seen it on the bolt underneath the patternmaker's table and said at the time that it was ugly. Now here it was, all sewn up, but it didn't look like much of a dress. It looked like a big swatch of fabric with sleeves and a giant collar. They'd told me it was a new kind of housedress, something to get women out of pants and back into dresses and I was all for that. I sure didn't like feeling weak, but I did like feeling feminine. I'd been wearing pants for so long that I was ready to start wearing dresses again.

I pushed my arms through the sleeves, but the armholes were pretty tight. Then I looked down and found the long skinny ribbon of fabric that was the tie and the hole it was supposed to be laced into. I pulled the tie through, wrapped it around my waist, tied it into a soft bow and straightened the collar.

Wow! They were right about her; she knew what she was doing. That ugly piece of fabric was just beautiful once I had it on. It clung and flowed in all the right places. But the sleeves didn't feel right. I reached up, pretending I was putting the dishes away on an upper shelf or lifting a baby high into the air. They were too tight. Women with bigger arms wouldn't be able to reach much higher than their shoulders. I'd have to let her know about the sleeves.

Then I bent and crouched and turned, walked and danced, and sat and crossed my legs. The dress felt so comfortable, give or take a narrow sleeve or two.

But the bust would need some work. The surplus fabric in the front was too low. Large busted women like me would be showing way too much cleavage, and for small breasted woman, they'd show no cleavage at all. The dress would need some tweaks, but I could already tell it wasn't just a housedress. It was a dress any woman would love to wear, whether to work or out to dinner.

How ingenious; there'd been wrap-around dresses before, but they were usually sleeveless and pretty much restricted to tennis outfits. I hadn't seen one designed with long sleeves and a collar, and certainly not so pretty. The sleeves were a real plus—I'd been telling the designers that older women don't like to show their arms; they needed to make more long-sleeved dresses. And since it was a wrap dress, it would be comfortable on anyone, once some adjustments were made.

I could already tell what all the fuss had been about; she was indeed a rising star.

After changing out of the dress, I returned it to Giorgio, the patternmaker, and gave him my specifications for what he needed to do to make it fit better. He thanked me and assured me he'd give it to the best sample hand we had, Francesca, and I left for the day.

When I returned the next morning, the dress would be corrected and I'd try it on again. I couldn't wait to see the magic that Giorgio would do with the corrections I gave them. He could barely speak English, but I knew he'd work wonders. And I couldn't wait to meet the designer. I'd heard she was a total powerhouse and didn't take shit from anybody. She had even been married to a prince. Her name was Diane von Furstenberg.

The next morning was a hectic one. It was a bright, crisp September day and I was already up and at it by the crack of dawn, getting the kids ready for school. While I had my mind on my work, I still had to be a mom to my kids and a wife to my husband so I just focused on getting breakfast on the table, combing the kids' hair and packing everybody's lunch, the smile stretched across my face as if this morning routine was the highlight of my day. And sometimes it was. But not today; this was an important day for me, but still I did my best to be pleasant to everyone so their own days would start out well.

I had already picked out the dress I was going to wear that day, a lovely orange and pink paisley tunic that showed my curves and legs. If I ran into Diane von Furstenberg in the elevator or somewhere else before I got started with the fittings, I wanted to impress her. I wanted her to see that I was supportive of her idea that women needed to get back into dresses.

"You're looking beautiful this morning," Angelo said as he pulled me into his body and gave me a hungry kiss before he rushed out the door. Angelo was usually gone by the time I woke up, off to film the big news story of the day. He was running a bit late this morning, so I knew he had to hurry out the door.

I returned his kiss as I scrambled the eggs, then I scooped them onto plates, buttered the toast, poured the juice and hollered for Michael and Shelley to get to the table, breakfast was ready, all in one fluid motion and in high heels as if I was filming a mid-century commercial for a new Frigidaire.

I gave Angelo one last, quick kiss and straightened his tie as he headed out the door.

"You're so sweet," he said, "what did I ever do to deserve you?"

"I'll show you when you get home," I said with a wink, sending him off as quickly as I could.

I don't think Angelo really understood that my sweetness was just to conceal the fear I was coming to feel inside. I was desperate at keeping the peace and I guess that's the reason why I let him and the elders at the Kingdom Hall have so much power over me. I'd reached the point by then that I wouldn't do anything without their approval. If I wanted to accept an assignment out of town, I asked for their permission. If I wanted to buy something expensive with my own money, I asked for their permission. If I wanted to make a new friend, I asked for their permission.

I was just like my mom, after all; we'd both become experts at deception. The deception kept the anger at bay; it kept us safe; it gave us control. But sometimes it left me feeling trapped inside my own solitude, as if there was no way out, as if I no longer existed and had been replaced with a character I played, day after day, year after year.

But then again, I really had changed over the past few years. Over the years since I'd been working in New York, I'd learned not to smile in the streets. Everybody was so friendly in New Hampshire that there were always plenty of people to talk to just by walking outside. But it was a whole different story when I moved to the city. As much as I'd been admonished to smile more, once I began working in New York, just as I'd learned not to smile at the bag lady (who I continued to pass nearly every day) I learned that if you smiled at anybody, you would rarely get a smile in return. Everybody had places to go and things to do. Smiling at a man would be perceived as a come-on. Smiling at a woman made her nervous. And after Angelo had explained to me that the reason the bag lady had screamed at me so much when I'd approached her was because she lived a rough life on the streets and people would steal from her what little she had, I understood that my smile could be perceived as a ruse, just as easily as it could invite a return smile. It hadn't taken me long to learn to walk with my head down so I wouldn't have to look in the eyes of anyone who passed by; I wouldn't have to smile. I'd learned to harden my heart.

I had also become much more sure of myself at work and didn't feel the need to sugarcoat my words like I did at home. I'd even grown to like being called, "The Coat Hanger with the Mouth." What had once been hurled as an insult had become a source of pride. My opinions finally mattered. Why couldn't I be as confident at home as I was at work, I wondered.

But I knew the answer. The answer was, if I spoke up with as much conviction at home, my marriage wouldn't last. I loved Angelo and he loved me. But as our romance had turned to marriage, a marriage under the dutiful watch of the elders, I was coming to realize that he wanted a traditional wife. He didn't mind my career and even seemed to like it, but the longer we were with the Witnesses, the more he wanted to be in charge at home. He wanted his wife to pose no threat. To love, honor and obey.

But there was no more time to think about that. It was going to be such an interesting day. I had to get to the garment district where I was going to meet this rising new star of the designer world. She was coming in to see how her latest creation looked on the fit model from the Model Service Agency—and I was that fit model. I'd landed the job when I was working for a major coat house, and they'd taken on some of her coats. I was the fit model for her coats, but I hadn't yet met her in person. With all the buzz about that dress, however, she wanted to be sure it was perfect. She was going to check out the fit herself.

After I got Michael and Shelley off to school, I headed for the bus that would take me into the city. It would only take about 45 minutes to reach the Big Apple, and I spent those 45 minutes anxiously thinking about the dress and the woman who'd designed it. I sure hoped my suggestions worked. Of course, I knew they would—by this point I'd been at the game long enough to know what I was talking about, but still, I was nervous. I didn't work for many women designers, and I was excited to have the chance to work with one who was rising so rapidly in her field.

I walked up to Seventh Avenue, passing the ornery bag lady and giving her my biggest smile—I was in such a happy mood that it even prompted a smile in return. When I entered the building where I'd be working for the day, the elevator operator greeted me with his familiar courtesy.

"Good morning," I said to him, my smile still stretched across my face. "How are you this morning?"

He smiled back, clearly pleased to be acknowledged. His was a thankless job; he was paid to be invisible and I had no doubt that wore away at his soul, day by day. "Good morning, ma'am," he answered, "I'm doing just fine, how are you? Where can I take you?"

"Eleventh floor, please," I answered, standing as tall as I could in my three inch heels, my head held high. It was going to be a good day, I just knew it.

When I reached the 11th floor, I wished the elevator operator a wonderful day and walked through the showroom. The place was already buzzing with excitement as I walked down the long hallway to the patternmaker's room. I just had to see that dress on the dummy! I wasn't usually so excited about a dress, but this was Diane von Furstenberg's dress—and it wasn't like any dress I'd seen before.

When I entered Giorgio's pattern-making room, there it was, perfectly tied and hung on the dummy that had been made to replicate my own body. The dress looked magnificent. I couldn't believe that such an ugly green and white print could look so fabulous turned into a dress. Diane was clearly a genius at picking out prints—I was so wrong to say I didn't like the print. I could tell right away that she had vision—and that her vision said something about where she wanted to take the modern American woman. The dress wasn't just feminine—it had a power all its own. And it was practical and comfortable. I was so tired of sheath dresses that felt stiff and confining, or those dreadful seventies pantsuits that felt like fiberglass shrouds. This was a dress any woman could wear and feel good about herself—and ready to take on the world!

I took the dress off the dummy and hurried to my dressing room to try it on. This time, there was no problem with the sleeves or the bust— it had been cut perfectly. I walked out of the fitting room and gave the biggest smile ever to Giorgio and Francesca.

"You've done a great job," I said, twirling around so they could admire their work. "When will she be here?"

"She is here soon," Giorgio said, admiring me. "*Bellissima!* You are *bellissima* in green dress!"

Everyone on the floor agreed, this dress was a stunner. We were all very pleased with our work and now all that was left to do was wait for Ms. von Furstenberg herself to arrive and approve what we had done.

Twenty minutes later, I could hear her coming down the hallway, her footsteps unmistakably assertive and determined. I liked her already.

When she walked through the door with her beautiful long black hair flowing freely and dressed in a pantsuit and stunning ostrich boots, I felt like I couldn't get my breath. Here I was, a grown woman, and I was feeling like a teenager with a crush on the high school quarterback. She smiled broadly the moment she saw me, recognizing her dress, of course, and came straight toward me, reaching out her hand as she introduced herself.

As I reached out to shake her hand, however, my own hand started trembling and I felt queasy. I had never before been so nervous with a designer and I couldn't believe I was losing control of myself right in front of Diane von Furstenberg herself!

I was now looking at and speaking to the most powerful woman I'd ever met—someone with a commanding presence who was totally in control and had the power to make things happen. She was smart, tough and dedicated. She was also still smiling and admiring her beautiful dress on me.

"Oh, just look at you," she said in her famed Belgian accent, "you are so sexy. My dress looks like it was made for you!"

"Well, actually, it was," I stammered. "But the way you've designed it, it's going to fit every woman who wears it. I just love it!"

"And I love the way you look in it," she said. "You're so beautiful. You've done a wonderful job with my dress."

I knew in that instant that we had hit a home run with her. The dress was everything she'd imagined it would be—and I was the lucky girl wrapped up in it.

Throughout that year I did many fashion shows for Diane and fitted many of her designs. She always showed up to work dressed in pants, but as for her wrap dress, it became so successful that it even made the cover of *Newsweek* in 1978 and to this day it is in the Costume Institute at the Metropolitan Museum of Art. It was sold in so many different prints that a lot of other models had the opportunity to get involved with the continuing creation of her iconic dress—and I am happy to say that I was there in the beginning when the whole thing started.

It was a remarkable year. I may not have finished high school but working for Diane that year taught me more than any design school ever could. For the first time, I fit in with an inspiring group of profes-sionals—many of them women.

The times truly were changing. It was already 1974, the Water-gate investigation had just brought a president down, and women were becoming more powerful. We no longer had to align ourselves with men to get ahead. We had birth control now, and our new First Lady, Betty Ford, was supporting the Equal Rights Amendment, which I felt we were sure to win. We were making a difference working together—and we were choosing what we wanted to wear, not wearing what we were told by men we should be wearing.

Unless those men were elders from the Kingdom Hall. I relished the freedom I was gaining through my work and through the women's liberation movement, while doing my best to deny that every decision in my life was being made for me by the elders. I told myself they were protecting me, just as I had told myself that Dick was protecting me when more often than not he was abusing me, if not physically, then emotionally. Angelo wasn't abusing me, but I could tell he was growing increasingly disappointed in me, with every step toward independence.

I struggled to reconcile the dual life I was living, the independence that came with my career and the dependence that came with my reli-gion. I thought by working for a powerful woman, I'd be freed of all that tension. I thought her power might empower me.

But it wouldn't take long before I came to discover that working for a powerful woman didn't always leave me feeling powerful: In order to make it in such a cutthroat industry, Diane had to be tough. I was learning, however, that it's not easy working for a tough woman. As much as I respected Diane and her strengths, it got harder and harder to be the Coat Hanger with the Mouth when I was fitting for her. I was becoming the Coat Hanger Afraid to Open her Mouth, lest it be silenced with a glare or a few sharp, accented words.

Falling in line—I was learning—was something a woman does not do just with men, but with anyone in power.

It was up to me to find my own power. I just had no idea how to do that.

Chapter 14

Wear Me Down

Mine wasn't the only career taking off. By the late seventies, I was firmly established as a New York model, while Angelo was increasingly getting recognized by television producers and before long, he was interviewing the rich and famous every day. My shyness was all but gone and I felt confident walking up to his offices on 56th Street, which were right below the MGM studios. I loved watching him film the celebrities, but the minute the camera was off and I was introduced, I felt more like an awkward Lucille Ball than a confident and poised fashion model.

One afternoon I walked into Angelo's office and had a chance to meet the news reporter whose desk was next to his. She was a stunning woman whose mother, Ingrid Bergman, was considered one of the world's greatest beauties. Isabella Rossellini was as beautiful as her mother, with the same flawless skin, though she didn't wear any makeup at all. I was struck less by her beauty, however, than by her kindness and sensitivity. For someone who had been raised under the public eye all her life, she had a rare combination of warmth and beauty that I was instantly drawn to.

As for worrying about my husband working beside such a beauty all day long, I had no doubt that he loved me. I could feel his love for me the minute he walked into the room. He was a true Italian—always respectful to me. I had learned a thing or two about cheating men with Dick. I'd learned to spot the signs and the lies, and never once did I have reason to worry with Angelo. Our marriage was stressed by this point, there's no doubt about it. But our love for each other was as strong as ever.

It just happened that that evening Angelo was filming a new club opening. The club was called Xenon, and since he knew how much I loved to dance, he suggested I join him.

"Yes, you should come," Isabella said. "We'll go together, because I want to write a piece about it myself."

Angelo agreed. "It's going to be different than Studio 54. They're expecting more of the fashion crowd. You'll love it. Andy Warhol will be there, and maybe even Michael Jackson. It will be fun and glamorous!"

How could I say no? Besides, I was always looking for new ideas to pass on to my designers. If it was going to be as glamorous as they suggested, what better to do that evening than attend the opening with someone like Isabella Rossellini. She wasn't yet famous in her own right, but her charm was magnetic and it was a welcomed relief to go out with someone who wasn't a Jehovah's Witness and wouldn't be watching my behavior with a worried eye all night.

Early that evening, Isabella, Angelo and I, and the rest of the crew headed off for Xenon. Leaving Angelo and the crew to unpack their equipment, Isabella and I went straight for the door to the club. Our press passes got us into the club with no trouble at all, and we found ourselves leaving the bright summer evening for a darkness lit up by neon and throbbing music. A mural of neon looking like something Peter Max had designed lit up the stage and a bright neon X illuminated the dance floor. We were surrounded by black couches, mirrored tables, and light silver walls. Go-go dancing cages were open to all, and as the throbbing electronic beat of Donna Summer's "Rumor Has It" deafened us, we stood transfixed, watching one particular woman having a ball dancing in the cage. We stood there watching this big busted go-go dancer wearing nothing more than a thong, poking each other in the ribs and giggling like school girls. I guess not even a European like Isabella had ever seen anything quite like it.

Instead of being shocked, I found it amusing as I watched her gyrate and grind to the beat of the music, but as she hooked her thumbs into her thong I grew uncomfortable. Then, in an instant, we both had the surprise of our life as she wiggled the thong down revealing—a penis! By the look on Isabella's face, she was as surprised as I was, and that was the first time both of us learned what a transvestite was. Even to this day I remember Isabella in her paisley dress and espadrille shoes turning around and blushing. Then she hurried to look for the camera crew—not to escape the image, but to capture it on film!

They were crazy, exciting times with my days spent modeling for top designers, my evenings spent taking care of my home and kids, and my weekends a surreal mix of being a Jehovah's Witness by day and going to the night clubs and fashion shows at night. In barely more than half a decade I had gone from wearing jeans and no makeup, to changing my wardrobe every year so my clients would see that I knew the latest fashions. The seventies had passed in an instant, and as the early eighties and all its fashion catastrophes burst on the scene, I took stock of all I'd learned and did my best to avoid falling victim to the decade.

When it came to my own wardrobe, I preferred the simplicity of Ralph Lauren or Anne Klein, struggling to strike the perfect balance between style and fashion. Style is knowing how to wear something, creating a personal image that communicates who we are to the world—something I struggled with as my own identity continued to confuse me. But fashion—knowing how to look contemporary and embracing the latest looks—was something that had become much easier for me to master.

As I made friends with the buyers, they began to ask me to go shopping on Fridays, check out the stock and count the various garments, then to return on Mondays, count them again and determine which styles people were buying. That would help guide them in knowing what to stock for their own stores.

I wanted to please the buyers, but I also didn't have the time for such exhausting work, so I soon made friends with the saleswomen who would tell me what had been sold over the weekend. Sometimes I'd slip into the dressing room, put on the latest garments and take pictures of it, then take the photos to the patternmakers and designers. As for what fabrics they'd be made in, I knew most of the fabric sellers by then and when I saw a fabric that was particularly popular, I'd let the designers know and the dresses, pants or whatever could be designed in these fabrics—unless the Gambinos or Meyer Lansky had other ideas, in which case we had to use their fabrics.

I had learned so much that I didn't even realize how much I knew. But what I wasn't learning as quickly was the part of life that is supposed to come to us naturally—being a mother and a wife. My kids were growing and forming personalities of their own. Michael was entering his teenage years and his rebellion grew focused on Angelo. My beautiful, sweet little boy was becoming a man and he had an attitude that was right on schedule with most teenagers. And my beautiful, sweet husband didn't understand this attitude. All I was hearing from Angelo was, "Couldn't you teach your son in a way that would make it easier for someone else to love him? He's going to have to go out there in the world and work someday and you're treating him like he's still your baby boy!"

It was true I still considered Michael my baby boy, but it wasn't true that I wasn't preparing him for the real world or recognizing he was maturing. Angelo's words hurt me deeply, because they made it clear that there was indeed a boundary between my children and their stepfather. He loved them, I knew, but there was a line to his love that would never be there for a parent. Yet his words made me think, and realize that all in all, however much they hurt, Angelo's words were words of wisdom. I had always felt guilty for taking Michael away from his dad and as a result, I probably caved in to my son's demands and desires a little too easily. And working so many hours, I tried to compensate by trying to please my children, perhaps more than was good for them. I knew Angelo was right, but I didn't know how to negotiate such testosterone-fueled battles that seemed to be driving us all mad.

At least I knew that for all his frustration, Angelo was on my side. Just as he respected me, he taught my kids to respect their mother. After Michael had given me a hard time over some undoubtedly trivial issue, Angelo told him, "There are only two people who will ever die for you. One is Christ, who has already done it. And the other is your mom. So be careful how you speak to her."

Michael got the message after that. He began treating me better, but his battles with Angelo raged on.

It was at about this time that our dear friends Joe and Lela moved away. We had bonded closely with their family and they had become a great source of support. Without them, I felt as if we were floundering, trying to swim upstream with every new day. I don't know if this was the catalyst to push the pendulum in the other direction, but once it started to swing in the other direction, there was no stopping it. With Joe and Lela and their five kids gone from our lives, Angelo wanted to fill the emptiness with children—his children.

I will never forget the day he sat me down and told me the words that would change my life—our lives—forever.

"I want us to have a baby, Darlene," he told me.

I looked into his dark eyes, and there was no mistaking how serious he was. I had also believed he was as serious when he told me five years before, when he had asked me to marry him, "I love you, Darlene, and your kids are my kids. I don't need kids of my own."

When my head had cleared from his words of wanting a child, I reminded him of the words he had said when he proposed. Then he said the next words that shattered our world altogether.

"I thought I could wear you down."

Wear me down? After all I had been through with Dick, the many months on welfare, just taking the risk of ending up raising another child alone, the very thought that for all this time he had been "wearing me down"? It was all just too much. I just couldn't imagine giving up my career—and my income—to find myself depending on a man to take care of us. My head spun with confusion.

Angelo, the husband of my dreams, was just another man in my life trying to wear me down to get what he needed from me, I thought. Run, Darlene! Run like hell and take your babies with you! That was all I could imagine doing in response to his words. But they weren't babies anymore. They had happy lives now, in New Jersey. Running off with them wasn't an option.

Yet having a baby wasn't an option either. Not only would my career come to an abrupt end if I got pregnant and my figure changed, but Angelo's career was really taking off and he was spending a lot of time working. The more successful he became, the more time I would be alone with a small child—something he had no way of understanding.

No, no, no! my soul screamed. After a minute, I realized it wasn't just my soul screaming the words—those were the words that were coming out of my mouth. Those were the words I said back to Angelo. And they echoed in my head for months later.

We tried to stay on our familiar path that we had already created in our home, but it had become a rocky path. It became harder and harder to visit our friends with small children, and among the Jehovah's Witnesses and the Catholic Italians, it seemed that everyone had children and more on the way. It became clear to me that if I stayed married to Angelo, he would never experience this joy for himself. How could I keep telling him that I loved him yet still not give him what his soul desired—a child of his own? Or could I?

He was a good man, and he deserved better from me. Maybe, just maybe, I could do this for him. Determined to keep my marriage together and to give the man I loved the gift that he so desperately wanted, I stopped taking my birth control pills. I would give him his dream. It was not necessarily my dream, in fact, it was my nightmare, but it was his dream.

Yet those words he had spoken never quite left my mind.

"I thought I could wear you down."

Every month when my period came, I felt a wave of relief. I wanted Angelo to be happy, but I couldn't imagine another child. I had no doubt that I would love it, but I had no doubt that I would hate giving up my career and finding myself caring for a baby while trying to get my teenagers prepared for adulthood. The life I'd created for myself would be over, and the life that Angelo—and the elders—created for me would be the one I'd have to live with. I'd never been so relieved to have menstrual cramps.

Then one day, my period didn't show up. I waited day after day, hoping in my heart I wasn't pregnant. Angelo had just left for Canada with his camera crew to film a sporting event and didn't know when he'd be back home. I felt his absence like a sign of what was up ahead. Alone. My husband far away, busy with his career. We had no cell phones, no internet to keep us connected. He might as well have gone to Saturn.

Being alone also gave me time to think about what was going on in our marriage. His control was getting to the point that none of us was happy. I wasn't the traditional wife that he wanted and though he didn't seem to mind me modeling, he was embarrassed by it. He thought that people looked down on models, thinking we're all conceited airheads. He didn't think I was that, but I could feel his embarrassment at times.

The years of going to the Kingdom Hall and welcoming the elders and other Witnesses into our home had changed him. He wanted to be the head of the house now, and while along with that came his increasing devotion to me, my role was increasingly subordinated. I felt less like his partner and more like his second mate. Inferior. Subservient.

Michael was getting older and spending a lot of time with his friends. He would be gone and out of the house soon, and Shelley and I would remain at home, our lives revolving around the baby, her own life no doubt filled with boyfriends and preparing for college.

The family that Angelo wanted so badly was in his view expanding our social world. In my view, it was shrinking mine smaller and smaller.

I wasn't feeling well so I curled up in bed and wallowed in my fantasies and misery and self-pity. I saw only diapers and heard only wails.

Then Michael peeked his head into the room and asked if he could go to the new *Rocky* movie with his friends. He'd grown up so fast.

We'd seen the first two *Rocky* movies together. Now his mom was the last person he wanted to see any movie with! I understood, but that didn't keep me from falling deeper into an abyss of loneliness and anxiety. What kind of future had I agreed to? How had I let myself go from finally achieving success, to giving it all up to please my husband and demonstrate my subservience to a religion I had never quite accepted?

As I lay in bed, Shelley, now 14 and developing rapidly, kept checking in on me. She had always been the perfect child and even now as she began to enter the teen years, she still felt close enough to me that she would confide in me about boys. I wasn't too worried, because the boys she was meeting were mostly Witnesses, and they'd been taught to treat a girl right. But they also got married so damn young—no doubt because they were so horny from all that good behavior—and I didn't want Shelley to jump into a marriage too soon, as I had. She was definitely college material, and already on the honor roll. But college was frowned on by the Witnesses because they were convinced the end of the world was coming and there'd be a new Heaven and a new Earth. Who needs college if that's what's in store? Better to preach and round up more believers to be saved.

It was this view that was the biggest red flag for me. So many of the things they were teaching I believed in, like no war, no violence, husbands should put the needs of the family ahead of themselves. But keeping my children out of college was a red flag I couldn't ignore. Yet Angelo wanted her to be a good Witness. He wanted her to prepare herself for marriage and become a devoted disciple. The tension was growing greater with every trip to the Kingdom Hall. We were all so sick of the fighting.

By the next morning, I realized that my misery was more than just in my head. I wasn't feeling well at all. Michael came into the room all excited about the movie and as he told me scene after scene, I realized how mature he had become, while still seeing my little boy in all his enthusiasm. He didn't say he was leaving, but I felt it.

After he left I just lay there and cried because I was slowly realizing the blissfully happy life I'd been telling myself we were living hadn't been happy for some time. We were all unhappy and a new baby would not fix our problems. I must have spent the whole day in bed crying until I made myself even sicker. By the next morning, the pain in my stomach that I'd assumed was just my anxiety had grown so intense that I knew something was wrong. My suspicions turned to alarm when I began bleeding heavily and knew I had to get to a doctor.

I rolled out of bed and drove to his office and as I waited to be seen the pain became so intense I could hardly stand. The minute the doctor saw me, he scheduled an emergency D&C. Any chance of a child living would be swept away with the scraping of my uterus.

I didn't even have the power to give life to the child Angelo so desperately wanted.

When it was over, I couldn't escape my shame. I felt as if I had somehow aborted this child with my thoughts. The trauma had been so powerful that a pregnancy couldn't survive it. The depression I allowed myself to sink into could not sustain life. I felt I'd betrayed Angelo. I'd been disloyal to him, to my kids, and to our friends who could sense my profound unhappiness. I'd grown so unhappy that I had no idea what to do. My family had become so dysfunctional that not even a baby wanted to be borne into it. I had to make a hard decision that would set Angelo free.

Chapter 15

Babydoll

Telling Angelo I was considering a divorce wasn't easy, but telling the elders was even harder. For me and Angelo, the pain was deep and it was personal. We cried, we hugged, we fought, we made love. But mostly we just moved deeper into ourselves, the distance between us growing daily.

Telling the elders, however, invited a whole new level of scrutiny, judgment and admonishment into our lives—especially into my life.

"Do you realize what you're saying?" David, one of the elders asked me.

I poured him a second cup of coffee, returned to my seat at the kitchen table, and nodded.

"Yes sir, I do, but don't worry. My children will still be coming to the meetings. I make enough money to take care of them and I have to let Angelo go his own way. He needs kids of his own and I'm just not willing to get pregnant again."

His face darkened. I'd seen that face so many times on so many men. My father, when I'd tried to tell him about the makeup I'd stolen and he'd assumed that I'd gotten myself pregnant (as if pregnancy is something a girl does all by herself). Dick, when he'd seen customers coming on to me at the diner. My attorney, when he saw me arrive at his home with my children. And now this old man who'd probably never had to change a diaper his whole life, who'd probably never vacuumed a carpet, cooked a meal, done the dishes, cleaned up a child's vomit, packed his children's lunches, shopped for their clothes and school supplies, maybe even never helped them with their homework, much less grown one of them inside his body and pushed it through his pelvis until it felt like he was being torn in half. Yet most of all, not since he'd become an adult had he ever had to ask his spouse for money, ask his spouse for permission to go out, asked his spouse if he could buy a pair of shoes or take a class or get a job or take the kids out to McDonald's. He might have cherished women, but he would never in a million years choose to live the life he expected us to live.

"Has there been any adultery?"

"No sir, of course not. Angelo would never cheat on me."

He scowled. "And you?"

"No! I've been completely faithful to Angelo. That's not our problem."

"In that case," he said, finishing his coffee and rising to leave. "We cannot permit you to divorce. That would be against God's law. I suggest you reconsider." He walked to the door, bid me goodbye and was gone.

"Suggest you reconsider." That was his way of telling me that if I did not do as I was commanded—which was not divorce my husband, which meant bearing another child—then I would face the consequences. And the consequences meant being shunned. Not just me, but my children, as well.

I was furious. I had only come to the Kingdom Hall in the first place so my children would have roots in a community that was built on love, and if we were shunned by the church for me leaving my husband, they would lose all the friends they'd made over the last few years. I certainly wasn't feeling their love now. Instead, another man was telling me what I had to do to be accepted. If anything, his "suggestion" deepened my conviction to divorce.

The elders came to my home one after another over the next few months to try to talk me out of divorcing Angelo, but I had become too angry to discuss the matter. Shelley was already feeling the chill of their disapproval every time we attended one of their meetings at the Kingdom Hall. As for me, clearly, they sought my banishment altogether. One by one our friends fell away. Walking into the Kingdom Hall all eyes fell upon us and quickly turned away. We were outcasts. Invisible. We'd been erased.

I felt as if I were being spiritually raped. They were stripping me of their supposed godly love and support. They were letting me know that I was not the kind of woman to be cherished. My children were not the type of children to be recognized and treated with dignity and humanity. All the red flags I had ignored years before turned from flags to a rocket's red glare—they were not godly, they were not Christian, they were not loving or forgiving or even capable of basic human kindness. They may have opposed war on the battlefield, but they didn't oppose spiritual violence. They relished it.

"You know what you're doing, don't you?" I asked Gerald, another elder sent to put me in my place and compel me to be obedient.

"Yes, we are trying to counsel you," he replied, in that condescending tone that means to say, "because you're too weak and foolish and incompetent to make a decision for yourself."

"No, what you're doing is trying to make me cheat on Angelo."

Bewildered, he sputtered and spit up a laugh as if I'd just told him he was turning me into a rabbit. "Now, you're talking madness, Darlene, you really need spiritual help."

"No, I need legal help. I need a divorce attorney. Because if I went out and cheated on Angelo, you'd grant me permission to get divorced. And then all I'd have to do is turn around and repent, and then we'd be welcomed back and treated like people again. Isn't that how it works?"

"Don't be ridiculous, Darlene. You know it's not as simple as that."

"But eventually, that's what would happen, isn't that right?"

His silence acknowledged the truth I was speaking. If I divorced my husband to free him to have children of his own, I was a sinner not to be forgiven. If I screwed this fat, ugly elder right then and there then repented, I'd be loved. *Well, screw you,* I thought. *Screw you.*

Like the elder before him, he walked out the door, having failed in his effort to "counsel" some sense into me.

If Angelo and I had had any chance of making our marriage work, the Witnesses shattered that chance with their demands for obedience. Reluctantly, we agreed to divorce, but not until Michael graduated from high school, which was only a year away.

Once we'd made that decision, it gave me the power to speak up. I may have been the Coat Hanger with the Mouth at work, but at home I'd become the coat hanger—for others to hang their needs and demands on. I had learned that to have a happy marriage and be a part of the Witness community, I had to let Angelo and the elders make my decisions for me. Now I began making decisions for myself and my children. And Angelo didn't like that one bit.

"You've been getting a smart-assed mouth ever since you started making all that money!" he shouted. "You're not a first-class woman, anymore!"

His words hit me just as hard as any fist.

"You've become a second-class man!" He stormed out of the house and I just stared at the back of the door. I was no longer his sweet girl, it appeared.

Sweet girl. That was what my mother had been to my father. Even after he beat her, even after the fights that shattered their lives every weekend, even after his drinking had cost her son the lower half of his body. My father was the military hero. He gave the orders. She learned to obey those orders, to remain sweet and quiet.

But maybe she wasn't as sweet and quiet after all. Maybe she was just as fractured and scared inside as I was, but nobody could see it because like me, she had become an expert at keeping the peace. Just as I had learned as a child around my father, and later as a wife when I was married to Dick, she had learned to live her life in fear that her husband would explode at any moment. Maybe her sweetness wasn't a form of obedience, but a form of resistance. It was strategic.

Angelo never beat me, but I'd lived my life so obediently that he never had to. I didn't even notice the ways that I accepted others taking control. I let him become the master of the house, but deep inside

I resented it. I didn't want a master. I wanted an equal partner. The love and devotion he felt for me may have been just love and devotion for that obedient wife, the one I'd played for years. Now that I was no longer playing that role, he viewed me as a man.

Was that so bad? By this point, I felt that every man, including Angelo, held the keys to my cage. By becoming a man, so to speak, might I liberate myself from that cage? Maybe I could learn a thing or two by channeling the man inside of me. Wasn't that what so many men thought we were doing when we went to work each day and came home with the money we'd earned? Taking a man's job away from him? Wearing the pants in the family? Well, whatever it was, it was time to put on those pants and earn more money.

I would soon be a single mother once again.

As fortune would have it, while I waited for Michael to finish up school and start my life over again, I was chosen to be one of the models to do the loungewear show for Diane von Furstenberg. I was proud to represent her new loungewear line but I had concerns because it was being filmed. What if Angelo saw me parading on stage in underwear? Would that turn our already tense living situation into an absolute hell?

All I could do was push the thoughts out of my mind. If Angelo saw me and got upset, well, that would be his problem. I had a job to do. And that job wasn't so much wearing the pants in the family as it was wearing the panties—and selling them. So I signed on to do a show for Diane and kept my mouth shut at home. The money I'd be making would be mine and it would go to our new home.

I was selected to do the finale. It was an important role and one that only went to a trusted, experienced model. I'd be wearing a babydoll nightgown, a short, two-piece set with matching panties that couldn't have been sexier.

As I was getting dressed, my mind was on the elders. They'd been keeping such a watch on me that I worried they might even turn up at the show and I would find them sitting in the audience. Although I'd spiritually and emotionally severed ties with them, I continued to attend the meetings with Angelo and the kids, despite the chilling reception we received. They were my friends, friends of many years. Maybe it was easy for them to turn away from me, but it was far more difficult for me to turn away from them. I kept hoping for acceptance, even if it was acceptance by people I was coming to disrespect profoundly.

As I got ready in the dressing room backstage, the thought of their sitting in judgment of me had me so rattled that I couldn't shake the feeling of being ashamed. Like the wet T-shirt contest that I'd so enjoyed doing, but worried so much could lead to losing my children, now I worried that being seen on stage in a babydoll nightgown could lead to who knows what accusations? I had become so conditioned to fearing their judgment that now, divorcing Angelo and preparing to leave the Witnesses—or effectively being cast out—I still feared their judgment.

I listened closely for my cue and when it came, I slipped on the robe and stepped onto the runway. It wasn't an ordinary runway, however. When you reached the end, it was shaped like a T, and we were to walk to the left to show the audience the garments from one side, then to the right to show the garments from the other side. Then we were to return to the center and stand still, where a spotlight would shine upon us, illuminating the beautiful fabrics. That was where I'd remove the robe to reveal the sheer babydoll beneath it. The bodice was covered with lacework and wouldn't show my breasts, but the lower half was sheer and everyone would see the sexy panties underneath. I prayed to God that there were no elders in the audience!

As I walked toward the audience, each step a subtly provocative one, I realized with horror that in my nervousness and hurry to get on stage I'd forgotten something—the panties! I couldn't remove the robe—they'd see a lot more than I was getting paid to show off! So as the announcer detailed the features of the stunning set, I slid the robe down my shoulders, but instead of removing it, I tied it around my waist, turned and returned up the runway heading straight to the dressing room as fast as I could.

So much for wearing the pants in the family. I couldn't even wear the panties in it!

No one from the Kingdom Hall ever saw my embarrassing show. Nor did Angelo. But I stopped doing lingerie shows after that, even though they paid well. I was just too afraid of being caught doing one.

The more I thought about that decision, however, the more I knew that their control over me had gone too far. How much more did I need to take before I stopped attending the Kingdom Hall altogether?

A bit more, it turned out.

As the next few months passed, we all got ready for Michael's graduation. I wanted him to have a special day to remember so I invited his father and Brenda—yes, they were still married, believe it or not—to join us for the festivities at our home. Shelley, more than anyone, was excited to see her dad. Even though she saw him during the summer, it wasn't enough for her. She needed him. She didn't know about how he'd treated me. Angelo and I had agreed not to bring up the past or talk badly about their father, and we'd abided by that decision. She had a right to her relationship with her father.

He arrived alone, Brenda having declined the invitation. Although I wasn't exactly happy to see him, I have to admit that the day went relatively well. I was so proud of my son. He did something that I hadn't done—he'd finished school. Dick and I were quite civil to each other, but I wasn't at all pleased to see that he barely interacted with Shelley at all. She was heartbroken, and I was infuriated that he was treating her just as he'd treated me—oblivious to her existence. Nonetheless, I was determined not to say anything during the party. I'd save that for when I had a moment alone with him.

That moment came when it was time for him to leave. I walked him to his car, and as he turned and took one last look at our beautiful home, the Mercedes in the driveway, pool in the backyard, and landscaping that cost more than our house in New Hampshire, he said, "You did quite well for yourself, Darlene. Our kids are growing up real nice and you've got a beautiful home."

"Thank you," I said. "Because you showed me I could do it all without you. Also, tell Brenda again that I said thank you." I turned around and walked into my beautiful home and hugged my beautiful kids, and even kissed my beautiful soon to be second ex-husband.

Not long after that day, I asked Angelo for the divorce we'd been delaying. He'd been hoping he could wear me down on that point, as well, but he knew our marriage was over. We still loved each other, but our lives and dreams were heading in different directions. I could never be my own self as long as we stayed married, and he could never have the children he so deeply wanted. It killed both of us as I watched him pack his clothes. Dick and I had divorced because we didn't love each other. Angelo and I were divorcing because we did.

Later that evening I took Michael and Shelley out to dinner and explained to them what was going on. Shelley was sad, but Michael, who'd been trained into manhood by the Witnesses, was furious.

"Mom, if you loved God as much as you say you do, then you would have made your marriage work!"

His words struck a blow, but an even bigger blow came a couple of months later when he packed his own bags and moved back to New Hampshire to live with Dick and Brenda.

"Dad's promised me a good job, and there's nothing left for me here," he said, still angry, but excited for the possibilities his father had dangled before him to get him set on his future.

I cried not so much for the loss of my son, as I knew that was coming, but for what I knew was coming for Michael. His father wouldn't keep that promise. And he didn't. After arriving in New Hampshire, Michael set out on adulthood on his own, turning to me for help when he needed it, and knowing I'd never let him down.

As for Shelley and me, we went back to the Kingdom Hall a few more times, but we were treated with silence. Then one night, listening to the elders talk about God's Kingdom and the love Jesus showed by telling us, "Believe all things! Hope all things! Endure all things! Because Love never fails!" I realized that Shelley and I were enduring everything all by ourselves. No one there loved us. What did we need these people for?

I took my daughter's hand, stood up and said loudly, "How dare you speak words when you don't even know the meaning of them?" We turned around and walked out.

We were free.

Elsie Parris - Mom - An English Lady

Clyde Parris - War Hero

My Brother Danny
My First Wounded Warrior

One of My First Professional Shots

Mediterranean Allied Air Forces
Prior to the European Tank Command

Eisenhower Jacket - Four Purple
Hearts among Other Military
Honors

View of Lower Manhattan, Taken from My
Brooklyn Window Three Days After 9/11

A Native American's Resting
Place

My Coast Guard Evacuation from the
Westerdam Hay House Cruise

Cover of Carol Nashe Directory
Circa 1972

"Spec Sheet" - Model Service Agency,
NYC

My Dummy

Model Service Agency Photo - Circa 1980

Admiring My Dummy

Garment Center Advertisement

Fabrics

Patternmaker

Garment Center Statue of Jewish Patternmaker

Gassing Up in Queens, NY

Professional Photo Shot

Machu Picchu in the Background

Betty and I Discussing the Climb

My Precious Daughter Still
Checks on Me Every Day!

Andrea - My Friend, Fellow Traveler
and Healer

Every Mom Needs One of These!

Mother and Daughter

Mom and Son After Mountain Ride

My Real Accomplishment

A Family Tradition Continues—Mike and Cari Ride On!

Today

My Husband Edward

Betty and Edward

Andrea and "The Boss", Yelana,
My Dear Friends

Betty Ann and Me

Chapter 16

Fifty Cents Short

I couldn't move my arms. I tried lifting my arm over my head and I couldn't get it past my own eyebrows. Something was wrong.

I peeled off the dress and still standing in my slip, I stepped out of the dressing room and handed it back to the designer.

"This dress doesn't fit."

"Of course, it fits," he countered, "you need to lose weight, baby."

I looked at him, long shaggy hair and all. He was a short, good looking guy about my age with a loud, Bronx-accented voice, totally full of himself and already one of the hottest designers in the country. He might know how to design a pretty dress with his pen and paper, I thought, but he has no idea how women are shaped. The dress he'd had me try on had been designed for someone with breasts the size of soccer balls and arms skinnier than chopsticks. No one would ever wear it.

"My arms are perfectly fine. I'm a size eight and this dress is not a size eight. It's cut badly. I couldn't even raise my arms."

He threw his tape measure across the room and cursed, hollering for another model to replace me.

"Get rid of her! Bring me someone thinner!" he howled to his staff.

"You can get someone thinner," I calmly told him, "or you can get someone who will help you sell this dress. Which do you prefer?"

He stared at me, his face flickering from anger to disgust to amusement in the time it took me to lower my arched brows. That's when I knew I had him. He would listen to me and fix the dress so that it would fit the average woman.

"Oh, right," he said, chuckling, "You're that coat hanger with a mouth."

Yes, I was. They could drape clothes on me all day long, but they were going to hear my opinion about those clothes. I was now a seasoned pro and that's why they were paying me—to open my mouth and tell them how women wear their clothes, not to shut up and just look pretty in them. And this designer was going to listen.

I'd met him when I was working for Lerner's. His name was Max Hart. We were at the showroom in the garment center when he came in with a new dress he wanted to sell to Lenny. I tried the dress on and he loved the way it fit me and the way I moved in it, and Lenny was quick to buy it. Later that day, Lenny called me into his office.

"You sure impressed Max, Darlene," he told me. "In fact, he wants to hire you himself."

"That's great, Lenny," I said, thrilled to have the work. "I hope you don't mind if I accept."

"Of course, not. I won't have any more work for you until the next season, and I know you have a family to support." He paused, and I could tell by the look on his face that there was something on his mind.

"What is it, Lenny? If you don't want me taking the work, just say so. I value you and don't want to take a job that would get in the way of our relationship." Lerner's was providing me enough steady work that I didn't want to do anything that would jeopardize the working relationship I had with Lenny, who was one of their top buyers. If Lenny didn't want me working for this guy, for whatever reason, I could always find more work. Clients were no longer in short supply.

"No, it isn't that," he said. "I don't have any problems with you taking the work. But just be careful. This guy is fifty cents short."

I didn't know what he meant by "fifty cents short," and I was too embarrassed to ask, so I just nodded confidently like I got the picture.

"Don't worry, Lenny," I said, "I can handle him."

"I'm sure you can, Darlene," Lenny said, smiling with pride. We'd forged a good relationship over the years and I always knew Lenny had my back and he knew I had his. Even better, he was one of the few buyers I worked with who genuinely loved his wife and wouldn't pull any crap with me. He kept his hands to himself and his head on his shoulders and that was rare in the fashion world. So I gratefully accepted the business card that Lenny handed me and went home.

The work involved private fittings for the fall collection that the designer, Max (a.k.a. "Fifty Cents Short") wanted to get into all the Lerner stores. He figured that given my close relationship to Lenny, hiring me would assure him that he had a foot in the door. And he knew I could do the job.

I took the subway to the garment district and knew the minute I emerged from the underground that his place was going to be shabby. The street was rundown and the smells of rotting garbage and human piss were a stark contrast from the glorious world of fashion that was tucked behind some of those doors.

I found the address and sure enough, it was a dreary building, but I rang the buzzer and was let into a dark entryway that hadn't seen a broom or a coat of paint in decades. I couldn't imagine carrying those beautiful dresses in and out of such a dirty, rundown environment, but it wasn't the first time I'd been in such a building for a fitting. Unfazed, I took the elevator to the ninth floor where I'd been told I'd find the showroom.

The showroom wasn't bad. It was small, but clean and bright, and the usual chairs and mirrors had been strategically arranged so the buyers could admire the girls modeling the clothes they had come to buy. I walked straight to the back where the production area was, where I found the typically frenzied backroom lined with bolts of colorful fabric, tables jammed together with old Italian men hard at work at the machines, and a variety of men in business suits or blue jeans and silk shirts running back and forth.

One of the first things I spotted was a patternmaker hard at work pinning the muslin and drape on a young busty model. Large breasts on a fitting model are there for one reason and one reason only—to entertain the men. Most women just aren't that busty, so clothes cut to fit a woman with big breasts won't fit most women—and that means they won't sell. But that was their problem, not mine, and apparently the patternmaker wasn't seeing it as a problem. The model was dripping with sensual delight as his hands groped her breasts and butt as if they were his very own play toys.

I'd stumbled upon that scene so many times it no longer fazed me. The old guys knew the young models were hungry for work and wouldn't risk their careers by objecting. And the young models knew if they complained they'd be out of work—after all, wasn't that just what had happened to me when I'd encountered that buyer at the hotel dressed in nothing but a towel? So a lot of them not only put up with it, they encouraged it, knowing that if they satisfied the client they'd get callbacks.

But not me. I was in my thirties already and I had children to support. Having grown up under the reign of my drunken father, I'd learned a thing or two about navigating bad-behaving men. You can't attack their pride, but neither can you let them attack yours. And you have to stay alert because they can change in an instant. I was on high alert.

I asked for Max Hart, and was sent to the back of the room where I saw him dressed like John Travolta, gold chains and all, shouting at some man in a suit.

"Come on, baby, you know I'm gonna blow this whole show out of the water! You know that, don't you?" He slapped the guy on the back and kept on walking. "How's the kids? They still in school? That's fantastic, baby, they're great kids."

"What's this crap?" He'd left the guy in the suit and was already onto someone else, a scared-looking woman holding a dress. "I told you I wanted to see some cleavage! Show me the tits! This neckline looks like something my mother would wear! No, even she wouldn't wear it. Get this out of here. Bring me back something sexy!"

"Excuse me," I said, wondering if the drape of my own neckline was sufficiently sexy to impress him.

"What!?" He spun around, and in an instant, the irritation slid off his face and in its place was a look of unmistakable approval. "Well, *hello*, baby! What's *your* name?"

"I'm Darlene Young," I said, extending my hand. I was in no mood for his theatrics, and the serious look on my face spoke volumes. "I'm your fit model. From Lerners?"

"Darlene, baby!" He opened his arms open wide as if waiting for a hug. I smiled, taking a step back. In an instant, he was on me, and right there in the pattern room he sank his lips on top of mine, his wet tongue like a giant, writhing slug in my mouth.

I didn't even think. I just instinctively hauled off and punched him in the stomach.

He doubled over with a loud grunt and looked up to me, clearly stunned.

"I'll give you a good fit, not a good fuck," I told him calmly, looking him straight in the eyes.

The patternmaker and his model gasped, momentarily pausing their groping session, though I didn't fail to note that the patternmaker's hand remained firmly planted on the model's ass.

Then I turned around and went straight into the back where I knew the fitting room would be. I was still going to work. I didn't want the man, but I did want the job.

I wasn't afraid he would fire me. He already knew my work was good, and I was smart enough to know that those men would mess around with the models all they wanted, but if they wanted to make money, they needed a fitting model with a mouth—one who would make them the money to pay for all their divorces.

When Max Hart came into the fitting room, I could tell he felt a mix of shame—for himself—and respect—for me. He wasn't used to having a model stand up to him. But before he could say a word, I laid out my terms.

"I'll work for you to do the fittings, but you have to keep that other model out there, with the patternmaker, because he's having a good time with her, and he's not going to have a good time with me. I'll do the fitting once he's gone."

He stared at me as if deciding whether or not to toss me out the ninth floor window, then nodded and we got to work.

I tried on the dress. The hem was a new kind, not like any I'd seen before. It was jagged, but I realized right away just how sexy that hemline was. It was just enough post-sixties to feel casual, and just provocative enough that any woman would feel so sexy in it she wouldn't hesitate to wear it in the evening to a nightclub or a party.

I walked out of the changing room and took my perch on the showroom stage.

Max walked back and forth, staring at the hem, lifting his eyes occasionally to the cleavage, motioning with his hand for me to turn.

Finally, after a silence that had lingered far too long, he shouted, "It's a winner!"

He threw his arms up in the air in a victory pose, when I said, "It's too tight."

"Too tight? What the hell do *you* know? It's perfect!"

"No, I can't move. I could never dance in this dress. Do I have the correct goods?"

The goods meant the fabric. A lot of what we tried on was a muslin sheer or some other fabric they had on hand for the sample, but the final fabric would be something else entirely. It was important to know what the fabric would be so I could tell if the final product would be a good fit.

"Yeah, the goods are good. What's your problem?"

"I need to see the spec sheet," I told him. The spec sheet would tell me the measurements that had been specified for the garment. If it was measured to spec, it shouldn't be so tight. My guess was that it hadn't been cut to spec, but I wouldn't know that without seeing the spec sheet for myself.

"Fuck. Who the hell are you to review my specs?"

"I'm the coat hanger with mouth that you asked for. And my mouth is telling you that if a woman can't dance in your dresses, she's not going to buy them."

He stared at me, a look that screamed anger. Then he turned and shouted to the floor, "I love this woman! Did you hear her? Let's make this dress even better! Let's make this dress dance!" Then he turned to me and hollered, "I love ya, baby! Now take it off. We'll look at the specs later. I have another one I want to see on you. And if you can't dance in that, then, baby, you just can't dance!"

"Oh, I can dance," I said, unsmiling.

"I'll bet you can!"

When he didn't get a response, he tried one more time.

"Come on, baby, show me a smile!"

"I'm not going to show you anything you can't handle," I replied, thinking of his slimy tongue in my mouth. I still wanted to spit it out.

He scowled, and tossed me another dress. "Here, put this on." Then he turned and started shouting at someone else. "Who's writing your paycheck? Come on, get moving! Make me some dresses!"

By Friday, I'd been pinned and paraded in dozens of dresses and our relationship was all business. I bent and stretched and turned and squatted and sat and crossed my legs in each and every one of them, showing him where the dress needed more give and where it needed to be more snug. He was coming to see that the punch in the gut had been worth it, and he was getting his money's worth by having me on his team. And if that punch in the gut and my big mouth hadn't been sufficiently clear, that afternoon, Lenny happened to walk through the showroom to check out the new stock. The minute he saw me, he gave me a great big hug—just as Max happened to walk in and see our embrace.

"Hey, Lenny," he said, clearly impressed. "I didn't know you were coming by. Your girl is a real find; she's been helping us out a lot. You picked a pro!"

I could tell from his leer and his tone that Max thought there was something going on between Lenny and me, and later he even commented that we were "very close." But I didn't correct him. As long as he thought I was Lenny's mistress, he'd leave me alone. Every vendor wants their dresses in Lerner's shops, so Max backed off—and he spread the word about me and Lenny. That annoyed me, but it served me well. People left me alone after that and not having to fend off their advances, I could do my job.

As for Max, his business started growing and kept on growing until he had over a hundred employees, and soon he was out of that dreary old building and into a series of bigger and better ones. But it wasn't an overnight success. For the longest time we didn't have a production man, so we all chipped in and did everything ourselves, even if it wasn't in our job description. As a result, I worried that changes I might suggest for a garment wouldn't be made, or wouldn't be made properly, so I had the factories send me a sample of the garment they would be working on each morning.

I had a rack set outside my dressing room where each factory rep was instructed to hang the garment. That way I could catch a mistake before they got too far into production. Often the mistakes weren't in the sewing. They might have the wrong goods, or fabric, or the cutting room may have laid the fabric wrong when they put the pattern on top to cut the garment. Whatever it was, I would walk into work, grab the garment, try it on, and give the go-ahead or tell them to stop and fix the problem—thereby saving Max a ton of money he otherwise would have lost in faulty production.

Finally, after many months of working like this, Max hired a production man who'd dropped out of Harvard Law School and decided to make it big in the fashion industry. We were assured he was smart and clever and would really shake things up, but as far as I was concerned he was tough and short tempered and easily pissed off. Hardly what we needed.

At any rate, the morning he was hired, I came into work to find my rack had been moved, so I went and got it and moved it back to my dressing room and started to try on the dresses. Apparently, however, I'd displeased the new production man who felt it was *his* job to check production. I was just a coat hanger.

When I heard him yelling and screaming, I went to his office to see what was going on.

"From now on, when you want to try on a dress you come to me, understand?"

Before I could say a word, he continued. "And once you've got it on, you come back here to my office so I can see how it looks on you. I want to be sure that the shoulder pads or zippers are the ones we ordered, and not something the factories have substituted with some cheap crap so they can make more money!"

"I'm sorry," I began, trying to explain, "I just moved the rack because—"

Before I could finish the sentence, he slammed his fist down on his desk and bellowed, "I don't care *why!* From now on you will do as I say. I am *the king* around here and you'd better get used to it!"

I had to turn my head so he wouldn't catch me smiling, then I turned back to him, stifling a laugh and said, "I agree with you. You are the king."

He smiled. He'd put me in my place.

I went on. "And a king is a ruler and a ruler is twelve inches and twelve inches is a really big prick. And you, sir, are indeed the biggest prick I ever met."

He stood there stunned for a moment, then laughed pretty hard and I walked out of the room.

The next day, the head of the Fashion Institute of Technology was having a walk-through of our company. The Fashion Institute was a school for training upcoming designers, and Max Hart was already the buzz in the business. On this particular day we had a rep from one of the factories in Queens coming in. The factory was called Mie, which was pronounced "my," and it was run by a Chinese man who did not speak English very well. We couldn't pronounce his name very well so we called him Dick, which was as close to his name as our ears could discern.

Max had also hired an assistant for the new production man, a woman who happened to be eight months pregnant, and since the production man was new to the business, he had a difficult time communicating with Dick, so he had this assistant call the Mie factory every morning to check on production.

Well, on this particular morning, the Fashion Institute was bringing in a group of young students and taking them on a tour through the back production area when suddenly the students gasped and giggled as the production man began screaming at the top of his lungs to his new assistant.

"It's your job to take care of Mie Dick every morning!" he bellowed.

The poor woman came running out of her office in tears—her big, pregnant belly making the scene all the more hilarious, after everyone heard him tell her it was her job to take care of "my dick!"

Such were the chaotic early days of Max's company. Eventually his small little company became quite well known—and Max bought himself a penthouse on Broadway.

Fifty cents short, he wasn't.

Chapter 17

Zorba

While my work picked up, my spirits didn't. I missed Angelo. The divorce had been quick and fair but emotionally rough. If it had taught me one thing, it was that I could survive without a man. Shelley and I were becoming a team. She was a teenager now and for the first time, it was just the two of us—and we were both busy. She was focused on her school and friends, and I was focused on my work.

I was working for Max Hart regularly, and while it wasn't clear who was backing him, it wasn't uncommon to see a bunch of serious-looking men in suits going back and forth—and in the garment center, serious-looking men in suits had to be taken seriously. Or else. As a result, only certain fabrics could be used, only certain brands of shoulder pads or zippers or trim could be purchased. Max used whatever he had to in his designs, and he always seemed to have the financing he needed to keep production up.

That wasn't all he kept up. I got into the habit of dressing in his office, where he often kept the TV on during the day. One day, as I was dressing, I noticed a hospital scene with nurses caring for a patient. Wanting to catch up on *General Hospital*, a popular soap opera of the day, I kept glancing at the show each time I had to change. I didn't pay it much attention, but by the second or third time I peeled off my clothes, I saw the nurse was doing the same! My jaw dropped when I realized it was a porn film that I was watching!

Max may have been the most colorful of my clients, but he wasn't the only one I was working for. By this point I was working with the best designers in the garment district—not only Diane von Furstenberg, but Ralph Lauren, Anne Klein, and Calvin Klein, and I worked with buyers from all the major department stores. I was no longer the timid small town girl waiting tables. I was a successful model, one of the top fit models in New York City, and if I could make it in the Big Apple, I knew I could make it anywhere. I was also well paid and able to afford my own home. I didn't have to beg any man to let me keep my home. I didn't have to beg any man to not chase me out of the city. And I didn't have to beg any man to not make me have children.

But I sure missed Angelo. There were nights I had to stop myself from reaching for the phone just to share my day with him or see how he was doing. If he hadn't wanted children so badly, I could have stayed happily married to him the rest of my life. Yes, we'd had issues, but don't all marriages? We had become such good friends and lovers that losing that connection was a great loss. There was no mistaking that I loved him, and his absence in my life left an emptiness that no amount of work or preoccupation could fill.

My loneliness wasn't enough to get me out of the house and dating again, though. Dating was out of the question. The only men I'd ever dated I'd ended up marrying, and I didn't want to put Shelley or myself through that again. It was much easier to talk with the men I worked with. We were in the same industry, we faced the same pressures, we saw each other every day, and we all had children growing up, so we always asked each other for advice.

One of the guys, a patternmaker from Greece I'll call Zorba, on account of his charm, was always having trouble with his kids. He had a girl and a boy and they were both quite young when they lost their mother to cancer five years before. The only person Zorba had to help him was his mother-in-law. He described her as an angry, spiteful old Greek lady who had filled his kids with lies about him. There was always some Greek tragedy going on in his life, and since I was always boasting of how well Shelley was doing in school, he increasingly came to me for advice, or more often, just for me to listen. His own daughter, Zoe, was in her teens and had taken her mother's death hard. Like Brenda, Zoe had become a handful. She was skipping school, chasing boys and taking off to her grandmother's house every chance she got. She would not listen to her father and was setting a bad example for her younger brother, Johnny.

"Can you meet with her, Darlene?" Zorba finally asked me one day. "She's not going to listen to her old father. She needs a woman she can look up to who will talk some sense in her. Will you please do me this one favor?"

The last time someone had asked me for this favor, I'd ended up with a teenager in my bed beside my husband. The request didn't bode well, but seeing as I had no husband, and Zorba was such a nice, attentive man—and handsome as well—I figured it wouldn't do any harm.

"Okay," I said, "She might not listen to me either, but I'm willing to give it a shot. I can't imagine losing a mother at such a young age, and I'm sure she's a good girl who just needs some maternal guidance."

"*Efharisto!*" he said, thanking me in Greek. "*Ela!* Come. I'll buy you lunch and we can talk. You will really like Zoe, I know it. And she's going to love you. You like *souvlakia?*"

Before I knew it, we were sitting in a Greek café, sipping thick, sweet coffee and crafting our game plan.

I began to meet Zorba for lunch regularly, and we cooked up a plan to explain to Zoe that her father wanted me to give her advice on pursuing a modeling career. I agreed to take the subway from our home in New Jersey to Astoria in Queens and meet her at a coffee shop.

I was surprised at how much I was looking forward to it. By this point in my life, with a son graduated from high school and a daughter soon to be, along with a successful career that paid well enough that I could support myself, I felt that I did have some wisdom to share with a young, impressionable girl. I could relate to her rebellion and rest-lessness and the grief she felt for the loss of her mother. Although I'd never lost a mother, the impact of my little brother Danny's accident on our family had taught me that life can deliver a devastating blow at any moment, and the grief of such a loss can last a lifetime. I genuinely wanted to help this young girl.

When I got there, she was waiting, and I could see right away that if she wanted to make it in modeling, she clearly could. She had strik-ing features, and she was really quite charming. She still had a lot of growing up to do, but to look at her, you'd think she was much older by the way she dressed. I wondered who bought her school clothes and couldn't imagine either her Greek grandmother or her father picking out such a short skirt and sexy top for a 16 year old, but I kept my mouth shut about her clothes, since I knew that would only alienate her.

I introduced myself and after a few awkward minutes, we both seemed to relax. We ended up talking for hours about her life, her mom, and her goals for the future. Although the discussion about modeling was a ruse, the advice I shared was not—and if she followed that advice, and did want to be a model, or whatever she put her mind to, I knew she could succeed. She just needed to get her life set on the right course before she found herself heading in a direction she would regret. I didn't want to see this lovely young girl mess up her life, or make some of the mistakes I had made. I did want to see her learn from some of my successes, however. So I urged her to finish school, pressing on her the importance of an education. I also let her know that buckling down and working hard wouldn't just provide her with a diploma, but it would also show prospective employers that she was willing to work hard to reach her goals and that meant she would work hard for any modeling agency that hired her.

"But you never finished school," she pointed out, "and you've done well."

"Yes, but not finishing school is something I've regretted my whole life. Fortunately, I've been lucky. But I also had to work much harder. I had to build my career while raising my children and that wasn't easy. If I'd finished school instead, there's no telling where I'd be in my career. And if I hadn't married so young, I wouldn't have found myself married to the wrong man and treated so badly. My first marriage did so much damage to my self-esteem that it was only by the grace of God that I've made it this far."

Zoe seemed to take that in, and as she pondered my advice, I added, "One more thing. Because I didn't finish school, I spent years depending on men to help me survive. For years, I couldn't make enough to support myself and had to count on my first husband to support me. There weren't a lot of opportunities for women when I was growing up, but you're entering a whole new world. There are powerful women who are shaping their own destiny now and they don't have to depend on anyone else to give it to them. In my generation, if a woman didn't come from a wealthy family, she didn't go to college. And if she did, she had two choices. She could be a teacher or a nurse. But that was about it. Now women are going to college—and modeling on the side. If you do that, you have the best of both worlds. So if you want to be successful and have your own life where you don't have to depend on anybody, you need to finish school. And if you want to go into modeling, then you need to learn the tools of the trade."

She nodded. "That makes sense. I don't want to end up poor or married to a loser. Okay, Darlene, I'll finish school. I'm not making any promises about what I'll do after that, but I'll get through the next two years and then decide. You know, my dad was right about you. You're really cool."

"And I think you're pretty cool, too, Zoe," I told her, feeling so grateful that I'd had the opportunity to help nudge a young woman toward independence and success. There had been no women mentors for me growing up, so being able to be one for someone else brought me such joy and pride.

As the evening came to an end, we agreed to talk again in the future about her goals. As for me, I just wanted to get home to my own daughter. I had a whole new appreciation for Shelley. She always worked hard in school, made good friends, and never gave me one minute of worry. I was just so proud of her after all that she had gone through with losing her father to divorce, and then her stepfather. Talking to Zoe made me realize how vulnerable young girls are, and how fortunate both Shelley and I were that she hadn't been making bad decisions along the way. My little girl was becoming a woman right in front of my eyes and I now realized that it wouldn't be long before she was dating. I had better spend more time with her explaining the facts of life, I realized, before she met a boy who would be more than willing to show them to her!

The fear of not having enough money to take care of my children still haunted me. I had never forgotten the brutal days on welfare and I was never going to let that happen again. However, a modeling career was not exactly one to count on, once I started getting older. I knew that socking away some money was a priority. But being available for my daughter was also a priority, I was coming to realize, so I figured being home for her mattered more. I therefore made the difficult decision to cut back on my bookings. I needed to work less, and be a mom more.

So one afternoon I left work early to surprise my daughter who was so used to her mom working long hours. We were both still dealing with our new lifestyle after Michael had moved back with Dick, and Angelo and I had gotten divorced. I knew it was hard on her, too, and wanted her to know that I would always be there for her.

You can imagine my surprise when I walked into my home and instead of finding it empty with my daughter in school, I came face-to-face with my daughter sitting next to a young man on the sofa. They were only watching TV, but between the looks on their faces it was obvious that they were more than just friends.

The contrast between them couldn't have been greater. There was Shelley, dressed in a grey pleated skirt and pink sweater, looking like she was ready to pledge to a sorority. Next to her was a long-haired guy in sweat pants who looked like he hadn't showered in days. He slouched on the sofa with his butt perched on the edge, his legs spread three feet apart as if sitting upright was too much trouble. He was only in high school himself, but he might as well have had Underachiever tattooed to his forehead. Fortunately, he scrambled to his feet, and introduced himself.

"Hey, I'm Craig," he said, "Shelley and me was just taking a break from homework. I told her we'd better finish it up pretty soon or Mr. Hollenbeck would be pissed. Ain't that right, Shel?"

Shelley nodded and he added, "Yeah, well, we can do it some other time, I got things to do. Nice meeting you, Mrs. Young. I think that's real cool, you being a model and all. Maybe Shelley can do that some-day. That be cool, wouldn't it, Shel," he said, turning toward her, "you making lots of money like your mom?"

Then he flashed me an awkward but sexy grin, muttered goodbye, and walked out the door like he was the coolest cat we'd ever encoun-tered. We were all relieved by his departure. In just those few words, that grin, and that walk, I could see he was the type who assumed that just because he'd been born with a penis, he expected to have the upper hand with anyone who had been born without one. It wasn't confidence he exuded, so much as a sense of being in charge—and not by way of any skillset, that was for sure.

I had spent years with men like that. First a husband, then the men I served when I waited tables, the men I served when I modeled their clothes, the men I served when I let them pin their garments on me. I really liked a lot of men, and I had sure loved Angelo, but I couldn't help but know that there was a type of man who would run all over a woman every chance he got—and that type was more the norm than the exception. And now here was my daughter falling for the same type of charmer who would crush her dreams of going to college and move her into that cage I was trying so desperately to keep her out of. He would convince her not to go to college because that would mean she would outgrow him and his ego would not be able to handle that. I saw it all like I was watching a movie trailer play before my eyes and there was nothing I could do but keep an eye on him and see where the relationship was going.

I was so familiar with manipulative charmers by this point that I could spot one a mile away. What was far more difficult, I was about to discover, was spotting them up close. It turned out that the little ruse Zorba had cooked up to get his daughter to listen to me wasn't the only ruse he had planned. But it was going to take me a good long time to realize what I'd gotten myself into, before I could get myself out of it.

Chapter 18

Beware of Greeks
Bearing Luggage

S helley and I had been out shopping and by the time we made it home it was late and we were both ready for bed. As we pulled into the driveway of our house, I saw a car parked out front. I got out of the car cautiously, and then I recognized him. It was Zorba.

I had never told him where I lived. I had never given him my address. The thought that he would just show up like that gave me a chill, but before I could say a word, he was rushing toward me practically sobbing.

"Darlene, you have to help me! Please, I don't know who else to turn to!"

He was a wreck, and my worries about how he knew where I lived were quickly replaced with concern. Something was terribly wrong.

"Zorba! What is it? What's wrong?"

He threw himself at me, hugging me and sobbing as if he'd just received the most devastating news. "It's Zoe! She's gone!"

"Gone?" I gasped. I imagined the worst in that instant, but he quickly replied.

"She's run away. To her *ya-ya's*," he frantically blurted out. She'd gone to her grandmother's. Okay.

"I'm sure she'll be fine, Zorba," I said, trying to calm him down and get him inside. "Come on, let's go inside and I'll make you a drink."

We went inside, I introduced him to Shelley, and poured him a glass of wine. "Now, tell me what happened."

He managed to get out a story about their having a fight and she took off for her grandmother's house in Astoria several days before and she had stopped going to school. He had gone there several times in hopes of bringing her home, but each time his former mother-in-law told him she was out with friends and had no plans to return to school.

"The old goat wants Zoe to stay with her forever! She thinks she can replace the daughter she lost to cancer by having Zoe move in and take care of her for the rest of her life! Please, Darlene, help me! I can't let this happen to my daughter!"

We sat up talking late into the night and my heart broke for him. He had already lost his wife and now his daughter was not only rebelling, but she had run away, dropped out of school, and her grandmother was helping her do it. It sounded terrible, and I wanted so badly to help.

Seeing as it was so late and he'd had plenty to drink, I made up the couch for him and let him sleep over. The next day after work, I headed over to Astoria to find Zoe. As I walked up the street nearing the address Zorba had given me, I saw her sitting with her grandmother on the front porch. Seeing me wave and Zoe recognize me, the old woman leaned over and whispered something into her ear. Then she rose, glared at me and went into the house, leaving me with Zoe.

After a bit of reluctance, Zoe finally opened up and poured out her heart, sobbing about missing her mother. She said living with her grandmother was like having a mother and she needed a female voice in her life right now. She also felt great comfort going with her grandmother to the church her mother used to go to.

"Your dad probably doesn't have the words to heal your pain, right now, Zoe," I told her softly. "He can't even heal his own pain and the loss of someone he loved so much. Maybe you could ask him to go to church with you. That might be just what he needs, too, something to believe in. Come on, let's get off these steps and take a walk to your church right now!"

That was all the prompting she needed and as Zoe and I walked to church, she opened up about all the pain she felt having lost her mother and being the only girl with a brother who got on her nerves and a father who didn't understand her.

She wanted to know what church I went to, and rather than tell her about the Jehovah's Witnesses and that long story, I just told her I looked at spiritualism differently. "I believe God resides more in our hearts than inside a manmade structure, like a church," I explained. "But I do believe in God and I respect all churches as long as they don't teach hatred or violence toward other people's belief systems."

My words seemed to calm her and Zoe spent the rest of the walk in an amicable silence, but as we drew closer to her home, she burst into tears again.

"Why did God make my mom suffer for so long? The church says that suffering is because someone's violated God's law but my mom was good. She didn't deserve to suffer. And my grandma tells me to forget about my dad because he hates the church now!"

Her confusion was the confusion of the ages, the incomprehensible contradictions between what religions teach about punishing sinners, and what those of us who suffer learn to reconcile inside ourselves. I thought about how I felt so guilty for my little brother's paralysis after the woman at the rectory had said he would be okay if I'd been a good girl. I knew I had sinned, and for years I had told myself my brother's suffering was my fault. And now Zoe was trying to make sense of her mother's suffering, while struggling to love her father who had left the church when his wife died. I felt my heart break open with love for Zoe and wished that I could cradle her in my heart until all her pain was gone.

But all I could do was offer some words of comfort and encourage her to remember all the wonderful things about her mother.

By the time I got home, my heart had opened not just to Zoe, but to her poor, broken father whose own heart and spirit had been so terribly damaged.

I became so preoccupied with work and keeping my eye on Shelley, that I wasn't paying much attention. Things seemed pretty quiet for the next few months and I was spending lots more time with Shelley, just as I'd hoped. We had a lot of fun together and although she continued to see Craig, and I thought he was a sneak and just didn't like him at all, I grew to accept him because he made Shelley laugh. And he was charming—just like Zorba, who started coming around more and more. Both men were quite charming and said all the things a girl likes to hear, so our spirits were up. I encouraged Zorba to bring his kids over on the weekends, thinking it would keep Shelley's mind off Craig and help his kids, as well—especially if Shelley could be a good influence on Zoe and keep her on the right track.

It wasn't long before we started to feel like a family and I felt safe around Zorba. He didn't want to get married and definitely didn't want to have any more children. He took me to beautiful restaurants and sang to me and took me out dancing once in a while. He was just so damn romantic that I found myself addicted to this charming Greek man. We both worked in the same industry—me as a model and him as a patternmaker—and lived in the same town. Everything seemed to fall into place and I eased into being his lover as comfortably as if he'd been there all along.

Then things started to get complicated. One day he showed up at my house with all of his clothes. He explained that he had been forced to leave his apartment because he had not paid his rent. He had all kinds of excuses, and those red flags started flaring, but it was like seeing my best friend in need and what could I do? He had sent Zoe and her brother Johnny to their grandmother's house and asked if he could please stay with me, just for a little while.

I knew it was a bad idea right away, but I couldn't bring myself to say no. I felt as if just by his asking, I was being told this is what we were going to do. All those years of becoming my own woman, gaining independence and my own income, and in a heartbeat, I was once again reduced to that young girl from Tilton, New Hampshire, who let men make the decisions.

I reluctantly agreed that he could stay in the playroom downstairs, but wondered how in the world I was going to explain it to Shelley. Still, I thought it wouldn't last long and he'd be gone and we'd be back to normal.

But two weeks later, his son Johnny moved in. Johnny was only twelve and missed his dad terribly. When he looked at me with his big brown eyes and asked if he could stay with us and go to school there, I melted. I couldn't possibly reject that little boy. So I agreed, and our family of two, became a family of four, with Zoe still at her grandmother's house, but visiting us on weekends. Without even realizing it, I found myself a mother to Zorba's kids.

After telling Angelo I couldn't do it again.

As you can imagine, once he had woven himself into my life and home, Zorba was showering me with affection and telling me how much he loved me. He confessed that he'd loved me for months but knew I wasn't ready for love so he'd kept his feelings a secret. But now that we were finally together, he couldn't keep them secret a moment longer. He wanted to marry me.

And I fell for it. The thought of falling in love with a romantic, handsome Greek man with the body of a Greek god was enough to have me singing in the daytime and swooning in the nighttime. And he seemed just as happy if not more so.

And why shouldn't he have been? Once he put a giant diamond on my hand—something neither of my previous husbands had done—he had me cooking the meals, cleaning the house, watching his kids—and making all the money. He didn't lift a finger.

Everything was moving so fast. I wasn't ready for marriage, but I also didn't think it was good for the kids to have us just living together. Besides, the girls, Zoe and Shelley, were thrilled at planning our wedding. The more Zorba pressed me to make a date, and the more Zoe said she'd leave her grandmother's and come stay with us as soon as we were married, the more pressure I felt to just get it done and over with. I didn't even have time to think about it—it just seemed like my life was moving so quickly that my only role was to catch up with it.

That's how I ended up married to Zorba. And that's how he persuaded me, right after we'd married, to sell the home I'd bought for me and Shelley, the home I loved so much, and move to Astoria—where Zoe was, still living with her grandmother.

Shelley was graduating from high school and the more Zorba and his kids pressured me to sell the house, the more I convinced myself it would be the catalyst to break up Shelley and Craig. Craig had dropped out of school and his parents were kicking him out. It was only a matter of time before he'd be pressuring Shelley to come live with him in some crappy apartment while he worked at the local grocery store stocking the shelves. Moving to Astoria was probably just what I needed to do, like it or not.

Yes, it would be a fresh start for all of us. I would look for a townhouse with a gym and a swimming pool, which Shelley would love. The long distance would be enough for Craig to give up on Shelley or Shelley to give up on Craig, Zorba would get his daughter back and Johnny would get to live with his sister once again. I had to stop thinking of what I wanted this time, and think about others. This is what our family needed.

It didn't take long for my beautiful home to sell. I found myself on the day of closing wondering what in the hell I'd been thinking. But it was too late; I had no choice but to sign the papers, accept the check and turn over the deed to my home. On the day the moving truck showed up, I looked at Shelley's face as they took her piano away—because it wouldn't fit into our new house—and wondered, *what the hell did I just do?* My daughter had lost her home, her piano, and all of her friends. And for what? For the controlling selfish wishes of my new, so-called husband.

If I had known what was up ahead, I would have bolted right then and there.

The words of a friend who had warned me about Zorba came rushing through me as I stood there, watching them load the moving truck.

I was in the thralls of new love and had ignored her then, but now the words that had gone in one ear and out the other came roaring back into both ears.

"This man only dates attractive women with money, Darlene, and you have it so watch out. Zorba's very charming and handsome and he can be very persuasive. Watch out."

Was it too late to watch out?

I put a smile on my face, the smile I'd been trained to wear over the years, and looked at my handsome husband. "I guess that's everything," I said.

"Yes, everything is set," he said. "*Ela!* Come on, let's go." He opened the car doors for me and Shelley.

We got into the car, and fastened our seat belts.

We were in for a wild ride.

Chapter 19

My Big Fat Greek Marriage

W e hadn't been in the new home for long before the stealing
started. Money disappeared regularly, from my wallet, from
Zorba's, from Shelley's, or personal things disappeared
from our rooms. Zoe claimed it was disappearing from her wallet, as
well, but I'd learned to spot a liar. She was lying.

When she began lying about Shelley, claiming my daughter was
the thief, I had finally had enough. I knew Shelley wasn't a thief—and
I knew that Zorba's daughter was. But he wasn't about to consider the
possibility. He was as convinced it was Shelley as I was that it was Zoe,
but I'd seen enough of Zoe's antics to know that she was doing it. Zorba
believed anything he told her, though. He never held her accountable
for anything.

As for me, I wasn't as angry with her as I was concerned. I wanted
to understand why she kept stealing, but every effort I made to raise the
issue just led to a battle with Zorba. Soon the fighting was constant.

It was Shelley who was suffering the greatest. She felt frustrated,
scared, and alone in the new home and because she shared a room with
Zoe, she found herself always having to hide her personal belongings,
and having to defend herself against the accusations that she was the

one doing the stealing. Instead of feeling like a part of our new family, she came to feel like an outcast.

On top of it all, the move had indeed turned out to put a screeching halt to her relationship with Craig. The strain of the move had led them to fighting so much that when I wasn't fighting Zorba, I was breaking up Shelley and Craig's fights. We'd gone from a home that was a sanctuary to a home that was a battleground and we were losing the battle. Rather than being relieved Craig was gone, it just became one more indication of all my daughter had lost by my marriage to Zorba.

Fortunately, I'd become wise enough over the years that I'd learned to take charge of my own finances. I'd had no money when I was married to Dick, and what little we'd accumulated during our marriage all went to him. I'd let Angelo handle all the finances in that marriage, even turning over all my paychecks, and it was only thanks to the fact that he was a good man that he never ripped me off. I came out of that marriage with a decent savings account. All that money plus the money I made from selling our home went into my own bank account, in my name, not Zorba's. I had a hunch early on that I'd be needing it. Every day since I'd said, "I do," I found myself saying, *what did* I do?

One day it all came to a head after Zoe had sat down on Shelley's bed while she was menstruating and not wearing any protection. Her beautiful pink satin bedspread was stained beyond repair, and we knew she had done it on purpose. That's when Shelley had had enough.

"Mom," she told me, "I called Craig and we've decided that I'm going to move back to New Jersey and live with him."

Her words felt like the sky had cracked apart and crashed down on me. My little girl was leaving me—and far worse, she was moving in with a guy I knew to be going nowhere in his life. All because I'd married Zorba.

Before I'd even had time to absorb what was happening, Craig arrived at the door. It was clear that they'd been back together for some time and been making plans for this departure. But to his credit, Craig asked for my blessing in their reconciliation, and though I knew he was the wrong man for a girl with Shelley's determination, I gave my blessing. They wanted to build their own life together. And Shelley needed to get out of our house. She needed her own space, and I couldn't blame her. She had had enough.

A few weeks later, a moving truck came and moved out all of her things. The tension between us was palpable. She was still angry that I'd sold our home. She felt as if I'd replaced her with Zorba and his family. She felt driven out.

We both tried to be strong as we kissed each other goodbye, but as soon as she left, I ran upstairs to hide in the bathroom. I crawled into my shower where no one could hear my sobs. I cried and cried and cried. I cried for losing my daughter. I cried for marrying Zorba. I cried for my daughter feeling pushed out of my life. I cried for being left alone with a man who only wanted to fight. I cried because I wished they'd taken me with them.

Why hadn't I just gotten us a little apartment and moved out months before? My eighteen-year-old daughter had more courage than I did. Why couldn't I just leave? Why did I think I owed it to Zorba to stay just because I'd married him? Why did I think I had to stay so his children wouldn't feel like they lost another mother? I had left Angelo because I didn't want any more kids, and now here I was, taking care of somebody else's kids. How had that happened?

Those were the thoughts that kept running through my head, when I heard the shower door open. Zoe stepped inside the shower, crouched down alongside me, and held me as I sobbed. She was trying to comfort me, for once showing a tender side that had been buried since the day Zorba and I had married. But I didn't want her embrace. I was furious with her. Not wanting to hurt her, I stopped my crying and just fell into my pain. I told myself that I had to endure what I had created. I just didn't realize how long I would endure it, how long I would punish myself by living with the mistake I had made. Instead, I told myself it would get better.

It was months before I heard from Shelley again. She remained angry with me, and I suspected that Craig encouraged her anger. Isolating Shelley would help him to control her. In the meantime, I had two troubled kids to deal with. Zoe was continuing to steal, and with Shelley gone, the blame for the thefts fell to Johnny. She was also skipping school, and encouraging Johnny to do so as well. By getting him into trouble, it would be easier for us to believe he was also stealing. I worried that the way things were going, Johnny would end up on the same path as Zoe, so I suggested to Zorba that we send him to a private school. There, he would be free of his sister's influence, and be on the path to college. Zorba liked the idea, but when Zoe found out about it, she threw a fit. She knew if Johnny was away, she'd be hard pressed to conceal her antics. Naturally, she begged her father to reconsider. Naturally, he caved in. She always got what she wanted with him, and my views were irrelevant.

"No, Darlene, I've made up my mind," he told me. "Zoe's right. He should stay with us."

"Zoe's always right in your eyes!" I screamed, but before I could utter another word he grabbed me by the throat and threw me down on the bed. Just then, Johnny walked through the door and saw what was going on and Zorba stepped back. I didn't want the poor boy to see such a scene but I was thankful that he had. His dad was seeing blood and it was my blood he was after.

I got up, straightened my clothes, and went to my closet. I got out a bag and set it on the bed and began packing. That's when Zorba was sorry. That's when he pleaded. And that's when I gave in. Not because I forgave him. Not because I believed him when he said it would never happen again. I gave in because I didn't want to abandon Johnny. He needed me. And I gave in because I realized I had no place on earth to go.

A few days after everything had settled down, I called Shelley and invited her to come by for the weekend. Zoe would be at her grandmother's and we could have a peaceful dinner together and maybe sit by the pool to get some sun. Even though I knew she was still angry, I also knew that Shelley was missing me, too, and it was time to catch up on our lives.

When Saturday came around, I ran downstairs to see my baby girl. Oh my God, it felt so good just to hold her! Even better, Zoe wasn't there, and wouldn't be back until it was time for Shelley to leave the following day. The four of us—Shelley, Johnny, Zorba, and I—spent the next 24 hours having a really nice time with no drama and no battles. It was so relaxing and I felt so happy to be back with my daughter. I missed Michael terribly, as well, but he had established his own life while I was still aching from the cruel and abrupt departure by Shelley. The visit was exactly what I'd needed.

Just as I was putting dessert on the table before Shelley had to return home, Zoe came through the door. I invited her to join us, and felt the chill of her presence the moment she sat down. The tension was so great a single word could have shattered it, but we managed to get through it with forced smiles and polite chitchat.

As Shelley readied to leave, my instinct told me to check my wallet. I knew that if Zoe was going to steal any money, she'd do it while Shelley was there so that she could blame her. So I went to my room where I kept my purse, counted my money, then walked Shelley to the car. I kept hugging her and chatting with her, as if I could somehow stall her long enough to keep her with me forever, but eventually I had to let my little girl go. Then I went back inside and straight to my bedroom and opened my wallet. It was empty.

Zoe had taken every last dollar, and Shelley had been with me every second since I'd last counted it. I went back downstairs and told Zorba what had happened.

"You're a fool for not seeing what your own child is!" he thundered, refusing to believe it had been Zoe. I repeated the fact that Shelley couldn't have taken it because she'd been with me every minute since I'd counted it. I then watched him get off the couch, boiling with anger, and charge at me.

But this time, I didn't flinch. I wasn't afraid. And I wasn't backing down.

As his shoulder pulled back and he readied for the punch, I delivered a punch of my own.

"Zoe is moving out," was all I had to say to defuse his blow. "She's going to have to live with her grandmother. I'm done with all this bullshit."

Then I turned and walked away, leaving him alone with his rage and his children.

It's funny how when you reach the limit of what you'll tolerate from someone, you can find all kinds of excuses for not just exceeding that limit, but for becoming all the more convinced you owe them even more of yourself. That was what happened with Zorba. Once Zoe was gone and living with her grandmother, I had a whole new burst of confidence and threw myself into my marriage. Like the poor fool who falls for a con artist and then convinces themselves that rather than call the cops, they'll give the con man even more money, I convinced myself that I had made a commitment when I'd married Zorba and I wasn't going to back out just because things got rough. I was going to make my marriage work. But I was too naïve to realize that the dynamics of their lives were already in full bloom before I came into the picture. Zoe or not, the drama was constant, the battles were constant. My efforts to bring peace to the family became as annoying as the buzz of mosquitoes, so it wasn't long before every time I walked into the room, Zorba and Johnny began speaking in Greek. If Zoe was visiting, there wasn't a word of English. I was being shunned in my very own home.

Well, I reasoned, if I was going to be a part of the family, then I'd have to learn something about their culture—and their language. So I set out to do just that. Discreetly. They didn't have to know that I was learning Greek. It wasn't long before the continual conversation in Greek that was intended to shut me out, instead only served to accelerate my learning. Eventually, I could just sit back pretending I didn't understand a word, when the truth was, I was understanding quite clearly.

And that is how I came to know that my dear husband was planning on leaving me and returning to Greece, just as soon as he'd saved enough money. No wonder when he lost his job, he was devastated. But I was as eager for him to be gone as he was, so I helped him to find work as a patternmaker in the garment center, with one of my best accounts—Max Hart.

Zorba was happy with the new job. Max was one of the most influential men in the dress market with so many connections in the industry that if Zorba did a good job, he could be set for life—or at least, until he hightailed it to Greece.

Unfortunately, while the job kept Zorba happy and his temper down, it meant that not only did I have to deal with him at home, but I had to deal with him at work, as well. I was responsible for the fit of the garments and if they needed corrections to the cut, Zorba wouldn't listen to me.

"I know what I'm doing, Darlene!" he'd snap. "I've been a pattern-maker all my life. You're just a clothes hanger. Go put on some clothes!"

He had no idea the role I played in turning his patterns into good fits. If I kept my mouth shut and didn't mention the corrections, then the clothes wouldn't fit well and that meant they wouldn't sell well. All I could hope was that during market week, when the buyers were around, he would stay in the backroom working on his patterns while I worked in the showroom with the buyers. I had an excellent reputation working with them and I didn't need my husband spoiling it.

One day during market week, I came into the showroom while a buyer was boasting of his days in Vietnam. His name was Tom.

"I had this one whore I always went to," he was telling a bunch of male buyers who were lapping up every word. "And I never had to pay her. I'd just threaten to blow her damn head off if she ever bit me or tried to say no!"

As half the men roared with laughter and the other half squirmed in silence, I tried to think of something to say, but was just too stunned. I turned around and left the showroom, and the silence that settled as I did so made it clear that everyone knew why I was leaving. I made up my mind then and there that I'd stay away from that guy.

When I got home that night, I told Zorba about the incident, and my decision to avoid the buyer.

"You'd better be nice to that man, Darlene, because he holds both of our careers in his hands. One word, one look of disapproval could end it all. All he needs to do is start complaining about your fits not selling well in his stores and they'll get a different model. For once, try to keep your mouth shut."

I was stunned that Zorba would say such a thing, but as his words sunk in, so did something else—the truth they contained. It had never dawned on me before that someone could retaliate like that, but Zorba was right. I was so good at telling my clients how to get the right fit for a garment before it hit any of the department stores that I never worried about how they could kill my career because they didn't like me. I knew buyers liked to have their egos stroked and I'd become pretty good at doing that. When they were rude I'd keep them laughing with an innocent joke and change the subject. They were only around for market week, after all, so they'd be gone and back to their wives in a day or two and that would be that.

But this time, it was different. This time, a buyer had confessed to raping a woman and threatening to kill her. And this time, I hadn't made any light joke about the matter—I'd walked out.

Sure enough, it wasn't long before Max called me to his office.

"Look, baby," he said, in his typical New Yorker bad boy way, "I know you know your stuff, but it looks like we've got a problem."

"What's wrong, Max?" I asked him, a bit nervous, but not overly concerned. I figured it was something minor. "Was there a problem with one of my fits?"

"Yeah, it looks that way. One of those prom dresses you fit during market week isn't selling. I got a call from the buyer and he ain't happy. He's coming in next week to have you try it on in front of him. Make sure he leaves happy, okay?"

"Sure, Max, I'll do my best."

"I don't want your best, baby, I want better than that. Got it?"

"Yeah, Max, got it!"

I got it alright. It was Tom, the piece of shit who bragged about raping women in Vietnam. Zorba was right—he was gunning for me. Well, I figured, this is going to be the first hit on my career.

I was scheduled to fit for him the following Tuesday and I felt anxious beyond belief. I wasn't used to being so nervous with buyers, but I knew that no matter how good a job I did, he'd let Max know it was no good. Despite my nerves, when Tom arrived, I was as pleasant and professional as I could possibly be.

"I thought the dress was lovely and the fit was fabulous," I assured him. "What seems to be the problem? I'm happy to do whatever I can to fix it."

"Yeah, well we'll see about that. It's too sheer on top. You can see right through it. Try it on. I want to see if it's see-through on you."

By this point in my career, I was so accustomed to dressing and undressing in front of buyers and patternmakers that I didn't think twice about whether or not they could see through the garments. With this guy, though, I knew I was being punished and the entire purpose of the fitting was to subject me to his power over my body. But like the prostitute in Vietnam, objecting would be worse than complying. So I just smiled and said, "I'd be happy to help you. We'll see if that's really the problem and whatever it is, we can fix it."

I put on the prom dress, and it looked great. Then I walked over to the window of the showroom so there would be plenty of light falling on the dress. I didn't see any problem; it wasn't at all too sheer for a teenage girl. But he sure did.

"No, it's not fine," he said, "I can see your nipples. That's why it's not selling. You should have noticed that before. I thought they said you were some kind of pro at this thing."

"I am," I assured him. "But I'll talk to Max and we can add a second lining and the problem will be solved."

"Yeah? Well how's that going to fix my problem with all that inventory?" he growled. He was badgering me as if I was trying to fight with him, when all I was doing was trying to agree with everything he said.

"I'll have Max pick up the inventory and correct the lot," I told him. That made him laugh.

"You're pretty quick with the answers, aren't you? Okay, then, I'll take you up on that. Have him pick it all up and line them all."

Again, I smiled and assured him all would be fine. Of course, it wouldn't be fine with Max. It was going to cost him money—money he couldn't make up by charging the buyer more than he'd already paid. Max wasn't going to be happy.

"Hey, baby, it ain't your fault," Max said when I told him about it. "It's the patternmaker who fucked up. Who is he?"

The patternmaker, it turned out, was my husband. The fact that it was the only dress that Zorba had worked on for that particular buyer was no coincidence either. Tom knew I was married to him, so he decided to gun down not just my career, but my husband's as well. And I had no choice but to tell Zorba.

Naturally, he was furious. He didn't handle criticism well at all, and blamed it all on me.

"I am not responsible for picking the fabric for any of the dresses that go through here," I told him, unwilling to be the fall guy. "If I really felt the fabric was that sheer, I would have said something, but in the end, it's always the patternmaker who makes the final call."

"Yeah, well, if you hadn't been such a bitch around him in the first place, this never would have happened," he said.

I was being blamed by my own husband for walking away when a man boasted about raping a woman at gunpoint. What should I have done, stuck around and laughed with the guys?

Zorba wouldn't let up and we argued all night long. He kept saying it was all my fault, and I must have changed the piece goods after he had finished making the pattern. By the next day, he took our argument to the other patternmakers, and told them how I'd gotten him into trouble by switching the fabric on him.

What he didn't realize, however, was that these other patternmakers were the Italians I had been working with for years and over those years we'd formed a tight bond. I would let them know in Italian when Max was around or in a bad mood and they appreciated the heads-up. I always had their backs and they always had mine and were very loyal to me. So when Zorba started bad-mouthing me, they not only assured him that I always gave them a good reorder fit and spoke up every time I saw something wrong, but they also tipped me off about what my dear husband was saying about me behind my back—and it wasn't good.

Zorba was more interested in damaging my reputation than sticking up for me, and that betrayal felt worse in many ways than all the many betrayals I'd suffered with Dick during my first marriage. Zorba may not have been cheating with another woman, but he was willing to sink my career if he thought it would help his own.

As for Tom, he stopped complaining about the dress after the second lining was added, but he continued to come around every Tuesday. I made sure that I was unavailable any time he was around, and did my best to stay clear of him. Zorba was right about one thing. This man could be trouble and because of my big mouth, I knew it would only be a matter of time before I told him off. So for once, I became the Coat Hanger with the Closed Mouth.

In the weeks that followed, not only was I under terrible stress fearing what Tom might say to Max to sabotage my career, but the longer I heard from the patternmakers about Zorba constantly bad-mouthing me, the more distant we became. I was grateful to the patternmakers for alerting me to his gossip, but it broke my heart wide open. Maybe that's just what I needed. I needed my wounds exposed before I could take the steps to heal them.

Even though I'd been skeptical about the church, first since my brother Danny's accident and the terrible thing the woman had said to me about he'd recover if I'd been "a good girl," then after my horrid experience with the Jehovah's Witnesses, I still had this need for my prayers to be heard. So I headed to church.

Zorba was a member of the Greek Orthodox Church so we would go there occasionally for Sunday service. I'd take communion with Zorba, but I could never bring myself to kiss the priest's hand after he laid the *antidoron* wafer in my mouth. I knew he regarded me as a heretic for not converting, so kissing the hand of a man who judged me was just not going to happen.

But needing to pray for my marriage, one day after work I set off for the beautiful old Greek church. I loved the holiness I felt in the church, and despite the priest's stern gaze that inevitably fell upon me when I went there, I knew I'd find solace in prayer.

As I walked up the steps, however, instead of relaxing I found myself growing stiff and my throat closing up. I knew I didn't belong there. But I so wanted to say that prayer that I opened the wide, heavy door and entered the chapel. It was empty. I slipped into the pew closest to the door and put my hands in my lap. In that instant, my mind became flooded with all the hurtful memories that had been churning inside me for years and I started to cry. I bowed my head in prayer.

I had barely begun my prayer to God when I felt movement beside me. I lifted my head and looked into the face of the priest whose eyes always held such scorn for me.

"May I help you?" he asked. It was not the tone of a compassionate priest who wanted to offer help. It was a tone that told me I didn't belong.

"No, thank you," I answered. "I just need a few minutes to say a quiet prayer and then I'll go."

As if I hadn't spoken at all, he repeated, "Can I help you?"

Again, in the same kind voice I'd used before, I said, "No, I'm fine. I just want to say a prayer to God and then I'll be leaving."

He continued to hover above me and would not leave me in peace. His presence was so unsettling that I felt I could not say my prayer until he was gone. As I waited, kneeling and my hands folded in prayer, he finally spoke again, saying at last what his eyes had told me every time I failed to kiss his hand. "You're not Greek Orthodox, are you?"

"No, I'm not," I replied, my voice now as stern as his. "But Jesus is Jewish and I hope you don't have a problem with that."

I knew I was being rude, but frankly, I was there to talk to Jesus, who was a Jew, not some Greek man with dirty sneakers, a long black robe and a huge cross laden with expensive jewels hanging around his neck. And, I thought, an ill-fitting one at that.

I knew my fits.

Without reply, he left, and I took some long breaths to calm myself before proceeding with my prayer. After a few minutes of meditation, I began my prayer again. But I had barely offered up my thanks to God before I again felt a presence beside me. I lifted my head and saw two policemen standing over me.

"Ma'am, you're going to have to leave," one of them said. "The priest wants to lock up and go home."

"I came here to say a prayer, and I've been unable to say it because I keep getting interrupted. After I've said my prayer without being interrupted, I will leave. It will only take a few minutes."

I bowed my head again and they repeated their command. "Ma'am, you're going to have to get up. The priest wants you to leave."

I lifted my head once again and asked, "Don't you feel silly standing over me while I try to say my prayer?"

It was a rhetorical question. My thoughts were no longer on my prayer. They were on their uniforms. I had never in my life gotten help from someone in uniform, whether it was the clergy, a policeman or my father who always talked about the power you get from putting on a uniform. What power? As far as I saw it, I was as good as anyone in a uniform, and in my line of work, I knew better than anyone that a uniform was just another costume.

When the police still didn't budge or respond, I added, "This is a sanctuary where people come to pray and find peace. This is where Jesus told us to come to pray. This is not a home where anyone, not even a priest, can tell people to leave."

But my words were wasted. Zorba rushed through the doors of the chapel and asked what was going on. The priest must have called him. It was ridiculous. I was not a threat, nor an outsider. He knew who I was and he knew my husband. But Zorba stood by me. When the police explained to him that I was causing trouble, he said, "Knowing my wife, she probably just said Jesus was Jewish and she wanted to pray to him."

Yep, the priest had filled him in. But I was proud of him in that moment. He stood by me when it mattered. I bowed my head and said my prayer quickly as they all stood above me, then I rose and walked home with my husband, feeling for the first time in weeks a sense of love for him.

We didn't talk much on the way home, but I could feel he would have a lot to say about it over dinner. That was okay. However much it might have irritated him, he had stood by me, and that meant a lot to me.

The first thing I did when we got home was head straight to the bedroom so I could get out of my work clothes. I had barely crossed the threshold when Zorba came up behind me, pushed me onto the bed, picked up his slipper, and hit me hard across the face.

"Don't you *ever* do that again!" he screamed. "You embarrassed me in front of the priest! How the hell am I ever going to be able to go back there with my kids?" He raised his hand to hit me again when Johnny came to the door. Once again, my stepson had saved me. Zorba left, and I stayed in the room for the rest of the night and just cried.

The next morning, when I got up to go to work, I saw that there was a dark bruise on my forehead. I couldn't let anyone see that. No matter what excuse I came up with, they'd pretty much guess the truth. So I got the scissors and cut some bangs, just like my mom used to do to hide the marks my dad left on her face. Women find all kinds of ways to hide the scars we pick up along the way, whether physical or psychological. We all do it.

I found the largest pair of sunglasses I owned, and walked out the door, hidden behind them.

And learned to say my prayers in private.

Chapter 20

Going Home

I was working when Shelley called. The first words out of my mouth were angry ones. She knew better than to call me at work. I was right in the middle of a show.

"Mom," she said, and I realized she was crying. "Aunt Julie called. Grandma died."

I exhaled. Shelley was okay. It was Dick's mom. I'd always liked her, but she was quite old and I hadn't seen her in years.

"Oh, honey, I'm so sorry. Is your dad okay?" Shelley wasn't especially close to her paternal grandmother, but close enough that I knew she needed comforting.

"Oh, no, Mom, it's not Grandma Young; it's Grandma Parris, Mom. She died today."

I screamed, a long, howling scream. My mother was dead.

Everything after that was a complete haze, from driving back to New Hampshire that day to preparing for her funeral with my sisters.

I do, however, remember that Zorba refused to accompany me. He didn't know my mother, he reasoned, so why should he attend her funeral?

His absence was both a relief and yet another cause to resent him. Even the most basic roles of a spouse were beyond him. I was the one who was there to support him, an obligation he didn't consider worth reciprocating. At the same time, not having him near was a blessing, just as long as I evaded the questions about where he was with some talk about urgent business he had to attend to.

Returning to Tilton was also mixed. I hadn't been home in years, and found it both alien and warmly familiar. I felt right at home and an outsider at the same time. For decades I'd been living in New York and now walking the few streets of Tilton where I still recognized everyone I ran into, left me feeling comforted and grateful I'd gotten out. Of course, there'd been some changes. A few new stoplights, an occasional new business, but for the most part, it was a town outside of time, a network of roads, most now paved, a handful of businesses, some taverns and churches and, of course, the American Legion Hall—where my dad drank, and Danny had his accident. The memories flooded me.

I remembered so much, from so long before, but I couldn't remember the last days my mom and I had spent together. The last time I'd been down I'd made her a birthday cake and waited for the gift I'd bought her to be delivered. She was so surprised when the truck pulled up and a brand-new bed came through the door. I even slept with her that night, just to be close to her. We talked for a long time that night about Danny, who had just gotten his own apartment, and how worried she was about him living independently. She was also so proud of how far he'd come—and relieved, because she'd been caring for him for so long. As she grew tired, she curled into a ball, and I did the same. I'll bet we were both thinking the same thing—that we would give anything to see Danny be able to bend his legs and curl into a ball, too.

If I saw my mother after that birthday, so long ago, I don't remember. I'd become so lost in my own life and work in New York. I just thought she'd always be there.

She had died of a sudden heart attack. There had been no indication she had a heart problem. She just dropped to the floor, dead.

My dad took her death pretty hard. They had spent their whole adult lives together, and as mean as he was to her, we never doubted his love for her for a minute. They were best friends, and he adored her—and she adored him, despite the way the war had changed him, leaving him an alcoholic, in chronic pain, with PTSD and head injuries that made it next to impossible to control his temper. They had tried their best to rebuild their lives after the war, raising five children, nearly losing their only son who ended up needing constant care and would never walk again. Their drinking, their battles, their misery—it all just worsened with time and once the kids were out on their own, it became harder and harder for my mother to hold up.

As much as my heart went out to him, however, I still blamed my dad for Danny's accident. It had been over twenty years now, but I'd still never invited him into my home since that day, I still kept him at a distance. I blamed him for Danny's suffering, and I blamed him for my own suffering, and I blamed him for my mother's suffering.

Even though in my mind her suffering had begun with Danny's accident, her death brought new memories to life. Now, I realized, she had been suffering almost as long as I could remember. One memory in particular, one that I had buried deeply away, came creeping back, like waves lapping at the shore as the tide slowly rises.

I was small, maybe about five or six years old, and for some reason, I'd come home from school early. Back then, particularly in a small town, it wasn't unusual for kids who had to go home early to just walk home. It was only a few blocks and everyone looked out for everyone else. There was always a mom waiting for us when we got back, and if for any reason that mom wasn't there, there was a neighbor we could go to. I never had to sit at school waiting for a parent to pick me up. This was one of those days, when something sent me home, a tummy ache, a sack lunch I'd forgotten, a change of clothes, something like that.

When I walked through the door, I smelled a powerful odor. It seemed to get stronger as I ran toward the kitchen, calling for my mom. When I got there, she was lying on the floor, unconscious.

"Mommy! Mommy!" I called, shaking my mother to wake her. But she wouldn't awake so I ran out the door for help.

She had tried to kill herself with the gas from the oven.

To this day, whenever I smell gas I feel a terrible fear.

As I grew older, and began to realize what my mother had done, I'd blamed my father. In my eyes, he was the cause of all our pain.

Now here he was, in his own grievous pain, in shock by the death of his wife. I stayed with him a few days after the funeral, and the visit was, for the first time, free of tension. But in its place was a reverberating ache that filled the air, swept through our veins and flooded every moment between us.

On the third day, as I was preparing him breakfast, I told him I had to leave. He looked so sad, so deeply sad. I had never seen him look fragile before, and now he looked as if he might shatter if I touched him.

I wondered what he was thinking. I knew what I was thinking. I was thinking about all the unnecessary fights between us, the years of anger and misunderstanding and the expectations we had each placed on the other to be people other than the people that we were. The demands we made on each other for perfection in a world of imperfection.

There was so much between us that was left unsaid.

I wondered when he last gave our mother a yellow rose. Her favorite. I recalled all the yellow roses he once gave her when I was little. Had he ever given one once she grew older?

Then my own shame hit me as I wondered when I last gave her a yellow rose.

We were all of us guilty of not giving our mother more understanding and love. She had spent so many years in such deep pain that we all grew distant from her, afraid that if we got too close to that pain it would swallow us alive.

And now she was gone. Beyond our reach to give her that love and understanding she so desperately needed.

As I left my father that morning, I had sense enough to reach out to him and acknowledge his pain. I stood in the doorway and hugged him, an embrace that felt, if anything, awkward. I wondered if he'd ever hugged me as a child. If so, I didn't remember it. He must have held me as a child, of course he had, I'd seen pictures.

If he had, his pain was so great that his hugs were replaced with fists and belts and angry words with every year that we grew older. He'd had five children and not one of us could help him through his pain.

As we stood there, hugging in that moment, I thought of a day when our family had all gone on a picnic, and our mom had packed us our favorite tuna sandwiches and some of her homemade cookies. I hadn't thought of that day ever since. Our dad had bought all us kids little paper planes to play with; they were yellow and orange and he showed us each how to fix the wings onto the bodies of the planes so they'd fly. We were delighted, and laughed so much and had such a good time that day. My dad stood beside me on a big rock and showed me how to fly the plane, and cheered me each time I threw it, even when it didn't soar like his did. I felt so happy and proud. I'm sure he hugged me that day, lifted me high up in his arms.

For some reason, I'd buried that memory, just as I had buried the memory of my mother trying to take her own life.

It was hard to remember my mother being unhappy when I was a child, and it had been equally hard to remember the good times I'd spent with my father. I'd created two distinct images of my parents that I had clung to over the years, my mother the joyful, dancing Ginger Rogers, and my father, the angry, drunken man. If any other memories dared challenge those images, I chased them away, determined to treasure the childhood I'd constructed in my mind. Mom was good and happy. Dad was bad and angry. There was no room for gas ovens or paper airplanes in that world. There was only room for the memories that confirmed the world I had created, a world both real and unreal, a world borne of trauma and damage.

My car seemed to be parked so far away as I took those last few steps down the driveway. After I started the car, I turned around to look at my dad. He was leaning against the frame of the door, his face telling me how much he wished I wouldn't leave. I smiled and waved, yet somehow, I knew that this would be the last time I would see him.

He died three months later.

"Lucky" Parris had withstood bombs and bullets, but he couldn't withstand the loss of his wife. He'd died of a broken heart.

Zorba sent me to his funeral alone, once again.

Chapter 21

They All Look Alike

As I suffered silently in my marriage, sunk into a deep depression but knowing I had to muster up the courage to get out, I kept myself busy with work. Max Hart brought me so much work that over the years I'd come to rather like him. He had a blunt way of talking, but then so did I. Most importantly, we were making each other a whole lot of money—money I was stashing away in my own personal bank account so that when I got up the nerve to leave Zorba, I'd be financially secure.

At any rate, it was in the midst of my miserable marriage that Max had a jumpsuit that wasn't selling. It didn't matter what store it was selling in, no one was buying it. And this wasn't a case of a nasty buyer. There really was a problem.

Tanya and I were surprised. Tanya was a Black plus-sized fit model who I'd worked alongside for dozens of fittings. She knew her stuff as well as I did, and we'd both tried on the jumpsuit and loved it. But for some reason, the women consumers trying it on did not. Both Tanya and I knew how to test drive the garments we wore to make sure that the cut, fabric and proportions were right. The problem wasn't with the fit models. Since we worked well with the patternmakers, as well as the designers, it wasn't likely that they had put out a poor design. The problem had to be coming from someplace else. Determined to solve the problem, Max had all the stores ship them back to the warehouse.

When they arrived, our production man, David, brought a few of the garments to the showroom for me and Tanya to try on. The minute we put them on, it was clear what the problem was. The fabric had obviously shrunk a lot more than the garment center standard for shrinkage. That had happened at the manufacturer's. The length of the torso was so short that every time I bent over I'd get a wedgie. When I tried reaching, as if I were reaching for something in the cupboard, the armhole ripped right open. It had shrunk so badly that the specs were worthless.

Max had rolls of this fabric in the factories overseas and pending orders to take care of. He had to deal with the problem or it would cost him a lot of money and damage his reputation. That meant a trip to Taiwan, where the fabric was made. He couldn't get rid of the fabric, so he had to come up with a whole new pattern based on the changes in shrunken fabric.

"I've got too much shit to deal with right here, I've got orders coming out of my ass and the last thing I need right now is to fly to Taiwan. Darlene, you, Tanya, David and Marco are going to have to handle it. Ever been to Taiwan?"

I hadn't and I loved the idea of going. The only problem was, our wonderful Italian patternmaker, Marco, did not want to go. The trip would take several weeks and he didn't want to leave his family for that long (while I couldn't wait to get away from Zorba!). Without a trained patternmaker, we wouldn't be able to correct the problem, so Marco—who barely spoke English—set out to teach me how to correct a pattern. Fortunately, having been married to Angelo, I knew enough Italian that Marco and I could communicate well enough for him to teach me how to fix the problem. After a few days of working with Marco, I had the corrections down pat. I could correct both my size, and the large size, which Tanya would fit. We were off!

Max had us all flown first class to Taipei, arranging to have us picked up at the airport and driven to our hotel to rest up before we got to work. We hadn't even gotten through customs before the adventure began. It seems that not many Black women went to Taiwan in the eighties, because no sooner had we gotten off the plane than we were rushed through security and another entrance where we wouldn't be seen—not because they were afraid of Tanya, but because seeing a big, Black, beautiful woman, they just assumed that she was Oprah Winfrey!

Tanya was showered with attention, and I especially loved seeing her get all the attention over some pretty white girl. They treated her like a queen, asked for her autograph and gushed about how much they loved her. We laughed the whole way, and long into the night and many a night after, just thinking about it—and it was all the more funny because Oprah wouldn't have been caught dead in the baby blue spandex that Tanya was wearing!

After being whisked into a waiting car, we headed for our hotel. The city was every bit as fast and bustling as New York and with as many skyscrapers and honking cars and screaming drivers. Even though we hadn't gotten much sleep on the long flight, after settling into our room, we had way too much energy and the whole day ahead of us so we decided to head straight to the factory and get to work.

We arranged for a car to take us and during the 45-minute drive, we got an education in poverty and wealth. Once past all the skyscrapers and fabulous stores and nightclubs and restaurants, we drove through some of the most extreme poverty I'd ever seen in my life. Many of the homes would have been condemned in our own country, and many of the factories looked far worse. I sure hoped that Max's factory would be in better shape than the ones we were driving past. I also hoped that by bringing work to the country, Max's factory would be helping to put food on the tables of these families so they could send their kids to school. I was still naïve to how much of that work was done by kids who never could go to school, because it was often their tiny fingers that were sewing many of the clothes sold in the States.

When the car pulled up in front of a clean and newer building, I was relieved. It was in much better condition than most we'd seen and when we went inside I saw that it was clean, well organized, and many of the employees had beds where they slept at night. I later learned that because so many lived in villages far away, the employees left their homes and families to work in the factories where they virtually lived. If their children didn't work in the factories along with them, they had to leave their children altogether. This harsh reality was something new. When I had started working in the fashion industry, the clothes were made by immigrants in factories in New York. While the conditions were sometimes poor, they were nothing like the brutal conditions of the sweatshops that were flourishing throughout Asia. With the cheap labor in Asia, the garment district was rapidly transforming. The Italian and Greek patternmakers, tailors and sample hands who the designers and models worked alongside of as a team, were being replaced with these impoverished Asians working half a world away in grueling conditions. Now here I was, standing in the midst of it all, ready to take the skills I'd learned from Marco and teach them to a Taiwanese team we'd never see again. I was still only vaguely aware that the entire industry was changing drastically. What was on my mind right then was saving those bolts of fabric—which meant doing a good job correcting the patterns.

We were introduced to Mr. Wang, a short, skinny man with thick glasses and fleshy lips who ran the factory. He welcomed us in his broken English, and as he did so he looked me up and down as if I was a bolt of fabric he was inspecting.

"Very nice, very nice," he said in a lecherous tone that I hadn't heard since my waitressing days. I wanted to tell him, in the crudest language imaginable, that the admiration wasn't mutual, but my job was to represent Max so I returned his leer with a cold smile just as David interjected and asked where the pattern cutting tables were located.

"Ah, yes, right this way," Mr. Wang said, escorting us past the rows of sewing machines where seamstresses were hard at work. I was amazed at the technology of the machines—I'd expected them to be ancient, but they were much more modern than anything I'd ever seen before. There were single-stitch, double-stitch, overlock and cover-stitch machines that were as sturdy as small trucks, four-thread overlock machines threaded with a rainbow of industrial threads, and even programmable sewing machines. These machines would outproduce our production in New York, there was no doubt. And so would these women, who were lined along the tables like ants at a picnic, hard at work.

As we passed them, their heads bent over their machines, Mr. Wang began calling out to some of them in Chinese. Although I didn't know a word of the language, I understood their meaning. The women's heads lowered even further, and as he brushed his hand through the hair of one young woman, his hand falling alongside her breast as he walked by her, I saw her face redden with shame. There was no doubt, this was a man who bullied and harassed the women who worked for him, someone who knew he could do whatever he wanted and no one would complain, because no one could afford to leave their jobs.

When we finally reached our work area, we quickly got to work measuring and cutting out the patterns. Mr. Wang would occasionally drop in to see how we were coming along, and always managed to find himself standing beside me, his hot, foul breath just inches away, his gaze practically fixed on my cleavage. I continued to ignore him and focus on the patterns, but couldn't help but eavesdrop as he yelled or flirted with one unfortunate woman after another just trying to do her job. Finally, after hours of measuring and cutting, when we were satisfied we'd had it right, we laid the patterns on the fabric for the sample hand to cut and sew together and called it a day.

By this time Tanya, David and I were pretty exhausted and quite hungry, so we decided to get something to eat. David asked Mr. Wang if he could suggest a nice restaurant, and as luck, or bad luck, would have it, Mr. Wang just happened to own a restaurant.

"I come with you," he said, "yes?"

"Yes," David answered. "We would be honored, Mr. Wang."

"I no go now, but finish work. You wait, yes?"

"Sure, I'll wait," David said, as Tanya and I rolled our eyes. We were hungry, and we were in no mood for waiting for the creepy Mr.

Wang. David caught the drift. "You girls go ahead and we'll catch up with you."

Relieved, Tanya and I bolted out the door, ready to play.

We took off for the restaurant and with time to kill, we figured there was no better way to relax than order a glass of wine. And then two glasses of wine. By the time David and Mr. Wang arrived, we had become much more forgiving of the lecherous Mr. Wang and found ourselves having a delightful time. We knew David quite well and he was always a gentleman and pleasant to be around. While Mr. Wang's friendliness was sometimes a bit too much, the evening went quickly and was filled with laughter.

"Come on, Darlene," Tanya finally said, "let's get out of here. I need some sleep."

"You're right," I agreed. "Tomorrow's another big day for us all. Besides, if I eat another dim sum, that pantsuit isn't going to fit me!"

We all left the restaurant drunk, happy and laughing. Tanya, David and I were confident that the patterns we'd made were accurate and everything would fit like a glove, and Max would be happy with our work. He had put his faith in us, and despite having had a bit too much wine, I wasn't about to let him down, especially given how much he'd paid to fly us all out there.

The next morning we were up at dawn and headed to the factory, our heads a bit foggy but our spirits clear and bright. Mr. Wang was already there, and the moment he saw me his eyes were crawling all over me as if he'd just purchased me. I brushed him off with a wisecrack and went straight to the sample hands' area. There they were, my size and Tanya's plus size, both dressed on the dummies and looking pretty good. Mine looked a little big, but all in all, I could tell it was going to work.

Tanya and I grabbed the garments off the dummy and ran into the bathroom to try them on. They may have had modern machinery, but they weren't so sophisticated that they had a dressing room, but we'd changed in stranger places. At least here we had our privacy, which wasn't always the case. In fact, by this point in my career I had put on and taken off so many garments in front of designers and patternmakers that I no longer even gave it a second thought—as long as they were professional, which most were. At any rate, I was just glad Mr. Wang wasn't on hand to watch us.

Tanya was right beside me and she had slipped into hers before I even had mine unzipped, and it looked so great on her that I moved faster to put mine on. The fit was perfect! I couldn't wait to show it off—my first pattern, one I'd corrected all by myself.

I went out on the floor and showed them how I could reach to the floor and tie my shoe—without splitting a seam—reach high to take a can off the shelf like I was shopping in the supermarket. I even tried a little dancing just to make them laugh. We were all having a wonderful time. I couldn't believe that I even called my job "work." I loved it!

With the new pattern approved, the factory could get to work producing the new cut, so we grabbed a copy of the new pattern to take to the next factory, where the process would be started all over again. With Tanya's and my roles completed, we gave that task to David, while Tanya and I headed back to the restaurant where we'd dined the night before, and once again, ordered a couple of glasses of wine to celebrate, and before long, the afternoon turned into the evening, David and Mr. Wang caught up with us, and we once again had a delightful evening.

But again, we knew that as successful as the day had been, our work was not yet finished—we had to follow up at the second factory in the morning. A car was brought around to the front of the restaurant and David, Tanya and I all climbed in and headed back to our hotel, while Mr. Wang got into his car, just behind us.

As we drove, I noticed that Mr. Wang's car was following us. I didn't give it much thought, at first, because I was so tired. But once the car dropped us off in front of the hotel, I noticed that Mr. Wang parked his car and was heading toward our hotel. Now this made me a little nervous because I had seen how he had handled the women who worked for him—he treated them with contempt, as if they were his property. He felt he could handle them any way he wanted. The way he'd been leering at me left me feeling just as vulnerable. I was not in a country where women had much say over the way they were treated, and I doubted my American citizenship would make much difference.

I wasn't taking any chances so I turned around and asked Tanya if I could stay in her room.

"Don't look back," I said, "but Mr. Wang's heading toward us."

She got it. She took me by the arm and whisked me into her room and locked the door.

Not ten minutes later, there was a knock on the door. Tanya opened it slowly and sure enough, there was Mr. Wang.

"I am here for Darlene," he said, as if I were a take-out order. "Go get her."

"I'm afraid not, Mr. Wang," she said, "It's too late. We're both going to bed."

"No, I no go. You get Darlene. Tell her Mr. Wang want her. I no leave."

All I can say is, there's nothing quite like an angry Black woman telling someone off! In her deep, throaty voice she bellowed, "I will sit my big black ass on your skinny white bones if you don't get your ass out of here, you old fool!" Then she slammed the door shut and we cracked up laughing.

Mr. Wang was no trouble after that. We were up at the crack of dawn, hard at work at the next factory for a whole new adventure.

By the time we flew back to the States three weeks later, we were exhausted, Max was thrilled, and the pantsuit became a hit. I had just one more thing to do. Get rid of Zorba.

Chapter 22

Buyer Beware

The fashion shows for the new fall line were coming up and that meant that all the buyers would be coming around from all over the country. Most of the buyers were men, married men, and away from their wives they were hornier than a Viking helmet. I'd be busy, not just keeping them in line, but fitting for the new lines. But what was really on my mind was finding an apartment in the city. I wanted to get away from Zorba, move into my own place for the first time in my life—no men, no kids, just me, a grown woman, ready to take care of herself.

For so long I'd been taking care of Zorba and his kids, and now I was in my forties and old enough not to take his crap any longer.

The turning point had been on a subway ride to work. I found myself sitting next to a woman I recognized from previous rides. She was reading a book, one I had seen her reading before. It was called, *The Road Less Traveled*, written by M. Scott Peck. The book had come out years before, in '78, but it was still popular.

As we sat chatting about the book, I commented that she must have liked it a lot to read it twice.

"It saved my life," she told me. "My first marriage was a disaster and I was in a shambles after that. I couldn't even trust my own thoughts. So I got some therapy, and this is the book my therapist recommended. It's really helped me."

I had no doubt that it had. She had a sense of peace and joy about her that was almost magical. It was hard to imagine her ever having been troubled.

We chatted some more about the wonderful husband she was now married to, and how happy her life was. I was glad she didn't ask me about my marriage—or why I was wearing such big sunglasses on the subway. I was once again concealing a bruise, and I had a hunch she knew, which is why she didn't ask about him.

As we rode along, her words about her bad marriage pierced my heart as if a splinter that had been lodged in it for years was finally loosening. I felt something stirring inside me, something in my gut telling me to pay attention. When I got off at my stop, instead of heading straight to work I ran into the first bookstore I could find and bought myself a copy. When I got home, I didn't just read it. I devoured it. I read it again, and again, dog-earing the pages and underlining everything that struck me as a special message meant just for me. This book was telling me something I needed to hear: "When you love something that is of value to you, you take care of it, you treasure it."

Angelo used to call me his treasure. He taught me what it felt like to feel truly loved. Zorba, on the other hand, didn't treasure me at all. He didn't take care of me—he expected me to take care of him and if I fell short, he damned sure made sure I knew he wasn't happy. He was a mean man, inside and out, and I never should have married him. I had married him because I felt I had to—for his children's sake. He was handsome and charming but as so many handsome and charming men are, the only one he was in love with was himself.

Like the woman on the subway, I no longer trusted my own thoughts, at least not when I was at home. At work I felt completely in control, completely confident. But at home, it was nothing but fighting and concealing—concealing my pain, concealing my sadness, concealing my anger, and concealing my bruises. As for whatever it was Zorba was concealing, I no longer even cared. He still didn't know that I could understand him when he was speaking Greek, but I no longer even paid attention. As long as he was talking to someone else, I didn't have to interact with him. Why the hell I hadn't left sooner, I just didn't know. Maybe I was punishing myself for having married him in the first place. Whatever it was, reading *The Road Less Traveled* got me thinking about true love—the true love I'd lost when I divorced Angelo and the true love that I wanted and deserved—and it got me thinking about the importance of finding a spiritual foundation.

I had strayed from the church as a young girl, after Danny's accident. And I had strayed again when I left the Witnesses—for good reason—and again I had found myself alienated when the priest from the Greek Orthodox Church had called the police on me for praying.

In place of a spiritual life, I had been living a material life. I was valued for my body, which was used to make and sell garments to decorate other bodies. Of course, I loved my work, and I loved the beautiful clothes I got to wear, but the truth was, I had no sense of who I was outside of a marriage or outside of a job. Every day was spent serving clients, serving husbands, serving buyers. There had to be something more.

No matter. I had to set those thoughts aside and focus on the upcoming shows. My thoughts were swirling like a snowstorm inside my head as I realized I was approaching 1400 Broadway—where my next booking was, and where Zorba was inside, cutting patterns. He was the last person in the world I wanted to run into, but he worked for one of my best clients, and that meant having to deal with him not just at home, but at work.

As I approached the building, my mind on not wanting to encounter my husband, I saw the old familiar face of Tom, the buyer who had boasted of raping the Vietnamese woman at gunpoint. Ever since that horrid encounter with him and his nasty payback over the prom dress he'd said was too sheer, every time I'd run into him, I'd share my concerns with Zorba about not trusting him. And every time, Zorba had the same response—"Be nice to him, Darlene. Your smart-assed mouth will only hurt your career one day. Or worse—it could end up hurting mine."

As Tom approached me, he put his hand on my shoulder and said, "Hi, Darlene! How are you doing?"

"Great, Tom!" I replied, my body stiffening, but my face lighting up in a smile that came on as automatically as a light switch. "How are you doing today?"

"Never been better," he said, as I stepped into the revolving door. He followed, and entering the lobby he added, almost as an afterthought, "Hey, Darlene, how would you like to get together and sit and talk for a bit? I've been seeing you around for years and we've never even had a real conversation."

I just smiled and lied to him. "Well, actually, I can't do that," I said, "I'm meeting a real estate agent later today. She's going to show me a place I'm thinking about renting." Just saying it made it feel more real, as if maybe there really was a real estate agent out there somewhere who would find me a sanctuary where Zorba would never once walk through the door.

"You're looking for a place? Maybe I can help you. I know a place that's coming up for rent in a few months and the owner's a friend of mine. If you want, I can give him a call and show you the place. You'd be the first to take a look at it."

Wow. It was like magic. All I had done was make a wish by lying about a real estate agent showing me an apartment, and now it was really coming true!

"I'd love to see it," I said, and just like that, Tom assured me he'd be in touch.

Everything was falling into place. And of all people, who would have ever guessed that Tom would be my savior? Maybe the universe was settling the score, and sending him to do me a favor for all the grief he'd caused me in the past. Maybe I had him wrong, all along. After all, that story he'd told was a war story. I'd seen what war did to men, just growing up with my father. Maybe I needed to learn not to judge a man by the things he'd done in war.

When my booking was over, I took the elevator to the lobby where I found Tom already waiting for me. I could tell right away that he was excited about something, and he wasted no time in telling me his good news.

"Want to see the place?" he asked, his eyes incandescent. "I've got the key, and my friend said I can show it to you."

"I'd love to see it, Tom," I told him, excited but with a lot I had to get done. "Can we do it tomorrow? I've got to get going." I had no more appointments for the day, but I did have things I needed to do to get ready for the shows.

His face turned into a little boy's pout; he was clearly disappointed. "I can't," he said, "I have to catch a train later tonight and head home. It's going on the market soon, so today's the only chance we're going to have before he lists it. Come on. You're going to love it, Darlene. It's right on Sixth Avenue and it even comes with a doorman!"

Sixth Avenue and a doorman? Well, I couldn't exactly say no to that! "Alright, let's go see it!" As we walked the fifteen minutes from the building where I worked to the apartment, I started to feel more relaxed around Tom. He told me that he was a single parent of a child who had been born with some severe physical disabilities, and might have to have supervision his entire life.

"That's why I never stay overnight here," he explained. "I need to get back to Brooklyn before my son's bedtime." His eyes were as soft and gentle as a puppy's and I started to see him in a new light. The war had damaged him, as it had my father, and now here he was caring for a disabled child.

Compassion flowed through me as I thought of what it must be like for him. Caring for a seriously disabled child was something I had watched my mother do for years with Danny. I shared the story of Danny's paralysis, and in hopes of encouraging him to be optimistic for his son's future, I told him about Danny having a job, going fishing— he'd even recently bought himself a boat.

When we reached the entrance to the building, he introduced me to the doorman, who clearly recognized Tom. No doubt he visited often, maybe stopping for naps before the long ride home, I figured. But my mind wasn't on Tom or the doorman. All I could think of was soon I would be looking at my brand new home.

We took the elevator up several floors, got off, and there it was. My new apartment. As we entered the living room, the cleaning lady who was preparing the apartment for showing greeted us warmly. Everything was falling into place—the pleasant doorman, the pleasant cleaning lady—and a spacious, light filled apartment just like I had dreamt of. It was just perfect. I ran from room to room, discovering all it had to offer. There was a staircase going down into the master bedroom, so I headed for it. As I turned around to tell Tom where I was going, I saw him give the cleaning lady some money and tell her to come back later to finish up. For the first time, I felt a wave of discomfort—that same familiar discomfort I'd felt around him before.

I had no time to think of it, however, because in an instant, Tom was on the staircase, right behind me. Not wanting him to be so close, I hurried down the stairs and into the bedroom. It was small, but had mirrors on both sides of the walls to make it look bigger. I was just taking it in, when the next thing I knew he had pushed me onto the bed and I felt the full weight of his two hundred and some pounds crushing me. As I tried to push him away, I started yelling at the top of my lungs for him to stop and let me up, but he put his arm across my throat to shut off my air. I dug my fingernails into his arm but I was soon fighting for any breath at all.

I couldn't breathe and my heart was pounding so hard I thought I'd pass out. I tried to speak, but with my air cut off, no sound came out. As I struggled to be free of his grip my head turned and I was sickened when I saw in the mirror what he was doing to me. With his right arm pressing hard on my throat, he used his left hand to reach between my legs. I released my grip on his arm and reached down to pull down my skirt, but it was too late. He was already doing what he had planned to do to me all along. The last thing I remember as the pressure grew greater on my throat was fighting for my last breath and digging my nails so deeply into his arm that I drew blood.

"Fucking bitch!" For an instant, he released the pressure on my neck and consciousness returned. "You got fucking blood on my shirt, you goddamned—"

I didn't wait for him to finish his curse. I had just enough time to make my move. I don't think he expected me to be as strong as I was because he didn't try to stop me when I dashed toward the stairs and ran up them three at a time, grabbing my bag in one fell swoop as I ran out the door.

The elevator was thankfully waiting and as I rode down, I noticed his semen all over my skirt, but I was crying too hard to even care. When I reached the lobby, I made sure the doorman had a good look at my face so that he could later identify me. I wasn't going to wait around to tell him what had happened. I just wanted to get out of that building as fast as I could and get to a doctor and get a rape test taken.

The rain had come down in the short time we were inside, and now it was pouring hard as I tried to flag a taxi. By the time I reached my gynecologist's office, I was so hysterical that he saw me immediately. As I lay on the exam table, I told him everything that had happened, sobbing and shaking as his fingers and swabs probed inside me.

After it was over, I went into the dressing room and put my clothes back on, still stained with semen. When I came out of the dressing room, my doctor was standing there.

"Darlene," he said, "I have some advice I'd like to share with you, if you don't mind."

"Oh, yes, please, I need all the advice I can get," I told him, just wanting someone, anyone, to make this all go away.

"You know I took care of Zorba's wife when she had cancer," he began, and I wondered where he was going with this strange twist.

"Yes, I know. Zorba's the one who recommended you. But what does—"

He cut me off before I could finish. "Zorba's a very emotional man, Darlene, all Greek men can be pretty passionate, you know. I'm just suggesting that before you go to the police, you go home and first tell Zorba the bad news. It's better that he hear it from you than he find out by being questioned by the police. They'll want to question him, you know, since he's your husband. They'll need to rule him out."

That wasn't what I wanted to hear, but maybe he was right. I mumbled something in agreement, and when he left the room, I sat there on the exam table, trying to pull myself together before I went home. This was going to be the longest ride home in my life—what was I going to say to him? How would he react? Would he feel any guilt for telling me to be nice to that piece of shit buyer? Would he go with me to the police station? Would he blame me for going into the apartment? What would I say about even looking at an apartment? My feelings were all over the place, careening through me like fireworks.

I needed someone to tell me what to do.

Chapter 23

Walk of Shame

It took forever to get home. Every stop of the subway was like a stop of time itself. People got on and got off, as if everything was normal. Did they even see me? If they did, they would have seen that I was naked. That's how it felt—as if my clothes were still ripped off me, as if every touch of a stranger leaning against me would be followed by hands clenching my flesh, body parts thrust inside me. I was terrified of anyone looking at my face, penetrating my eyes. I could not bear even that.

Walking up the stairs to my apartment took all my energy and there was so little left to take. I wanted to just crumple onto the stairs and lie there, waiting for someone to find me and gently, carefully, carry me back to my own bed where I could shut out the lights and the world and lie there, alone and untouched, safe and secure and hidden away forever.

But I could not collapse. Instead, I moved one foot in front of the other until I was standing in front of my door. Then I opened it. I walked inside, but Zorba wasn't there. I could hear voices coming from the hallway and walked to my bedroom and there he was, curled up in bed, still dressed in his work clothes, watching TV. He didn't glance up.

"Zorba," I said, "I need to talk."

"Well, you'll have to wait," he said, not even glancing at me. "I'm watching this bitch destroy a man's career!"

Zorba was watching the Clarence Thomas Supreme Court confirmation hearings.

"He's going to be the next Supreme Court Judge and here she comes along, just smearing him with her lies!" Zorba had worked himself up into one of his rants and I could see that there would be nothing I could do or say to calm him. "It's always some woman who stops a man from getting ahead! What a bitch."

I stepped into the bedroom and glanced at the TV. There she was, Anita Hill, dressed in a double-breasted turquoise suit. She was surrounded by flashbulbs from the crowd of reporters crowded around her—and before her was what looked like an endless table of male senators, questioning her. I swear I didn't see a single woman in that room, not even among the reporters. If there was one, it didn't register. All I saw was that one lone woman being questioned by all those men.

"How the hell can an educated woman do this to someone who's done nothing but try to help her in her career! She wasn't sexually harassed—anyone in their mind can see that!"

I dropped my head, perhaps not so much in shame as to just not see any more of it—not all those men, not Zorba, not the bedroom. I walked into the bathroom to take off my skirt. I'd try to talk to Zorba later about what had happened to me. This was clearly not the time to raise the subject.

Alone in the bathroom, I lifted my head and looked in the mirror. There was dried mascara all over my face and I wondered how Zorba hadn't noticed that. I wanted him to notice. I wanted my husband to see that I'd been crying—no, not crying—sobbing—and I wanted him to see that I was badly hurt. I needed him to see that.

I turned around, still dressed in the semen-stained skirt, opened the door and walked back into the bedroom. He was slouched across the black bedspread, its pattern of red roses crushed beneath his weight. I felt myself crushed beneath him. I just wanted him gone.

"Zorba," I said, as firmly and calmly as I could, "please shut off the TV. There's something important I need to tell you."

But he was still stuck in his rant.

"Not now, Darlene! This is important. If you gave a damn about anything else in the world besides your kids and your career you might want to pay attention! This is historical! Whatever it is you wanna bitch about, you can do it later!"

There was no way he was going to shut off the TV, so all I could do was shut off my mind. I turned my head toward the TV just as Anita Hill was trying to answer a senator's question. He clearly wasn't accepting her answers.

The minute she opened her mouth, I knew she was telling the truth. I listened to her speak, calmly, nervously, a Yale-educated attorney testifying before an all-male Senate that her boss at the Equal Employment Opportunity Commission had boasted to her of his interest in porn and made jokes about pubic hairs. Maybe those kinds of comments were tame in comparison to what some women went through—just ask us models, we'd heard way worse than that—but he was at the time the man in charge of investigating sexual harassment and misconduct in the workplace—and he was asking to be confirmed to a life-time appointment to the highest court in the land where he would be hearing all kinds of cases related to sexual harassment and misconduct. What she had to say was important.

I could tell that what she had to say wasn't being believed. She handled every question with grace and as I stood there in my skirt stained by my rapist, my husband oblivious to my presence, I found her testimony infallible—she wasn't changing it, she wasn't becoming emotional—I could see the pain written all over her face but her voice remained steady. There was no anger in her words; she was telling the truth, plain and simple. Yet here she was, cooperating in their hearings, and she was being mocked, interrogated, interrupted, disbelieved. It seemed as if among all those men there wasn't one of them who showed her any sympathy at all. Instead, she sat there being drilled by a bunch of men who obviously had the same opinion that my husband had—that she had no right to destroy a man's career. It was her career that ought to be destroyed instead.

That would be what I would face if I testified in court. I envisioned myself sitting in a courtroom trying to explain why I had felt afraid of this man for years. I could hear them asking me, "If it was true that you were afraid of him, why did you agree to go alone with him to his apartment?"

Like Anita Hill's harasser, my attacker was well respected in his field—he could get me fired with just a few carefully placed words to the right people. Models were replaceable; buyers were not.

I felt raped all over again, watching Anita Hill testify, watching the look of utter disgust on Zorba's face as she spoke. But if Anita Hill could endure it, so could I.

I returned to the bathroom, took off my skirt and panties and put them in a bag to take with me the next day when I went into the city. I would go to the police station the next morning and report what had happened to me. I wouldn't bother to tell Zorba; the police could tell him that his wife had been attacked. They'd probably want to question him about my state of mind when I returned home, anyway. He could tell them I was upset about something. He could tell them he was too busy watching Anita Hill "destroy a man's career" to find out what it was.

I was done with Zorba. I would move out just as soon as I found a place to live.

That night, after I took my shower, I slept alone on the couch. I didn't want anyone near me, especially Zorba. The next day I'd have my attacker arrested, and deal with the fallout then.

When I got up the next morning, Zorba had already left for work. I was grateful for that. He never had bothered to ask me what I was upset about; he hadn't even bothered to ask why I had slept on the couch.

After taking another shower, I headed out the door. My first stop would be to go to the police with my stained skirt and have Tom arrested. Going to the police station near where I worked would be easier on me, I reasoned, because I would recognize many of the officers who made their rounds in the garment center. There were always trucks unloading garments on the racks to be brought into the stores. The police patrolled the area to keep an eye out for thieves.

An hour later, I'd reached the garment center. As luck would have it, I ran into one of the officers going into the police station and asked him where the office was for reporting a crime. I was so scared of this man in uniform for some reason. Dressed in his uniform, he reminded me of my dad in his Eisenhower jacket—strong and powerful but potentially dangerous. And he reminded me of Tom, my attacker—he was a man with a gun and handcuffs on his hip and he could hurt me if that was what he wanted to do.

Of course, I knew he was a police officer there to protect me, and as a white woman, I hadn't had any experience with police abusing me as some women of color have endured. Still, there was something about the way he looked at me that put me on edge; I didn't feel safe with him as I should have. I felt scared. It was almost as if I had to give myself permission to speak before I could even open my mouth. When I did, in a voice so soft and uncertain, he looked me up and down.

"You want the Crime Victim Unit," he said. "Here, it's this way."

I followed him and told myself I was being ridiculous; he was a nice man, a police officer, and he was trying to help me. When I was introduced to an investigating officer in the Crime Victim Unit, I just blurted out what had happened, my words tumbling from my mouth in what felt like one long, endless ramble.

"I'm here because I was raped yesterday. A man I worked with took me to an empty apartment and he raped me. I went to the doctor and he told me to go home and tell my husband, so I did. But my husband was too busy to listen so I took a shower and went to bed. But I've brought my skirt and panties—my attacker's semen is all over it."

The minute I started telling him what had happened to me, I knew I'd made a mistake. He looked at me as if I were a mad woman. I noticed him watching my body, like he was sizing me up, which made my throat close up to keep me from saying anything more.

"Well, lady, your story's kinda hard to believe since you went home and took a shower before coming here. When girls are raped, they come to the police. They don't go home to their husbands and take a shower."

"But my doctor said—" Before I could finish, he cut me off.

"Your doctor probably didn't see anything to make him think you were raped. You got any bruises on the lower half of your body?" He looked down, toward my pelvis, and I turned red. "Cause if ya don't, it's just gonna look consensual, like you woke up this morning and changed your mind."

He spoke to me in a tone that made it clear he was suspicious about the whole thing and I felt my courage drain away and an overwhelming fear rush in. All I could think about was how could I have any marks on the lower half of my body if I was busy trying to get his arm off my throat before I passed out? I wanted to throw up, so I asked to be excused and hurried to the bathroom. Once I got there, I did throw up—and I kept throwing up until I was so weak I couldn't even walk anymore. How would I be able to repeat that story all over again?

As I walked out of the bathroom, I saw the officer I'd been speaking to talking to another officer who was leaning on the side of the door. There was no compassion or concern in his voice as he talked about me to the other policeman. They were talking about me as if I was some nut who'd wandered in off the street and they had to get rid of me. If there had been a woman police officer around, I would have walked over to her, but just like watching the Anita Hill testimony, all I saw were men.

The two officers had their backs to me, so I just turned around and walked out of the building as fast as I could, trying to remember if I'd even given them my name. If I had, would they come after me and accuse me of lying? I didn't know. I just knew I had to get out of there, get as far away from there as I could.

The whole experience, as brief as it was, had been so humiliating, and I could see that it would only get worse if I tried to press charges. I would not put myself through that again. So I just kept walking. And walking.

I knew then that I would forever remember the way I was treated by the police when I tried to report a crime. *No wonder so many women don't report crimes that happen to them*, I thought. *I sure wish I'd never tried to.*

I would just have to find another way to pay back my attacker. I wasn't going to let him get away with what he'd done to me. And I wasn't going to let him do it to anyone else again.

Chapter 24

Fighting Back

I had never taken a sick day, in all my years of modeling, and I was rarely even late for a fitting. Yet I felt as if those cops had finished off what the rapist hadn't. There seemed to be no line separating the violent rape and the indifference, disbelief and mockery that had followed. It was all one 24-hour long violation. I just wanted to go home, crawl into bed and shut out the world, but I knew I had to pull myself together because my accounts had deadlines to meet and I had bills to pay. It wasn't the fault of my clients if I was overwhelmed. They still needed the work to get done. So I stopped walking, got on the subway, and headed to my next appointment.

When I got home, Zorba still hadn't returned. I was grateful for that. I burned with resentment for him, not just for the way he'd treated me the night before, but for even saying in the first place that I should be nice to Tom because he could make problems for us. I'd told him about how I felt around Tom and the things Tom had said about holding a gun to a woman's head while he abused her, but Zorba didn't care. He was more concerned about himself.

The more I thought about Zorba, the more I despised him. I despised him for hitting me. I despised him for letting his thieving daughter frame Shelley and drive her out of the house. I despised him for treating me like his own personal servant. And I despised him for thinking Anita Hill was out to destroy some man's career. Why was any man's career more important than a woman's?

I had to stop thinking about my husband. It was filling my head and my heart and my soul with anger and pain. What I needed to do was focus. I needed to deal with Tom, before he raped somebody else.

I would destroy *his* career. I would call his boss and try to get him fired. Then he could feel what it was like to have his job threatened and his dignity destroyed. He probably even had a history of that sort of thing and if I told his boss what had happened, it might bring it all out into the open.

But first, I'd call Tom. I'd call that SOB and confront him with what he had done to me just to make him squirm in fear at the thought of being arrested. As my conviction to call him took root, I felt myself becoming more powerful. I had made a decision. I was taking an action. I wasn't sitting back and letting anyone victimize me. I picked up the phone, took a deep breath, and dialed.

"I'm sorry, but he isn't in," his secretary informed me. "He had to leave for China."

"China?" I said, incredulous. "I saw him just last night and he said he was going to Brooklyn. Are you sure he hasn't gone home?"

"No, he said an emergency came up with some shipping and he'd be gone for several weeks. Is there someone else who can help you?"

I hung up the phone, defeated. By the time he got back from China, any nail marks I'd left on his arm would have been healed, and any proof that I'd fought back would be gone. I sat down on the bed in disbelief. I was all out of ideas.

The door slammed. It was Zorba. His voice rang through the house like a furious beast.

He wanted to know what I was fixing him for dinner.

And to think we were fresh out of hemlock.

As the weeks passed, my anger, sadness and pain did not subside. If anything, the feelings grew worse. I had nightmares. I startled at the slightest thing. I couldn't stand Zorba getting near me. I couldn't stop thinking of Tom, and of what he had done to me. By the third week, I thought I might never see my attacker again. But I continued to see him constantly in my mind. I had to get help. So I found a therapist, a woman named Anne, and told her what had happened.

Anne encouraged me to confide in someone. She felt that keeping everything bottled up inside would keep me from healing.

"Is there someone in your family you can tell?" she asked.

"No," I said. I didn't want to tell my children what had happened. It would only cause them pain. And there was clearly no point in telling Zorba. He'd blame me, just as he did everything.

"A friend?" Since marrying Zorba, I had few friends. We didn't socialize. Like most abusive men, he had isolated me from my family and my friends.

I shook my head.

"What about someone at work? Is there someone you can tell there?"

Yes. There was. I could tell Brian. Brian was a client I'd worked for over the years and I really admired him. I had watched how he handled his daughters and it was clear that he loved and respected women.

And he was going through a horrific divorce. He understood pain. I was certain that he'd understand mine. So I called him, we met for drinks, and I poured out my story. He listened with a tenderness and empathy I hadn't seen in a man since I'd been married to Angelo.

"When I have a problem with a buyer not telling me the truth about an order," he told me, "I'll call them up to discuss it."

I shook my head vigorously. "No, I'll give him a piece of my mind when he gets back, but there's no discussing what he did to me."

"I know that. But I've been burned by these buyers so many times that I've learned to tape record the discussions. That way, when they change their story, I've got them. I've rarely had to use it, but it's assurance, just in case."

A tape recorder. Now there was an idea. Tom might be respected in the market, but if I could get him on tape admitting to attacking me, his own voice would be his downfall. I just had to get him to admit what he'd done to me.

Brian gave me a small tape recorder and showed me how to set it up in case Tom ever came near me again. Just knowing I had it with me made me feel much safer, and knowing I had a plan made me feel much stronger. I slipped it into my bag, and waited for the day Tom would show up.

As fortune would have it, that day arrived on my birthday. I couldn't have asked for a better gift. As I walked into the office of one of my accounts, my client told me there was a buyer who needed to speak to me because my fit wasn't selling well in stores. I immediately knew it was Tom. It was exactly how he'd responded after I'd heard him brag about raping the woman in Vietnam, and he'd claimed his prom dress wasn't selling because it was too sheer. I reached into my bag, and turned on my tape recorder. When I walked into my client's office, sure enough, Tom was sitting there.

I shut the door and walked closer to his chair so I could get every word on tape.

He didn't show any fear at all. He just started chatting as if nothing had ever happened. But his threat was unmistakable.

"Congratulations, Darlene! I see your husband is working here now. I certainly hope it works out well for him because this is one of the best dress houses in the market."

Just like the prom dress. He wanted me to know that he could and would make trouble, not just for me, but for Zorba.

Before I could even respond, he got out of his chair and walked toward me with a big smile across his face.

"I just wanted to let you know how sorry I am for how I behaved last month. I guess I just got a little carried away, because you're so beautiful. But I promise I'll never push myself on you like that again."

Still, I said nothing. The more he talked, the more I'd record.

"How about I take you out to dinner, to make it up to you?"

Take me out to dinner to make it up to me for raping me? Did he actually think I'd say yes? Instead, I looked him in the eyes and said, "Boy, did you pick the wrong day to come to me with your apology. What you did to me is called *rape* and I am *never* going to forget it."

His face flickered from the phony mask of charm he was wearing and I could see cracks in his façade as my words of truth sunk into him. Emboldened, I continued.

"In fact, today is my birthday and I am giving myself a gift, so hear my words closely." I paused and leaned in ever so slightly, and said, "Go fuck yourself, you lousy piece of shit!"

Then I turned and walked out the door, not even caring if my career would take a hit. My ability to fit a garment was well established, and I'd expose that rapist for what he was. The police might not find me credible, but in the fashion industry, people had learned to believe me.

Before I started talking, however, I needed some advice. I wanted to be strategic and I knew I was too emotional to be confident I wouldn't make a mistake. Should I go to his boss first? Or mine? Should I confide in his clients? Or would that backfire? I would expose him after I figured out the best course of action.

I felt my whole body flood with heat as the impact of what had just happened hit me—I had just confronted my rapist. For four weeks I had envisioned that moment, and when it came, it came so suddenly and out of the blue that I didn't even have time to think about it and now it was over and I had him admitting it on tape and I was shaking and I just had to get out of there as fast as I could and talk to someone and get some advice and there was only one person I wanted to talk to at that moment and that was Anne. My therapist. I needed someone to heal me. I called Anne and made an appointment for the next day. She would know what I should do.

The rest of the day went by very fast. Once again, having taken the action of confronting him and then making an appointment with Anne, I felt empowered. Tom had tried to bully me with emotional blackmail when he implied Zorba could lose his job, but it hadn't worked. I was not going to be his victim. Instead, I'd retained my self-respect. I'd won. When I got home that night, I poured myself a glass of wine and toasted my triumph.

My feelings of victory were short lived. When Zorba walked through the door, he was furious.

"They fired me!"

His words shattered my joy. Tom had struck back. Rather than go after me and risk me saying anything, he went after my husband, knowing it would be next to impossible for me to prove retaliation.

"The bastards fired me without any goddamned warning! They said my patternmaking wasn't up to standard because the dresses weren't selling! That's bullshit!"

I tried to console him, but he just pushed me away. "It's all your goddamned fault! You do the fittings. You're the one screwing up, not me! I know how to make a fucking pattern! You're just giving me the wrong specs!"

He ranted on and on about how it was all my fault, never guessing that this time, it actually was—because I'd confronted my rapist.

As angry as I was at Zorba for blaming me and, well, for being such a lousy husband, I felt an overwhelming empathy for what he was going through. He was older than me, already in his fifties and he'd just been fired from the best dress house in the industry. No one would hire him again. How would he support his son? I knew he'd fall into a deep depression and that would only make it worse. Now there was no way I could leave him.

The rest of the night as he screamed and howled, I kept my mouth shut, trapped in my own personal grief. Tom had struck back, and now my dreams of leaving Zorba were crushed. The darkness of the night wrapped itself around me like a shroud. A burial shroud.

I was late getting to my therapist's office. I'd missed the subway by seconds, and all I could think was Anne might cancel on me if I didn't get there in time. Fortunately, she was patiently waiting for me by the door. I hurried straight into her office and started talking my head off before I even sat in the chair. Even through my tears I was able to get the whole story out, while Anne kept repeating that the rape wasn't my fault.

"And it's not your fault that he lost his job. You need to move ahead with your plans to get out of that marriage, Darlene. He's abused you enough, and you've suffered enough."

She was right. It wasn't my fault, and staying with Zorba would only extend my suffering through the rest of my life. I walked out of her office determined to divorce Zorba. But by the time I got home that night, all my courage had been depleted. I couldn't shake the feeling that if I hadn't confronted Tom, Zorba would still have a job. I couldn't leave him with no way to make a living, no matter how much I resented him.

As for telling Tom's boss, Tom had made his point. If I did that, he'd come up with some other nasty act that would only knock me down again. He was a snake, a poisonous snake, and to survive I needed to back away. Defeated, but determined to survive, I'd back off.

I wanted so desperately to have the strength to fight back, to fight Tom and to fight Zorba. I wanted to be free of them both, but instead, I let them both entrap me in their misogynistic games. I spent the next few years in a deep depression, afraid of what Tom or some other buyer might do to me at work, afraid of what my husband might do to me at home. The rape had sunk me into a dark place, where I felt I had no control.

I hadn't become a victor, after all. I'd become a victim.

Chapter 25

Panties and Thongs

It was Thanksgiving, and the kids and grandkids were coming for dinner. I was so excited to see them. Shelley and Craig had married and had two children, a girl and a boy, and then Craig had left them all, never to see his kids again, never to pay a dime in child support. Michael had married and had two boys, and though I didn't see them as often as I saw Shelley and her kids, we all remained close. A holiday dinner with my kids and grandbabies was just what I needed to get out of the deep pit of self-pity and fear I'd plummeted into. Maybe it would only last a few days, but I'd learned to grab every moment of joy because as soon as it was gone, I'd find myself alone with Zorba, sunk deep in his own depression. Not even his boy, Johnny, could brighten our spirits. Our home had become a prison cell with each of us sentenced to solitary confinement behind its walls.

Shelley and I had planned the dinner—turkey, stuffing, mashed potatoes, sweet potatoes, Brussel sprouts, green beans, cranberry sauce, even *dolmades* and *spanakopita* for Zorba. And of course there would be cocktails and oysters to start off and pumpkin pie for dessert. We'd be cooking for days.

When I looked in my wallet, however, I realized I didn't have nearly enough money for groceries, and we were already at the grocery store.

"Don't worry, Mom," Shelley said. "There's a bank machine right outside."

"But I don't know how to use that," I told her. It was the mid-nineties, and everything had become electronic and computerized, and it was happening so quickly that I couldn't keep up.

"It's easy, you just put in your bank card and your passcode and then you can withdraw your money."

"What's my passcode?" I asked her, sounding like a doddering old lady.

"It's the code you selected when the bank gave you your card."

I was baffled. But after some back and forth discussion, Shelley got me to remember the most logical number I would have used, and when I tried it, it worked. The only problem was, it wouldn't give me any money.

"There must be some mistake," she said, "you can get up to two hundred dollars."

"It says there are no funds. But that's not right. I've got $80,000 in there."

Shelley peered at the screen, pushed some buttons for a balance inquiry, and said, "Mom, you've got to go straight to the bank. Something really is wrong."

We left the grocery store and hurried to the bank, where the teller informed me that earlier in the day my entire bank balance had been wired to Athens!

"That's my husband," I told her. "He doesn't have access to my account. How did that happen?"

Apparently it happened because he'd charmed a teller at the bank and persuaded her that as my husband, the money was also his. As soon as a supervisor realized what had happened, she knew they needed to stop the transfer.

"You're lucky we caught this," she said, while I thought, yeah, right, you didn't catch anything—I did. Your bank gave someone else my money. But I wasn't going to fight her. I just wanted my money back, so I asked her what they could do.

"He can't access the money for three days," she assured me, "so we still have time. Don't worry, we'll get your money back."

It took all afternoon, but eventually, they put the money back into my account, Shelley and I bought the groceries, and I went home to take a shower.

I was still in the shower when the shower curtain flew open. It was Zorba—madder than I'd ever seen him. Like Zoe had done years before, he stepped right into the shower, clothes and all, screaming that I'd taken "his" money, grabbing my hair, intent on beating me.

Thank God for wet skin, because I slipped out of his grip and ran out of the shower—and out of that horrible marriage, once and for all.

I was done. Done, done, done.

After I dried off, I reminded Zorba that he had a plane to catch for Athens.

Zorba was already packed and ready to go. He didn't leave with my money, but at least he left. There was just one thing he'd forgotten to take with him.

His son, Johnny.

I had a lot to be thankful for that Thanksgiving. Even though I was finally free to rebuild my life, however, my stepson took his father's leaving quite hard. His mother had died when he was so small, and I had been raising him almost as long as he could remember. I was really the only mother that he knew. Now his father had abandoned him. But Johnny was Zorba's responsibility, not mine. If Zorba was gone, Johnny could join his sister at their grandmother's. He didn't want to do that, though, because Zoe had bullied him so much. Still, I tried to convince him that going to his *ya-ya's* house was the best thing for him. Yet no matter how hard I tried, every step I took to get him to move there became a battle. Eventually, I just gave up. I accepted his need for a mother in his life and was confident that once he finished high school in a couple of years, his father would send for him. In the meantime, maybe we could be good for each other. I had never been alone in my life and this would be a good transition for us as we both entered adulthood—he when he reached eighteen, me in my late forties. Better late than never.

As the months went on, we fell into a routine that became comfortable for each of us. He had a mother to come home to, and I had another person in the house at night when I went to sleep. He seemed happy, and we cared about each other—I just wanted to be sure he grew into a better man than his father.

But our pleasant days together didn't last long. One weekend, after a long workweek that had kept me on my feet constantly, the only thing on my mind was a nap. Thinking a shower would be the best way to relax, I headed to the bathroom and jumped in the shower. The sun was coming through the window, making the whole experience more enjoyable. Resting my back against the cool tiles, I was enjoying the warm water running down my body, when my eye caught a beam of light coming through the bottom of the door. The sun was reflecting off a mirror—pushed under the door.

I grabbed my towel and yelled, "What the hell do you think you're doing, Johnny?" I yanked open the door, wrapped only in my towel, just in time to see him scurry away.

He may have been a horny teenager, but spying on his stepmother like that was not just disrespectful, it was disturbing. I was not going to feel violated in my own home.

If Johnny wouldn't leave, then I would. My instincts told me that it was only going to get worse and every time I'd ignored my instincts, I'd regretted it. I was no longer going to leave myself vulnerable to a potential problem, and this was indeed a potential problem. The next morning, I called Zorba in Athens, told him to come get his son, and packed my bags. I didn't want to remain in that house another night. And I didn't.

One of the clients I worked for was a woman named Janet, and she and I had become good friends. She was the one who had referred me to Anne, and sharing the same therapist, we'd come to confide in each other. So when I made up my mind to leave my house, it was only natural that I'd call Janet. Sure enough, not only was she there to support me, she even had an extra room in her apartment and I moved in.

I loved my new bedroom and was so grateful for the support and care she showed me. I started to smile again, and with the extra time on my hands, I joined a dance club—Anne had suggested it as a way to get me comfortable around men without having to be intimate. It turned out to be a great idea, and before I knew it, I was dancing up a storm, thoroughly enjoying myself. My parents had been great dancers, and I always thought of them as Ginger Rogers and Fred Astaire when I was little, and the dance genes had been passed to me. I looked forward to my dance nights out where I never knew who I would meet, but was always certain to enjoy myself. Life, it seemed, was getting better. The darkness of the last few years was fading and a new light was taking its place.

As for Zorba, he did return, and he began calling me regularly, hoping to get me back, but there was no way I was going to return to that cage of a marriage. Instead, I divorced him and began dating—nothing serious, just casual dates with pleasant men and no commitments.

Meanwhile, as my friendship with Janet grew, so did her interest in my personal life. Mutual friends and people at work began inquiring about things I'd told no one but Janet. She was telling them the personal confidences I'd shared. Although I confronted her and asked her to stop, she didn't, and as my client, she was not just my friend, she was my boss. It wasn't long before I found myself retreating to my bedroom, keeping my personal life private and not sharing any information with her. In other words, our relationship had become just like my marriages!

The last straw was when she began leaving post-it notes on my door with well-meaning advice. I'd had enough. She was treating me like a child, but as my boss, I felt I couldn't confront her. So I turned to Anne.

"Darlene," she asked me, after I'd explained my dilemma, "what color underpants do you have on?"

I smiled and answered, "I think pink. Yes, I'm wearing pink panties today."

Her voice became stern as she said something I'll never forget. "Darlene, did it ever dawn on you that it's none of my business what color underwear you're wearing?"

Wow. That hit me with a wallop. Then she continued.

"You don't have to answer every question someone asks you. No one respects your boundaries if you don't respect them. You've become used to living your life this way. When someone asks you a personal question or requests you do something that makes you feel uncomfortable, make your boundaries clear. Boundaries are a safe tool because they help you to recognize when people are well-intended and really care about you, or when they are only trying to deceive you to cause you harm."

"I never thought of it that way," I answered. "But you're right. I just want people to like me."

"I know, Darlene. You want to be liked by everyone, so you don't see the warning signs. And that makes you vulnerable to everyone—your stepson, your husbands, Tom, and now your roommate. Start putting up some boundaries. Once you do, you'll see that you've been playing a big part in this drama yourself."

"I guess it is my fault," I agreed.

"No! I am not saying that it is your fault you've been abused. What I'm saying is that you have the power to control your own life. You've had it all along. You just need to use that power to protect yourself. Begin by setting boundaries with Janet, and you'll start seeing how effective it can be when you make your boundaries clear."

Here I was, the Coat Hanger with a Mouth, and I had never learned to use that mouth in my personal life. The very quality that had helped me to rise in my career was a quality I left at work when I went home at the end of the day. I was living two different lives—the assertive fit model who could talk back to anyone at work, and the timid small-town girl who wouldn't dare speak up at home.

When I went home that night, I told Janet how I felt about her questions and her post-it notes, but at the same time, how much I valued our friendship. I didn't ask her to stop prying and talking about me at work. I told her I didn't like it, it was disrespectful, and if she wanted my friendship, she had to respect my boundaries. For the first time, she heard me. It was that easy.

I also decided to get my own apartment. I found one in Gramercy Park right off 21st Street and for the first time in my life, I found myself living alone. It wasn't easy at first—I had to have my sister, Julie, stay with me the first few weeks, and after Julie left, I had panic attacks—I felt so unsafe. Here I was, finally settling into the home of my own that I had dreamt of for years, and all I could do was cry. I would look in the mirror and all I saw were my imperfections, while others saw a flawless face that made them money in the showroom. I wasn't just a model, I was an actress. My entire life had been a role I was playing, from learning to smile back when I never knew how to smile, to feigning joy and confidence when what I really felt was miserable and helpless. I was still a victim, but a victim of my own making. I wanted to be a warrior like my brother, Danny. If anyone had a right to be angry and filled with self-pity, it was him. Instead, he would tell me that his braces weren't a problem—they held him up so he wouldn't fall. He didn't focus on what he *couldn't* do, he was proud of everything he *could* do. And he didn't stare in the mirror and tell himself how ugly he was. That was me, his sister, the model.

Finally, the absurdity of my skewed perceptions became so absurd that even I couldn't bear to listen to myself. If Danny could be happy with a life spent paralyzed, then I could stand on my own two feet and be happy in my new home alone. I began to reread *The Road Less Traveled* just to remind myself not to be a victim, and I took up meditation. I learned Qigong healing techniques and studied a range of alternative healings that brought me peace and energy and a tranquility I'd never known before.

Day by day, I adjusted to living alone, and the tears stopped. Besides, I was working so much that I was hardly ever at home. I was flying off to Taiwan, Singapore and Hong Kong so often my passport was falling to pieces. When I'd started in modeling, I thought it was a career that wouldn't last past my thirtieth birthday. That's when models are considered elderly. But my experience was entirely different. Each decade that passed seemed to bring me even more work. As for my figure, I was genetically blessed. I ate whatever I wanted and never even worked out—I was on the go so constantly that there wasn't time for any extra calories to hang around. My figure pushing fifty was the same figure I'd had in my twenties, and with all the experience I'd gotten, and the connections I'd made, the years just put me more in demand.

By this point, in addition to working for Max Hart, Janet and a slew of other clients, I had several department stores that used me to fit their private lines. One of the stores that I worked for regularly was Walmart. They had a mannequin made to match my measurements to use as their model for a new line of career pants, called George pants, which they were debuting. What I didn't tell them was that ever since that day when I was first starting out in New York and I put those shoulder pads in my underwear, I'd continued to pad my butt! Of course, by this time I'd upgraded to expensive butt pads, but no one knew, not even my agent. Even dressing and undressing in front of so many people for so many years, I'd managed to keep my secret, because the pads were sewn right into my underwear. They looked so good, in fact, that my agent, who didn't suspect a thing, sent me to Walmart headquarters in Arkansas for a showing. When I got there, they asked me to model some panties and thongs for their new line.

There was no getting out of it. I went into the dressing room and put on the first of the thongs, then stepped out into the showroom where a roomful of Walmart buyers and executives were gathered to see the new line. A voluptuous Latina woman with a backside as round as a peach preceded me. Then it was my turn and everyone's eyes lit up— they liked what they saw, and my stomach was still as flat as it had been twenty years before. Then they had me turn around. That's when they saw a butt even flatter than my stomach! That was the last time they ever asked me to put on a thong!

After returning to New York, my secret revealed, I headed to Times Square where my agent had her office. Miss Newman had retired, but I was with the same agency and was now represented by a savvy woman named Susan. It had been weeks since I'd been there and I needed to pick up a few checks. Besides, I got a kick out of showing up there because I'd become a bit of a legend among fit models, and I loved showing the new girls the ropes in the modeling field. I'd come a long way since dusting my eyelashes with flour!

As I reached the building, I said hi to my old friend, Roy, the elevator operator. He always greeted me and the other models with such respect that he felt like a father figure after all these years. As I got off at the tenth floor, Roy put his hand on my arm and said, "We've missed you around here, Darlene. Please don't be a stranger."

His kind words reminded me that I was not just respected, but that people liked me. I was more than just a coat hanger, with or without a mouth. I was someone people wanted to be around, someone people enjoyed talking with. I stepped into Susan's office with a confidence I hadn't felt in ages. Maybe I didn't need to pad my ass after all. Maybe I'd finally grown up.

So I did what grownups do, when they've saved their money. I bought a brownstone in Brooklyn Heights. Just for me.

Chapter 26

Underground

It was Danny's birthday, and we'd stayed up late on the phone talking, so it was no surprise when I overslept the next morning. I moved faster than usual, pushing myself to get some clothes on and get out the door. I lived just minutes from the N and R train, so if I hurried I wouldn't be late for my modeling appointments. As I was running down the stairs to the subway station, my phone rang. It was Shelley.

"Mom? Are you okay?"

"Of course, I'm okay, I'm just running late. Why? What's going on?"

"There's been an accident. A plane just crashed into one of the Twin Towers! Tower One!"

I was stunned. My route went right alongside the towers. And a plane crashed into it? That was horrible—a lot of people must have been killed. I told Shelley I'd talk to her later, I had to get to work, but wow, that was just terrible, I said.

"Mom, I'm worried about you, that's right by you."

"Don't worry, Shelley, I'll play it safe, and take the No. 2 train on Clark Street. It skirts the first tower and goes directly to Tower Two. I'll be fine."

Reluctantly, she said goodbye and made me promise to be careful, but wishing I'd just go home. Going home was not an option, though. Accident or no accident, I had fitting appointments and people were relying on me. I needed to get on that train.

I just managed to leap into the car when the doors shut and the train took off. After some time, however, the train stopped. We smelled smoke and everyone knew immediately that something terrible was happening, but we had no idea what it was. A sense of fear swept through the train and everyone was alert, our adrenalin pumping, but we all sat eerily still, vigilant to the slightest sound or movement. We sat there like that in the darkness for about an hour, as the subway car became stifling hot, and we all began to squirm. More disturbing, the smell grew more powerful, a smell none of us recognized. It became clear to all of us that we had to put our fears aside and come up with an exit plan. We were every age and nationality you could think of on that train, and some of the passengers didn't even speak English, but we all had to trust each other and work together to come up with a solution. In that stifling, frightening car, we became a family trapped in a metal can, breathing foul, hot air and barely able to even see each other. Yet somehow we knew we needed each other if we were going to get out of that scorching car alive.

Peering out the windows, it looked as if the train had stopped just short of the platform. If we could just get a door open, the strongest men on the train could lower us all onto the tracks. Then all we had to do was follow the hazy light just up ahead. The big danger was the third rail—the electrified rail that carried live current and could electrocute us if we stepped on it. Having no other alternative than escaping the suffocating car, we convinced ourselves that with the power out, the rail would not be electrified—still, I worried about the brave souls who would take the lead in bringing us to safety.

Suddenly, the doors of the subway flew open and everyone started to move. The sudden rush of fresh air awakened us to the fact that we needed to move fast, lest the doors close and we might be forever stuck inside that sardine can. As everyone pushed their way toward the doors,

I found myself backed up against the wall of the train, breathing that hot, humid subway air, now foul without ventilation. I began to lose consciousness, and feared I'd slide to the floor and be trampled. Then as if by a miracle, the face of a Russian man I knew from work appeared through the smoke, and I felt his arm slide around my waist to hold me up. He guided us to the nearest exit, and helped me down to the tracks, staying close by my side.

I had expected the air to get cooler as we got closer to the exit, but with every step we took, the air only got worse. No one had any idea what was going on. People were speculating that it was some kind of electrical fire, but all we could do was keep moving ahead, holding each other's hands in order to form a human chain as we moved through the tunnel and up onto the platform. If anyone fell, we could stop to help that person back up. The Russian man held my hand firmly in his grip and I clung to it because it was, quite literally, my lifeline.

A musical murmuring of prayer echoed through the tunnel in a melody of different languages, each of us praying to our personal God to guide us to safety. As we got closer to the exit, the chanting grew louder and I found great comfort in the chorus of prayer that made it clear that when we all walked out of that tunnel, it would not matter what religion we were or what traditions we celebrated. We were all survivors.

When we finally did reach the platform, the Russian man helped me up, and we all hurried to the stairs to climb out from the underground to see what was going on. But escape told us nothing. The air was so strangely acrid that I felt as if I'd entered a *Twilight Zone* episode. Swarms of terrified, confused people stood motionless on the streets, cellphones inoperable, staring blindly at televisions in shop windows, restaurants, bars, anyplace that had news of what was happening to us. I found a crowd gathered outside a storefront selling electronics and joined them, where I saw what they were staring at—a television. We stared, like millions throughout the nation, to the film playing over and over of the second tower being hit. The realization that we were under attack seeped into me with a slow but steady current that stunned me into silence. I wandered back out onto the streets and looked up to the Twin Towers, shattered and smoldering, clouds of black smoke pouring out of them. Then, in a horrific instant, I watched as the towers came down, filling the sky with a thick, swirling grey dust that fell on us like a shower of demonic rain.

My shock soon gave way to panic as I realized I needed to find a landline and call Shelley. All she knew was I had told her I was heading toward the second tower, just moments before it was hit. I had to get to work and call her.

I had to start walking. The garment district was at least forty-five minutes away and I had to get there. My kids didn't know if I was dead or alive. As I began to walk, every face I passed was as blank as my own. No one knew what was happening, or what would happen. We were shocked into silence, a silence that echoed with every step, when an ear-piercing roar shattered the silence and the sky filled with a stream of military jets.

I looked up and wondered, for the thousandth time, *What the hell is going on?* Bringing my eyes to ground level, I saw people running in torn, blood-soaked clothes. I realized they had been even closer to the towers than I had been, and many looked seriously injured. I quickened my pace, desperate to get as far away as I could and just as desperate to reach my children.

As I walked, I kept wondering who could do such a thing, who could kill so many people and for what reason? Would they continue to attack? Would I survive? I was terrified, and couldn't get away fast enough.

Thoughts of the cruelty of the world swept through me, bringing a wave of anger, and the faster I walked, the more my anger swelled as I thought not just of the people who had done this, but the institutions that had made their hatred and cruelty possible. I thought of the political institutions that had made battles for power a business, of the business institutions that had made greed into a religion, of the religious institutions that had made hatred of nonbelievers an act of virtue. All the hatred in the world had merged into this day, and no matter how hard I tried to comprehend the devastation, I just couldn't grasp it.

Yet what I could grasp was the kindness and unity we showed each other on the train. The people who shared neither race, nationality or religion had no thought of their differences as we worked together to survive. I thought of the Russian man who had saved me. His name was Ellea, and he was not a friend. I had seen him many times, fighting with his wife. Although I could not understand the Russian words, the anger in his voice told me he was being mean to her. She never fought back—she was so timid, in fact, that I would often come to her defense and yell at him to leave her alone. It was funny, but I could not yell back at my abusive husbands when they screamed at me as he did to his wife, yet I had no hesitance to defend other women. It was only in defending myself that I had been afraid.

And now, here was that same man, that same angry, mean man, putting his arm around my waist and guiding me to safety with such a gentle tenderness that his kindness was unmistakable. Like me, he was full of contradictions, capable of a kaleidoscope of emotions and actions that helped him to survive.

And he had helped me to survive. The man I so resented, had become my guardian angel at a time when I thought my life might end.

I had to get to my children! The more I realized how closely I had come to dying, how terrified I still was, the more I realized that every moment they didn't hear from me was an agonizing moment. I walked faster and faster, lost in my thoughts and my fears and my rage and the comfort I'd found from strangers.

By the time I reached the garment district, I was a wreck. Fortunately, Brian, my friend and boss, was there, and I couldn't have asked for a better pair of arms to fall into. I wanted him to hug me all day, but I had to call Shelley. Fortunately, Brian had a landline in his office.

The minute I heard her voice, I knew she was scared.

"Oh, thank God, Mom! We were so worried."

"I know, honey, but I'm fine, I just had to walk a long way." I didn't tell her about the subway, not wanting to upset her any further.

"Mom, I want you to come to New Jersey and stay with us here," she insisted.

I wanted to be back in my own home. Funny how I'd felt so unsafe living alone, but now that I was used to it, that's where I wanted to be because that was where I felt safest.

I loved my brownstone. It had been built in 1810 and had an old soul that brought me such a sense of peace. It was right off Montague Street and surrounded by beautiful, quaint little restaurants and boutiques, all shaded by an arbor of lovely trees that lined the streets. It even had a view—of the Statue of Liberty and the Twin Towers.

I shivered to think of what that view would now be—and what it would mean to me.

But I had to go back.

"No, Shelley, I'll be fine. I just want to get back home. I'll call you from there."

Just then, Brian interrupted us. "You can't go anywhere, Darlene, the city's been closed—there's no way out and no way in."

The city was closed? I'd never heard of such a thing and it was impossible to believe. But then, this entire day had been impossible to believe. At any rate, that settled the debate as to New Jersey, but I was still determined to go home. Since it looked like there wasn't going to be any work getting done that day, or any day in the near future, I bid Brian goodbye and set off.

I headed toward the Port Authority, hoping there would be bus service, but soon realized that was a useless plan. There were lines of scared, bloody and sobbing people all around. There were no busses, no cars, no trains. No one was going home. We would probably have to sleep right there on the floor. I was trapped on an island, an island under attack.

I had to get home.

My feet were throbbing, but I wasn't about to stand still. My home was about ten miles across the Brooklyn Bridge, but if the only way to get there was on foot, well, I reasoned, I probably walked about ten miles a day on my job. So I began walking toward downtown Manhattan.

I had been walking for several hours when I realized I had to pee badly, but no shops were open. They'd all shut down. Eventually I passed a construction site where the men had stopped working hours before.

They were just sitting around talking to each other and didn't seem to notice me passing by. Ordinarily, you could never walk onto a work site—and a woman couldn't pass one without a few catcalls—but this was no ordinary day. There were no rules. So I walked up to them and asked if I could pee in their port-a-john.

"Sure," one said to me, and everyone nodded respectfully. For a day, they'd dropped the whistling, the "babes" and the "honeys" and "sweethearts." For a day, we were all wounded and in need. These big, muscular men looked as scared as I was. I peed in the filthy, smelly john with gratitude and relief.

Further on in my journey, I came upon another group of men, sitting on old crates talking. I began to chat with them and learned that every one of them had lost someone they knew that morning, or they had just escaped death themselves. One had a son who worked in the towers, but had missed work that morning to take his wife and child to the pediatrician's. Another had just spoken to his nephew, just moments before he entered the building for his job interview. He died at the age of 22. The stories I heard were each more heartbreaking than the last, stories I would continue to hear from people for weeks, just an endless tale of lost lives and grief.

I stayed and cried with those men until I knew I had to get back up and continue my long walk home. And that meant walking back into the pitch dark smoke that still covered the lower part of Manhattan. Surely, I thought, there would be busses there that would take me across the Brooklyn Bridge. My feet hurt so badly I didn't think I could withstand another step.

I walked on, thinking of an old Jewish patternmaker, Mr. Fisher, who I'd worked with years before. One hot day as he was working on a pattern, he stopped to roll up his sleeves. I had often wondered why he wore those long sleeves on such hot days, and as he rolled them up, I saw the numbers tattooed on his arm that revealed the reason why. He was a Holocaust survivor.

"We will never forget," he told me, with eyes that had seen more than I could ever imagine.

Now I would never forget. My own tattoo wouldn't be written across my arm, but across my heart. I had finally witnessed just a glimpse of what my father had been through.

I muttered how sorry I was to my father, so sorry for not seeing his pain. "I am so sorry, so very sorry, Dad," I whispered to the heavens. "I see it now. Now I understand."

And in that dark moment, as I approached the blistering skies of Manhattan, still shrouded in a thick, dark soot, I felt a love for my father nudge my heart, a love I hadn't before felt. It had taken me half a lifetime to realize I needed to forgive him his war wounds, just as he had struggled to forgive me my looks, the looks he thought could not have come from him. Yet it was his war wounds that had made him the hero that he was, just as it was my looks that had made me the woman I now was.

It was time to cross the bridge. Not just the bridge that had divided me and my father across our lifetimes. That was a bridge I still needed to cross. First, the Brooklyn Bridge, the mile-long bridge across the East River that would take me to my home. There it was, at last. As I stepped toward it, having walked for hours through the rubble of my city while pondering the rubble of our lives, I had one thought above all others on my mind.

I never should have chosen a career that required wearing high heels.

Chapter 27

Eisenhower Jacket

Recovering from 9/11 wasn't coming easy. True, for weeks afterward we bonded together, friends and strangers alike, but the aftermath of the trauma lingered in our hearts and memories long after. Every morning, the moment I opened the blinds and saw the ravaged skyline, the Towers knocked out like front teeth from a perfect smile, I felt my heart both harden from anger and melt from grief. I so needed to heal.

I returned to meditation, Qigong, and energy healing, and I began learning about kinesiology, the study of how the body moves, and how our bodies absorb the pain and traumas of our lives. I dove into learning everything I could about alternative healing as I wrestled with finding peace and some sort of center to my unbalanced life. Over time, the darkness of September 11th began to lift and I felt an intensifying lightness and energy that restored my spirits.

I was also working harder than I'd ever worked before, and was traveling to Jakarta, Indonesia, regularly, as production had essentially stopped in the United States. Now everything was manufactured in Asia or Southeast Asia, and I'd watched as one by one, the Greek and Italian patternmakers and sample hands were laid off, never to be replaced. Even organized crime felt the blow, as the textile and trucking industries they once controlled began shutting down, and the men in black suits who once reigned over the textile trade moved on to the drug trade. The fashion industry had gone global, and fortunes were made and lost in the process.

My own fortunes, however, were growing. As I approached retirement, comfortably single throughout my fifties and at last at peace with my independence, my old designer friend and former roommate, Janet, called.

"Want to buy a yacht?" she asked, laughing.

At first, I assumed she was joking. And she was, sort of.

"Sorry, Janet," I answered, "I've made a lot of money, but not that much!"

"Well, it's actually a boat—I found a boat down on the Jersey Shore. We could go in on it together and dock it at the Brielle Yacht Club. We could have our own private weekend getaway. What do you think?"

What did I think? I thought it was brilliant. But I didn't want to sink too much money into something that could potentially be a money pit. So I suggested we ask our mutual friends Betty and Cheryl to join us. All were fashion or jewelry designers, all were successful, and all were single. Four girls and a boat, what could be more fun? I couldn't think of anything more healing and enjoyable than sitting on a boat, smelling the sea air and reading my books. I had just one rule—no men overnight. I wanted our boat to be a woman's space, and the others agreed. Our money paid and the papers signed, and we were the proud maritime owners of our own little "yacht."

Cheryl was a dream to get along with and we were soon leaving the city for Jersey Shores every weekend, not to return until Monday morning. Betty soon met a man from the yacht club and it wasn't long before she was there more often than we were. Betty had a fabulous figure, but she was terribly shy around men and always hiding herself under layers of clothing. Once on board the boat, however, she began to strip down to shorts and tank tops and it wasn't long before shy Betty had transformed into sexy Betty and her lusty sexuality came to life, all in a good, healthy way. As her romance grew, she spent less and less time on our small boat, and more and more time on her new boyfriend's larger, more private one.

Janet also found a man to preoccupy her time with, and it wasn't long before Cheryl's mom became sick and Cheryl didn't have time for the boat. That left me with the boat pretty much to myself, and the solitude was awesome. I'd sit back and read, drink some wine, read some more, chatting with my maritime neighbors until the sun went down. Then, after all the other boats had closed up for the night, I would put on my headphones, grab a cushion and sit on the boat dock. It was heaven. I had the sea rocking me to sleep and the smell of the ocean and call of the gulls to wake me in the morning.

It was a time of renewal, of loving myself instead of loving a man. I still dated, but with maturity came insight, and the better I felt about myself, the sooner I recognized when a man didn't treat me with respect—and I walked away. I was still putting myself out there, and hadn't written off men altogether, but for the first time in my life, I felt comfortable on my own. Somehow that spur-of-the-moment choice to buy that boat had been just what I needed—it had helped me not only to heal, but to feel in control and capable. If I could handle a boat, I could handle my life!

We kept the boat for four summers and I came down every spring of those four years to open the boat and didn't close it up until late in the fall when it was getting too cold to sleep on it. We probably would have kept it forever but Janet began breaking the rules and having men sleep over and before we knew it, gossip starting swirling at the yacht club that we were in the escort business. I wanted no part of that and Janet and I began fighting over the issue, so even though none of us wanted to sell it, it became apparent that it was time.

I was by myself on one of the last nights on the boat, when my sister Julie called. She told me that Danny had been diagnosed with cancer and had less than a year to live.

"He's frightened out of his mind, Darlene. You need to come home. He needs his family with him when he starts chemotherapy."

There was no question about my going home. I'd head straight for the city first thing in the morning and book the next flight out.

In the meantime, I hung up the phone, poured myself a glass of wine and just cried. I drank myself silly as I walked up and down the dock, thinking of my poor little brother and all the pain he'd suffered in his life. I was beside myself with grief and just cried and paced up and down until someone on a nearby boat had the good sense to call a friend to rescue me. Some of the other boat owners had been watching me, certain that I was going to fall off the pier and drown.

The woman sent to fetch me, Susan, was well known among the boat owners, and she arrived late at night, talked me into going home with her, and tucked me into bed. When I woke up the next morning, I wasn't sure where I was—my memory of the night before was, unsurprisingly, rather fuzzy. I got out of bed and wandered into the most lovely seaside cottage imaginable. Susan wasn't there—it turned out she had gone for her morning walk by the sea—but as I looked around, I fell absolutely in love with this charming home.

I made myself a well-needed cup of coffee and sat down in the sunroom, waiting for Susan to return, and wondering how in the world I would ever cope with losing my sweet little brother, Danny.

My son, Michael, met me at the airport and as we drove the hour-long drive to Tilton, we talked of Danny and how much each of us had wished we'd spent more time with him. Michael warned me that Danny had grown weak, but when we got to my parents' home, where Danny had moved after their deaths, I was stunned to see the frail, gaunt and hollow man that was my little brother. He was unrecognizable—until he smiled, and I knew my brother was still there, somewhere inside his dying body, his spirit as alive as ever.

I gave him the longest hug of my life, and then stepped back to watch as Michael hugged him. Watching them, I realized how big my son had grown. He was born big, but it seemed like just the day before I had been holding him in my arms. Now here he was, over six feet tall and 200 pounds, holding my frail brother and fighting back his tears. Michael was such a sensitive man, but his size gave him the appearance of power. He was forced to keep his pain inside because it's expected of men to save the world—and save us women along with it.

After Michael left to go home to his family, I made myself a cup of coffee and sat down beside my beautiful wounded warrior, my only brother. As we talked, it became clear that it wasn't death that Danny feared, it was going to hell. As death approached, the church's warnings of hell that had terrorized us as children had returned to terrify him.

"I'm just afraid that God won't let me into heaven, Darlene, and I'll spend eternity paying for my sins."

My rage at the church had never been greater. No God would ever send a boy like Danny to spend eternity in hell—and why was anyone taught that such a fate awaited them? Danny had lived his own private hell on earth, unable to walk, unable to ever enjoy sex or father a child, and yet through it all, he showed a greater strength than I had ever known in my life.

We sat in comforting silence for the longest time and as we did, I thought of all the years that Danny had spent paralyzed, yet it was me, the one who could walk with ease, could walk a runway and pivot like a pro, but was so afraid to take any real steps forward in her life. I was the one who had let life paralyze her. Danny had never done so. Danny had faced life with a determination to move forward every day that he awoke. Danny would never die. His body might go, but his energy would live on—and the lessons he had taught me, the lessons I'd so often forgotten about moving forward, would return to me with every step and stride ahead of me.

How I wished that Danny could take one last step before he died. It had seemed incomprehensible when we were told he'd never walk again that, in fact, he never would. And now he was dying, the years having passed. As I gazed at his frail, tender body I could see how fast the cancer was already spreading through his body. He would never make it another year.

For the next few months, I flew back and forth, Michael picking me up at the airport each time and each time, we shared the same sad conversation about our love for Danny and how hard he was struggling to survive. I had long talks with my brother, preparing him for death and assuring him that hell was not awaiting him, that he was only leaving his damaged body, his energy would live on.

At one point I even got an ice cube, placed it in his hand and let him watch as it melted, dripping its icy cold water onto his lap.

"You see, Danny, you are just like this ice. You are not going away. You are transforming into energy, a radiant, eternal energy."

Danny laughed. "Well, I just wish I could feel that energy on my pants right now! I'd give anything to feel that ice cold water on my legs!"

We laughed and hugged and cried as we talked about all that he had missed in life and all that he had lived. As the weeks passed, he grew weaker and struggled to breathe. Swallowing was getting hard and many times the food would just sit in his mouth until he could muster the strength to chew. His skin was pale and hung from the frame of his face like ill-fitting clothes. We no longer talked much. We would watch TV together and hold hands.

Each visit became harder, until one day, my sisters called to tell me he had slipped into a coma. They had been caring for him daily, cooking for him, changing and bathing him. Now he was in his last moments. I raced to the airport, and as I waited for my plane to arrive I stayed on the phone, talking to him, urging him not to be afraid, to let go, to pass through the veil and cross over. By the time I reached him, my sweet little brother was gone.

After the funeral, I returned home and put the Brooklyn brownstone on the market—like a gift from the angels, Susan had decided to sell her seaside cottage, and asked if I wanted to buy it. I was thrilled. There was no better place to heal from my grief, so once again, I moved.

Unpacking my many boxes of clothes, the designer wardrobes I'd accumulated over time, I came to one that stopped me cold. It was a large, cardboard box, dusty and heavy for its size. Inside was a gift that Danny had given me. I still recalled the moment he gave it to me, as if he were alive and speaking to me that very moment. He was in his truck, and I was standing beside it, talking to him through the driver's side window.

"Try it on, Darlene," Danny had said, reaching across the seat and lifting the large box. It was too big to fit through the window, so I opened the door and took it. "Maybe if you wear it, you'll feel the pride that Dad felt when he wore it. Maybe it'll help you understand him better."

I knew then what was inside the box and now, here it was again, as if Danny had sent it to me once again, this time from the heavens.

I lifted the lid and there it was. My father's Eisenhower jacket.

I pulled it out as carefully and tenderly as if it were one of Ron LoVece's wedding gowns. I slipped my arms into the sleeves, remembering how big it had been when I'd last tried it on at the age of eight. Once on, I adjusted the shoulders, buttoned it, and stood before the mirror. It no longer swallowed me, but embraced me. I thought of all the clothes I'd worn in my career. This was the first time I had found a jacket that didn't have to be cut to fit me—I was the one who had had to grow to fit into my father's Eisenhower jacket. My father had been right about its power.

The next day, I wore the jacket into work. As if by magic, heads turned. As soon as I stepped into the elevator, I was greeted by big smiles. As I entered the elevator, an old guy who recognized what those medals stood for saluted me. I began wearing the jacket regularly, and each time I walked down the street or entered a showroom, I'd find myself in long conversation with veterans. Some would launch into long stories about each medal and share their own war stories, urging me to put the jacket in a museum so the rest of the world could see it. Some even asked me if they could put it on and have their picture taken with it. For all the countless designer jackets I had worn as I walked down the streets of New York, none had ever had such a transformative quality. Then one day, I entered a crowded subway, looking for a place to sit.

An old man got up and, rising as tall as his ancient spine would let him, he saluted me—or I should say, he saluted my dad's jacket.

"Hey, you stupid old fool," some angry kid yelled at him, "do you know how many men had to die for her to wear that jacket?"

"Yeah, sit down!" one of his friends shouted to the old man. There were three of them, and as they began yelling at us, their delight at their own ignorance grew.

I walked over to them and, looking down, said, "Do you know how many times my father had to put his life on the line so you would be able to say anything you want in this country? You wouldn't be able to get away with disrespecting that dear man if men like my father hadn't fought for your right to do so. You are the ones who should feel ashamed."

I was prepared for a fight from them, but instead, one by one the other passengers rose, and gave me a standing ovation. The three cowards didn't say another word.

They didn't call me the Coat Hanger with a Mouth for nothing!

Chapter 28

Man from Mars

As the years went by, I continued dating, but I wasn't finding my perfect match. No wonder. I never made it past the third date—the third date always implied sex, so I would just get the hell out of Dodge before anything like that was expected of me. It wasn't that I was turned off by sex; it was just that sex always led to intimacy, intimacy always led to marriage, and marriage always led to disappointment. Besides, my life beside the sea couldn't be better—I was happier without a man than I'd been with a man. But the truth was, I did hope a good one would come along.

My friends would joke, "Hey, Darlene, have you found the perfect guy yet?"

And I would inevitably reply, "Yes, I have. He's tall, sexy, has beautiful silver hair and he's kind and a great lover!"

"So what's his name?" they'd ask, knowing I was putting them on.

"I don't know. He hasn't shown up yet. But he's out there somewhere, and the universe will send him to me at just the right time!"

That time came shortly after I retired at the age of sixty. My accountant had told me that I had more than enough invested to retire, and my feet were begging me to do so. I still loved the work, but the continual journey into the city and back each day was wearing me out. Now that I had a lovely cottage by the sea, I wanted to spend more time there. So I began working less, and enjoying life more, diving into my newfound love of alternative healing and the fabulous friends I'd made in that journey of self-discovery. I traveled to Machu Picchu in Peru, painted my new home with vibrant colors to which I'd added holistic healing oils, had crystal healing sessions, and just relished each of my days and evenings spent discovering a spiritual world I had become so divorced from in my years of fashion. The material world that had enriched me had been good to me, but the abuse and disrespect I'd suffered over the decades had taken a toll on me. I needed to find meaning in my life, a meaning that wasn't going to come with the next garment I fitted or the next buyer I charmed.

I was lying on a table in my friend Bernadette's studio when my life course took a turn. She must have been working on me for over a half hour with her loving energy as she opened up my chakras and cleansed my energies. At the end of the treatment, she ran a crystal pendulum up and down my body, and I was happy to watch the pendulum swing around each of my chakras. But when it got to my heart chakra, it stopped moving.

Bernadette looked at me and said, "Darlene, all your seven chakras are wide open except for one, and that's your heart chakra. The heart chakra is related to trust—there's something or someone you don't trust. May I open it for you?"

"Yes, of course," I said, trusting Bernadette. Whatever it was she was going to do to my chakra, I knew it wouldn't harm me. The truth was, my closed heart chakra was no mystery. I was still holding on to so much anger from the past. Anger for the husbands who'd mistreated me, the buyer who had raped me, the police officers who had mocked me, and still, the father who had failed me. I had come to forgive my wounded dad so much, but I couldn't deny that there was still anger there. It just wasn't enough to decide in my head to forgive him. My heart needed to open itself to forgiveness.

Bernadette placed some healing crystals along my body and murmured some healing prayers, and after I left I did feel better. I felt energized, awoken. I headed over to the Shipwreck, a bar near my home, where I was going to meet my friend Chad for a drink. Chad and I were old friends and he was a real gentleman, just the perfect guy to have a drink with and not feel any pressure.

As I walked into the Shipwreck, I saw that Chad hadn't yet arrived, so I sat near the end of the bar and chatted with the bartender. He knew me well from my old boat days when I came in for dinner. I always reminded him that no one was to buy me a drink—I didn't want to feel obligated to speak to some guy just because he'd bought me a drink. I could afford to buy for myself.

There were three gentlemen sitting at the bar and because I wanted to sit near the window to keep an eye out for Chad, I found myself sitting near them. The only problem was, every time I turned from the window toward the trio, I had to say something to them so I wouldn't appear rude. Before long, one of them asked if he could buy me a drink.

"No, thank you," I said politely, and turned back to the window. Just then, Chad pulled up and I watched as he parked his car near the window. I asked for my bar bill so I could look for a table.

"I'm sorry, Darlene," the bartender said. "It's already paid for." The mischievous smile on his face told me that he didn't care that he was breaking my rule. I followed his gaze, and saw that another of the men at the bar had paid for it.

As I got up to go to my table, I stopped to thank the tall, silver-haired handsome man. "But it wasn't necessary," I said kindly.

"I know," he answered, "I just thought my friend was being cheap not offering to buy you a drink," he said.

"He did offer, but didn't it occur to you that I could afford my own drink?" I extended my warmest smile, the smile I'd learned from Gloria Nash way back in my early modeling days, and began to walk away.

"I meant no harm," the man said, and as I tried to pull away he continued talking. At that point, Chad came through the door and walked over to us, and before I knew it, the three of us were chatting like old friends. The silver-haired gentleman introduced himself as Ed, though

I chose to call him Edward because it seemed a more dignified name for such a dignified man. As we left, Edward gave me his business card, but didn't ask for mine. That small gesture impressed me. It was up to me if I saw him again.

As I walked toward my car, I realized how nice this man had been. He had talked a lot about his kids and was obviously a devoted father. I continued to think about him after I got home and all through the night. There was nothing in the conversation that had sent up a red flag, and he had been nothing but respectful. So the next day, I called him and asked if he'd like to meet me that Saturday for a drink.

It was the first time in my life that I'd asked a man out! And it felt so right.

As Saturday came around, I spent a little extra time picking out something to wear. I wanted to look just right, because there was something special about this man. I had a feeling this guy would make it past the third date!

I'd chosen a restaurant near my home where we would meet. Not only was it close to home, in case I needed to make a quick exit, but I knew the bartender there, as well, and he always let me know if some guy was a lush or a louse. In this case, however, the moment Edward walked through the door he received the warmest welcome imaginable. Everyone knew him, it turned out, from the days he used to bring his mother there for dinner. That certainly impressed me!

The evening went so well. We spent most of the night talking about our families—he had four sons and as many grandchildren. He even asked me to dance. To this day I can still remember what it felt like when Edward put his hand on my back and brought me into position to waltz with him—it sent shivers up my spine!

A few months later, we were back at the same restaurant, when he got down on his knee, presented a beautiful diamond ring that my friend Betty had designed for him, and asked me to marry him. I had never been so thrilled to say yes!

We were married by the side of the sea in a beautiful ceremony with our friends and families beside us. I had been married three times before, but never had I been so happy, so nervous, or so certain. I was marrying the man of *my* dreams.

As the next few months went by, we learned a lot about each other. Edward's greatest pleasures were cooking, spending time with his boys, and working in his investment business. The more I got to know him, the more I fell in love not just with him, but with his family, one personality at a time.

He was learning a lot about me, as well. He saw how disturbed I became if we were watching TV and a rape scene came on, and he learned to turn the channel until it was over. Just as I had accepted his devotion to the Catholic Church, he accepted my devotion to spiritual teachings that had been alien to him. With each new thing we learned about each other, we grew closer.

Soon, however, the little differences that were so enchanting at first, became increasingly intolerable. I felt the subtle ways that he tried to control me, tried to tell me what to think or what to believe, and I rebelled. I wasn't going to let any man control me.

Our differences became misunderstandings and our misunderstandings became fights. We loved each other powerfully, but our fights were just as powerful. I wasn't adapting to his rules and the way I saw it, he had a lot of rules, and he resented my rules. We hadn't been married more than two months before I began sitting by the sea, pondering what went wrong.

It seemed like every man thought the same way, *But what, just exactly, is it that they think?* I wondered. After several weeks of fuming, I decided to give my new husband a gift—I bought him the book, *Men Are from Mars, Women Are from Venus.*

I walked into the kitchen, smiled at my beautiful husband and set the book in front of him. As I did so, I tried to explain to him that I loved him very much and because of that, I had a tremendous need to be understood.

"Seeing as you're not a woman," I continued, trying to lighten the moment as much as I could, "it's hard for you to understand how we think and this book explains it very well. Will you please read it?"

He looked up at me from the piles of papers he'd been working on and said, "I don't have to read that book, Darlene." Then he put his head down and went back to work.

Just like that, he'd refused to read it! I was livid. I took the book, grabbed a bottle of wine off the counter, and threw the book on the grill. Then I set it on fire and sat down to drink my wine, all the while muttering, "My marriage is screwed, my marriage is screwed . . ."

I must have sat out there for at least an hour drinking my wine and repeating my new mantra until it was encrypted into every memory cell of my body. My marriage was over. He wouldn't even read a goddamned book for me! I thought of going back inside and telling Ed exactly how I felt, but the words just stuck in my throat. Of course, all that wine didn't help my mood any. I wanted to go in there and yell at him and tell him how angry I was, but instead, I just sat and drank until the bottle was gone.

Every so often, Ed would peak his head out the window and I swore he was laughing, which only made me angrier.

Eventually, I gathered up my courage and went back inside. I knew I had to calm down or I would hurl every hurtful thing I could think of at my new husband. I was sober enough, at least, to realize how unfair that would have been to him. So without wanting to make a total fool of myself, I walked over to him, leaned on the counter to keep control of my tottering balance, and glared at him.

Finally, he lifted his head from his stack of papers and said, "I can see you burned the book."

"Yep," I replied, "our marriage is screwed. You won't even read the book."

"Darlene," he said, his eyes soft and full of love, "I don't have to read that book because I've already read it. Why do you think my sons have such successful marriages? It's because I gave each one of them that book years ago."

Boy, did I feel like a fool! I'd wasted all that time in a fit of rage for no reason!

The next day, I went out and bought the book again, but this time, I read the man's part. I had been so consumed with being understood, that I hadn't even considered understanding the man I'd married! As I read it, I began to learn that men don't talk like women do. We can talk and talk, but men usually don't say more than a few sentences before they stop talking. And what do we women do in response? We blame them for not listening!

The more I read the book, and the more I looked back on the many marriages and relationships with men that I had had, the more I realized that yes, men did try to control me. But not only did I let them, I also tried to control them. I had so wanted each man that I had married to conform to my world, to my rules, and to meet my needs, that I failed to reflect on my own controlling nature.

Of course, that didn't mean that it was okay for any of them to hit me, cheat on me or put me down. But finally, in my sixties, I began to look at my own role in my battles.

Just as growing into my father's Eisenhower jacket had taken me decades, growing into my marriage was going to take time. And this time, I'd found a man who was worth it. It was now up to me to become worthy of him.

Chapter 29

Basket Case

H ere I was on my fourth marriage, and only just beginning to gain insight into all the baggage that I had brought into it. As I worked less and examined my ego more—an ego shaped by decades of admiration for how I looked—I came to realize that I carried with me layers and layers of spiritual debris. No wonder I continually found myself engaged in battles with the men I married and had worked with! One after another played their own roles in the battles, that's true. But I was so buried under those layers of debris that I had spent my life trying on partners as if they were garments I was modeling.

Now that I finally had a partner who fit me perfectly, I was going to be damn sure I didn't blow it—or let him blow it!

With the extra time that retirement brought me I devoured books on healing, spirituality and self-knowledge. My circle of friends continued to grow as I attended conferences, workshops and seminars on these topics and every day seemed to shed another layer of my anger and resentment. I loved Edward more powerfully every day, and found a forgiveness for his imperfections that I had never felt with other husbands. But could I forgive myself for my own imperfections? I wasn't so sure. My entire career had been focused on perfection—presenting the perfect face, the perfect expression, walking the perfect walk, fitting each garment to perfection, maintaining the perfect figure. Imperfection, in the fashion and modeling world, is unacceptable.

But now I was out of that world—for the most part. I sure did miss it, and it wasn't long before I dipped my toes back into it, taking on the occasional modeling assignment just for kicks—if not the extra money. My main focus, however, was on my spiritual growth and learning to accept those imperfections in myself, to forgive myself my many faults and forgive others the same. Would I forgive my rapist? No, that would require attaining a spiritual plane beyond me. But with every breath, a new chakra opened, with every heartbeat, a new love for life bloomed. I was transforming. I was becoming a kinder, gentler person. I was becoming a lighter, happier woman. My smile was no longer the false smile I had learned to wear as a model. My smile was a radiant one, lit from within.

It was in the midst of this spiritual awakening that I learned of an upcoming cruise featuring some of my favorite authors and spiritual mentors. Edward was overwhelmed with work and couldn't go along, so I called Betty—she loved doing things at the last minute.

"A cruise? Sure, let's do it!" That's all it took to get her on board. Edward would drive us to the airport where we'd catch a flight to Miami, where Susan, the woman I'd bought the seaside cottage from, was now living. She and her husband would pick us up and take us to the ship and we'd be off!

For all the travel I'd done during my career, this was perhaps the most exciting trip I'd ever taken. Drifting out to sea with some of the top spiritual healers and writers of my generation, with nothing to do but learn and heal. Pure heaven.

Healing, it turned out, was something we both needed. Betty, a jewelry designer, had a high-pressure job in the diamond district and had a lot of orders to get out by Christmas. She appeared exhausted from the moment we left for the airport, and it wasn't long before I felt her exhaustion spread to me. I wasn't surprised—we'd always shared everything, from clothes to colds and this trip appeared to be no different.

"Don't worry, Darlene," she assured me. "All we really need is to sit in a lounge chair, smell the sea and feel the sun on our faces!"

"You're right, Betty," I agreed. "And wash it all down with some cocktails!"

We laughed and talked with excitement at the trip before us, determined to defy our less-than-excited aging bodies. On our first night on board the ship, we decided to celebrate and headed upstairs to the ship's lounge. The blue skies, warm sun and laughing seagulls—along with a couple of margaritas—were just the medicine we needed. As we placed our orders with the waitress, I felt a poke in my ribs from Betty. I turned and saw that she was looking at a woman sitting alone, drinking by herself at a corner table. She was one of the authors we'd come to see, someone I really admired.

"Go over there, Darlene—introduce yourself!" Betty urged.

I really wanted to, and I knew that Betty would do it in a heartbeat. But I also knew that, as one of the speakers booked for the cruise, this was her time to herself. I figured I'd have plenty of time to talk to her after her lecture the following day, and the truth was, I wasn't feeling all that well myself. I had been feeling an ache on my right side for some time and though I tried my best to ignore it, it continued to plague me. I really wanted a good night's sleep.

The next morning, the pain hadn't subsided. In fact, it became so bad that I skipped the morning's lectures and spent the whole morning resting in bed. After the first lecture, Betty came to check on me.

"I'm fine," I told her. "I probably ate something I shouldn't have. I'll be okay. I just need to rest some more."

Betty left, and returned after the second lecture, and I gave her the same assurance. This time, however, she wasn't buying it.

"No, you're not okay," Betty replied, "you look awful! You need to get to the ship's infirmary right away! I've never seen you looking so pale."

Betty was right, I did feel bad. As we talked, in fact, the pain had become a searing agony. By the time I reached the infirmary, the pain was out of control. The nurse took one look at me and told me she was calling the Coast Guard.

"You're running a high fever," she said, and asked me how long I'd been having the pains. "Have you ever had your appendix removed?"

"My appendix? No, I've never had it removed," I said, between grunts and cries of pain.

"You may be having an attack of appendicitis. You need to get to the nearest hospital right away."

The nearest hospital? We were out in the middle of the Atlantic Ocean! There was no hospital in sight.

As I drifted in and out of consciousness, the pain overtaking me in waves greater than those that were rocking the boat, the U.S. Coast Guard was called for an emergency medical evacuation. Betty never left my side, spending the hours calming me, and watching two dolphins playing outside the window, as if our guardians. She explained what was going on, step by step, repeating it often because the pain was making me delirious.

"The ship's changed course to meet up with the Coast Guard," she said. "They'll take you to the U.S. Naval Hospital in Guantanamo Bay."

So instead of spending ten days on the exciting cruise I'd envisioned, I was heading to Guantanamo Bay. *Life does throw curve balls when you least expect them,* I thought.

At some point I was strapped onto a gurney to ready me for the helicopter. As the helicopter approached, its roar deafening, the wind that it kicked up felt as if we'd entered a tumultuous storm. Yet I was nearly oblivious, barely hearing, barely seeing, losing all track of time. It seemed to take forever and the pain was agonizing.

"The helicopter can't land," Betty screamed through the noise, "they're going to have to lift you into it!"

"What?" I asked. I was so confused, but not at all scared. All I could think of was getting the pain to stop, whatever it took.

"Look up! See that basket? They're lowering it for you. They're going to put you in it and pull you up into the helicopter!"

Any other time in my life I would have been terrified. I never would have let anyone put me in a basket and hoist me into the sky, high above the ocean. But this was no ordinary day. Instead, I just said, "Okay."

Slowly I realized, the ship was awfully empty. "Where is everybody?" I screamed at Betty. It was so loud that we could barely hear each other, even though we were just inches away from each other.

"They've been told to stay in their rooms. They're watching the rescue on TV!"

"On TV?"

"Yeah, you're going to be on TV!" she laughed.

Well, how about that! After all those years on camera, it had come to this—Darlene Parris Young, basket case!

I have no memory of getting into the basket, but I recall being in it, trying to sit up so that I could see Betty, but I couldn't sit up. Then I felt it. The basket was lifting from the ship and ascending higher and higher into the air, swaying above the Atlantic Ocean. Still, I wasn't scared. I thought that if I rocked the basket hard enough, I could slip out from under the ropes and fall into the sea. The image was so enticing. I so wanted the pain to stop. I was so tired. I wanted to go home. I wanted to end my suffering, and the sea looked so calm. *Please, God, please let me die* . . . I prayed as I swayed over the ocean.

Then it happened. The pain stopped, suddenly and completely. My head became clearer and I felt incredibly light, as if my body and my past no longer anchored me to the earth. I began to soar, as a powerful, loving feeling swept through me. A constellation of tiny white lights twinkled above me, encouraging me to soar higher. I was returning home, slipping from my body but not my awareness. I felt the energy of my parents and my brother beside me, helping me to transform from my physical form to my spiritual form. I felt an incandescent joy as I left the sadness of my dying body. As if God's breath was breathing into me, I gradually felt as if I were blending into God's energy, and I surrendered to the melting feeling, melting and blending into all that is Divine.

Hands began to grab hold of me and a powerful force of wind blew against my face. They were not the hands of God but hands of men, pulling me into the helicopter, the wind from the propellers battering my face. An awareness of what I was leaving took hold of me. I became aware of my children, my grandchildren, my husband, and the sadness they would feel at my loss. I had to go back to them. I had to remain on earth with them.

And so I did. Two helicopter rides later, I found myself outside the emergency room of a hospital in Puerto Rico. When the staff reached me, I was once again strapped to a gurney and wheeled into the ER. A doctor came, looked me over, and frowned. He said something in Spanish, shaking his head, then left. He returned periodically, but no effort was made to treat me. They believed that I was dying.

I knew that I was not. I knew that I had made the decision not to die, but to live. And with the decision to live, came a return of the excruciating pain. I lay on the gurney, moaning in agony, knowing that I had been left for dead.

Then my cell phone rang.

It was my friend, Andrea, calling. All across the ocean, that phone had stayed inside my pocket, and now here it was, bringing me what I most needed—the sound of a friend's voice. And she was not just any friend. She was a powerful healer—and a kick-ass woman.

"No one speaks English here," I told her. "They think I'm going to die."

"You aren't going to die, Darlene!" Andrea ordered. "I speak Spanish. Get your doctor!"

I called out for a doctor and after they spoke with Andrea, I was rushed into another room for some CT scans. They discovered that my appendix had indeed perforated, sending poison throughout my body. It was too late to operate, and just a matter of time before the poison invaded my whole body.

As I waited for the poison to surge through me, I called Edward, not telling him the worse. But I told him enough that he was on the next flight to Puerto Rico. As I waited, the doctor continued to check on me occasionally but he made no effort to help me. I knew that I was not going to die, but that he needed to be replaced. Finally, I asked for a new doctor.

The next morning, my request was granted. A doctor who spoke English arrived and I immediately felt I was in good hands.

She concurred that it was too late to operate, but put me on a heavy dose of an antibiotic to stop the poison from spreading.

"I'm going to live," I told her, and she nodded, her smile barely perceptible.

After she left, Andrea called and gave me a healing over the phone, and across the many miles.

The next morning, when the doctor came to check on me, the look on her face was one of shock. I was sitting up in a lotus position, a huge smile on my face. She hurried away, only to return with the whole staff—all stunned to see me sitting up when I was expected to be dead.

"I told you I was going to live," I said. "So now can I please have something to eat?"

I was allowed my first food in days. It was orange Jell-O and it tasted as delicious as the finest souffle. I savored every bite, holding the cold, wobbly gelatin in my mouth to feel and taste its flavor and texture. I'd never tasted anything as exquisite.

By the time Edward arrived, I felt as if I were the star of the hospital. The cleaning staff turned their brooms and mops into dancing canes and performed a dance for me. Andrea called regularly and Betty miraculously appeared, to remain by my side. After a few more days, Edward was allowed to check me out of the hospital, and he booked us a room in a nearby hotel so I'd be close to the hospital.

We checked into our room for our long overdue honeymoon. It was perfect. The first thing I did was fling open the sliding glass doors to take in the view and there, over the ocean, was a magnificent double rainbow—and a dolphin swimming toward the horizon.

I was alive and in love and right where I needed to be. Life was perfect.

Chapter 30

Valentine's Day

alentine's Day was right around the corner, and I had no idea
what Edward would come up with. I'd been married to a Greek
and an Italian man, but neither could hold a candle to Edward
when it came to romance. Whatever it was he had planned, I knew it
would win my heart yet again.

He was always fussing over me about something. He showered me
with so many roses that I knew he was unlikely to do so on this day.
Finally, I came right out and asked him.

"What should we do for Valentine's Day?"

He put down his paper, took off his reading glasses, and smiled.
"Funny you should ask. I was thinking that, since you are always complaining that I never take you to the movies, we'd have a nice romantic
dinner out and then catch a film. How's that sound?"

It sounded perfect. "What should we see?" I asked him.

"I'll tell you what. You pick the restaurant, and I'll pick the movie.
The dinner can be anywhere, but the movie is going to be a surprise!"

You can imagine how surprised I was when the time came for the
movie. Instead of the romantic comedy I'd imagined, Edward chose
American Sniper!

I couldn't imagine a more inappropriate movie, and the last thing I wanted to see on Valentine's Day was a war movie. As much as I wanted to tell him so, I decided it wasn't a good idea. He wanted to see it, and Valentine's Day was as much about treating him as it was about treating me, so I decided to say nothing.

As we entered the theater, though, I was determined to have a bad time. I usually order a bag of popcorn, but this time I didn't even bother. I just bought a bottle of water and we went inside. The sooner it was over with, the better, I figured, realizing that my days of wine and roses were fading. Soon it would just be the days of wine and more wine!

As I watched the movie, however, I found myself drawn into it as if I was watching a film reel of my life. It was the story of a war hero, Chris Kyle, and his wife, Taya. She reminded me so much of my mother, loving her husband, worrying about him every day, understanding the pride for his country that sent him off to battle. When he returned home a war hero, Taya realized the extent of the emotional wounds that had shattered his soul. Just like Taya, my mother had witnessed the man she loved changed by war, yet stood by him knowing that he'd brought the war home with him.

I was riveted to every frame of that movie, my heart beating fast. I gripped my water bottle so tightly that it broke and I barely noticed I'd been drenched. The torment and pain of the men and women who fought our wars had never been more clear to me, and for the first time, I felt I truly understood why my father spent so much time at the American Legion Hall, why it was so hard for him to leave his drink and war buddies that day when Danny was waiting outside for him.

I left the theater feeling a tremendous love and forgiveness for my father. For all the times I'd been nudged toward forgiving him, my heart always seemed to stop short. Now there was no stopping it. I loved him with all my heart—and I felt a much better understanding of my mom and why she had never left him. She had fought her own private war in the shadow of my damaged father. There were no programs back then for veterans who returned with PTSD—there wasn't even an awareness of it, beyond some vague concept of "shell shock."

My parents' lives had been shocked by the war and that war had brought them a profound compassion for each other. I had never been able to feel that compassion until I saw it on the screen, performed by actors. Yet there it was, rising from my heart with a power unrestrained. I turned toward my husband and thanked him for giving my heart the gift it so badly needed that Valentine's Day. The gift of compassion and forgiveness.

In the years since that day, I have continued to love my father in a way I never did before, and that love has opened up a whole new understanding of who I am and where I've come from—an understanding that has made it possible to love my husband wholly and completely, without fear or anger or judgment. I look back upon my life and career and gaze upon the innocent yet angry girl I once was when I first entered the modeling world. I resented my appearance because I believed my father resented my appearance—and in defiance, I made good money off it.

I couldn't bring myself to smile, and once I did, it was a false smile, a smile that made me money, that charmed men, that softened the harshness of my words. I only really learned to smile once I walked away from the cameras and the runways and the showrooms and put the material world behind me and cast my gaze upon the spiritual world that had so long eluded me.

Now, as I enter my eightieth decade, I have never felt as young and alive and unafraid. Nor have I ever been as close to my children and grandchildren and stepchildren and loving husband. I am surrounded by the love of my family and friends, and in some ways, it took near death in a basket high above the ocean for me to realize how much we all need each other in this world.

And I still take the train into the city every now and then to fit a garment when my agent calls. I guess those calls will keep on coming, just as long as I don't gain or lose an inch—and keep my ass padded for good measure—just in case I land on it yet again!

Made in the USA
Coppell, TX
03 July 2020

30087774R10166